Contemporary Islamic Political Thought in Egypt

Contemporary Islamic Political Thought in Egypt

Reading Jamal al-Banna and Tariq al-Bishri in Autocratic Contexts

Ebtisam Aly Hussein

I.B.TAURIS
LONDON • NEW YORK • OXFORD • NEW DELHI • SYDNEY

I.B. TAURIS
Bloomsbury Publishing Plc, 50 Bedford Square, London, WC1B 3DP, UK
Bloomsbury Publishing Inc, 1385 Broadway, New York, NY 10018, USA
Bloomsbury Publishing Ireland, 29 Earlsfort Terrace, Dublin 2, D02 AY28, Ireland

BLOOMSBURY, I.B. TAURIS and the I.B. Tauris logo are
trademarks of Bloomsbury Publishing Plc

First published in Great Britain 2024
This paperback edition published 2025

Copyright © Ebtisam Aly Hussein, 2024

Ebtisam Aly Hussein has asserted her rights under the Copyright, Designs and
Patents Act, 1988, to be identified as Author of this work.

For legal purposes the Acknowledgements on p. viii constitute
an extension of this copyright page.

Series design by Adriana Brioso
Cover image © MTB/Getty Images

All rights reserved. No part of this publication may be: i) reproduced or transmitted in any form, electronic or mechanical, including photocopying, recording or by means of any information storage or retrieval system without prior permission in writing from the publishers; or ii) used or reproduced in any way for the training, development or operation of artificial intelligence (AI) technologies, including generative AI technologies. The rights holders expressly reserve this publication from the text and data mining exception as per Article 4(3) of the Digital Single Market Directive (EU) 2019/790.

Bloomsbury Publishing Inc does not have any control over, or responsibility for, any third-party websites referred to or in this book. All internet addresses given in this book were correct at the time of going to press. The author and publisher regret any inconvenience caused if addresses have changed or sites have ceased to exist, but can accept no responsibility for any such changes.

A catalogue record for this book is available from the British Library.

Library of Congress Cataloging-in-Publication Data
Names: Hussein, Ebtisam Aly, author.
Title: Contemporary Islamic political thought in Egypt : reading Jamal al-Banna
and Tariq al-Bishri in autocratic contexts / Ebtisam Aly Hussein.
Description: London ; New York, NY : I.B Tauris, 2024. |
Includes bibliographical references and index.
Identifiers: LCCN 2023036826 (print) | LCCN 2023036827 (ebook) |
ISBN 9780755653157 (hardback) | ISBN 9780755653157 (paperback) |
ISBN 9780755653164 (epub) | ISBN 9780755653171 (pdf) | ISBN 9780755653188
Subjects: LCSH: Bannā, Jamāl. | Bishrī, Tāriq. | Islam and politics. |
Islam and politics–Egypt. | Egypt–Politics and government.
Classification: LCC BP80.B352 H88 2024 (print) |
LCC BP80.B352 (ebook) | DDC 297.2/72–dc23/eng/20231023
LC record available at https://lccn.loc.gov/2023036826
LC ebook record available at https://lccn.loc.gov/2023036827

ISBN: HB: 978-0-7556-5315-7
PB: 978-0-7556-5319-5
ePDF: 978-0-7556-5317-1
eBook: 978-0-7556-5316-4

Typeset by Newgen KnowledgeWorks Pvt. Ltd., Chennai, India

For product safety related questions contact productsafety@bloomsbury.com.

To find out more about our authors and books visit www.bloomsbury.com
and sign up for our newsletters.

To my father
& those who carved their kindness in my memory

Contents

Acknowledgements viii
Technical notes ix

Introduction: From Orientalism to power over the public sphere 1
1 Contemporary Islamic political thought 15
2 Egypt: Surviving autocratic regimes 41
3 Jamal al-Banna on CIPT 81
4 Tariq al-Bishri on CIPT 123
Conclusion 163

Notes 171
Bibliography 187
Index 223

Acknowledgements

This manuscript became reality due to the support and cooperation of many people who were integral to the completion of my PhD dissertation, which is the basis of this book.

I would like to express my utmost gratitude and thankfulness to my two German PhD supervisors, who compelled me to thrive: Prof. Dr. Cilja Harders and Prof. Dr. Gudrun Krämer. They inspired me in many ways and I am still indebted to their efforts.

I also would like to thank all the people who made this book possible by sharing their time and knowledge for interviews during my fieldwork trips to Cairo.

Towards conducting the research resulting in this book, I received scholarships from the German Academic Exchange Service (DAAD) and Berlin Graduate School Muslim Cultures and Societies (BGSMCS).

Last but surely not least, I thank the two late Egyptian Islamic intellectuals: Jamal al-Banna and Tariq al-Bishri, who generously provided me with their intellectual production across decades and had the patience to answer all my questions regarding their ideas and stances.

Technical notes

The book uses the IJMES English transliteration rules for Arabic language. Throughout the body of the text, only words pertaining to Islamic terminology will be fully transliterated. Five terms pertaining to Islamic Thought are still used without transliteration throughout the text. These are *Hadith, Jihad, Ijtihad, Shura and Shari'a*; the use of these terms in this manner is based on similar literature published in English. All other Arabic names and terms will have the vowel (ʿ) and the vowel (ʾ) if it is necessary for proper pronunciation like with Qurʾan. Both in footnotes and in the bibliography, names of authors and titles of Arabic references will be fully transliterated though.

Technical notes

[illegible]

Introduction

From Orientalism to power over the public sphere

Scholarship on Islam is embedded in relativism; what Islam represents depends, and varies, much on various factors, such as the person, the time and the country where the answer is offered (Fyzee, 1963, 1). This translates, almost inevitably, into the centrality of interpretation and contextuality of the field called *Islamic*. Yet, Edward Said's seminal work *Orientalism* (1978) presented a serious, and in many ways controversial, implication of this contextuality. On multiple occasions, Said emphasized the role of human agency in depicting reality through his claim on an entrenched bias in the Orientalist literature on Islam and Muslim societies, emanating from a sense of Western superiority in the 'White Man' narrative. Although his Orientalism wasn't confined to Muslim societies, he initially had a strong focus on Western depictions of Islam (Said, 1978, 59–92), which later became even stronger, more elaborate and salient, in his book titled *Covering Islam* (1981). He showed great interest in the history of Western Imperialism, particularly how the knowledge brought *back* by European explorers, ethnographers, geologists and the like constructed Europe's awareness of others (Said, 1994, 189, 162, respectively). Meanwhile, Said's account on Orientalism is preoccupied with Europe's desire to dominate others (Aravamudan, 2012, 1). The strong appeal of the book was evinced by its translation into thirty-six languages (Jung, 2011, 17), and its logic of West/East juxtaposition inspired many writings on Islam and Islamist movements (see Bayat, 2013a, 6).

His appraisal was indirectly fortified through similar, though unidentical, accounts on the historical development of Orientalist scholarship in the West; tens of scholars wrote on the topic in, more or less, a reaction to *his* Orientalism (see Lemon, 2011; Sardar, 1999; Burney, 2012, 23–40). Muslim scholars generally reiterated Said's basic claims on Western domination through colonialism and the assumed bias of Orientalist studies on the East. From such a perspective, Orientalist scholarship was linked to positions created by colonizers to serve their own goals. Orientalists declared commitment to scientific methodology but their studies were allegedly jammed with fanaticism against Islam and Muslim societies (Shāma, 2012, 15). Their scholarship was regarded as based on inadequate knowledge of Qur'an and the life of the Prophet (Tibawi, 1976, 53), aimed at developing a sense of moral disappointment in the East, and among Muslims, towards a sense of Western superiority (al-Bahii, 1991, 431; al-Khaṭīb, 1982, 9–14).

Nonetheless, Orientalism doesn't fully capture the multiplicity of perspectives on the study of Islamic traditions and Muslim societies. It was widely criticized on the basis of adopting an instrumentalist notion of power and knowledge; namely, its inclination to place power and discourse exclusively on the side of colonizers as a blunt reduction of the subject. European concepts of modernity became a stereotypical, and an unconsciously applied, pattern by which post-colonial elites shaped their discourse and institutional framing of national modernization processes (see Bhaba, 1996, 42–4; Jung, 2011, 32), aside from the fact that his Orientalism was not strongly embedded in academic methods and techniques (Lewis, 1993, 115).

In my view, the core weakness of Said's Orientalism is that he put Western scholars who studied Arabs into one big pool (Little, 1979, 110–31), a problem that is most visible in the reality of Orientalist studies, which certainly deviated from Said's generalistic depictions. Tens of publications, by Western scholars, do not normatively address Islam and Muslim societies, neither defame nor raise doubt regarding the basic tenets of the faith of Islam, and consciously confine themselves to the scholarly enquiries about the meaning of texts and reality of Muslim societies (see Black, 2008; Krämer, 2013; Kalmar, 2012).

I decided to start my introduction from Said's Orientalism because its logic is visibly present in many of the writings falling under the field of Contemporary Islamic Political Thought (CIPT) today. In this sense, I approach it as *background knowledge* (Chilton, 2004). To be precise, scholarship on Islam and Muslim societies consists of studies of Islam and the larger *Islamicate*, comprising the faith as well as the larger social and cultural complex associated traditionally with Islam (Hodgson, 1974, 59) and much of this scholarship, by Islamic intellectuals, departs from Said's tenets, even if not in an explicit manner. His logic on Western superiority could be traced in tens, if not hundreds, of sources (see Said, 1978, 45; Said, 1994, 186; al-Azm, 1981, 5). Furthermore, Said, like several other scholars (see Wolf, 1984; Bayat, 2007, 89), put some weight on the role of humans in understanding history. All histories, to him, are partly imaginative and that the most important thing about history is not to discover it, rather to present it (Said, 1978, 55; Barsamian, 1994, 53–4). Acknowledging this element of subjectivity and perception into the construction of *truth* is constitutive to both CIPT intellectual production as well as my accounts on the latter.

In four related chapters, I attempt to read the massive production of two contemporary Islamic intellectuals from Egypt, namely, Jamal al-Banna and Tariq al-Bishri. Through a comparative lens, which is largely missing in CIPT, I seek to highlight the centrality of the commonly used mainstream and tajdīd (renewal) duality in writings in this field, a duality that surpasses the limits of CIPT in a particular country or region. Yet, because of its focus on two Egyptian Islamic intellectuals, who are embedded in their contexts in various ways, findings of this research can only be prudently considered to CIPT across the Muslim world. For, in each region, country, culture and language, CIPT is intricately moulded through its contexts, even when it aspires to engage at a universal level. Through the book's thematic focus and case selection, I hope to strike a balance between the content of writings by Islamic intellectuals and the particular contexts in which they contribute their writings. However, I don't, at any occasion, claim to offer a critical interpretation of CIPT as an epistemological realm. Through this book, I simply try to offer a different, context-embedded and systematic reading of CIPT authorship, one that could be employed to, comparatively, read the writings of other Ismalic intellectuals in the future.

One of the key obstacles I encountered conducting this research was deciding what *the* Islamic intellectual connotes, which actually relates to this duality of mainstream and tajdīd. For instance, in their claim to offer tajdīd, intellectuals like Jamal al-Banna, Mohamed Saʿid al-ʿAshmawi,[1] Hasan Hanafi[2] and Nasr Hamid Abu Zaid[3] (see Krämer, 2000a, 137) incite with their not-mainstream[4] contributions huge debates on the nature and qualification of the Islamic intellectual (see Kamrava, 2006, 13–21) or *who speaks for Islam* (see Krämer and Schmidtke, 2006; Esposito and Mogahed, 2007, 27–8). Mainstream[5] would connote the juridical and intellectual CIPT authorship complying to the established body of Sunni heritage, in the manner that is depicted in Chapter 1. In reading the writings of al-Banna and al-Bishri, who come from diverse family, educational, professional backgrounds and ideological orientations, I try to touch upon this duality and emphasize the diversity comprised in CIPT. Meanwhile, in the real world, presenting oneself as Islamic doesn't exclude offering parallel, often overlapping, accounts on politics (see Ṭabliyya, 2000, 210; al-Tiftizānī,

1997, 63–81). This is integral to reading their work and will become quite clear in Chapters 3 and 4 when the intellectuals' writings on CIPT are addressed and analysed.

To my bewilderment, it was quite challenging to find a definition to answer this question: Who is an intellectual? It's truly puzzling why some people are labelled intellectuals. Till this very day, a definitive role of the intellectual is a matter of significant disagreement. The *role* of intellectuals, through their work, could contribute to the construction of national or communal identity (Kahn-Paycha, 2000); it may also be that of civilizational revival or renaissance (al-Shūbāshī, 2013), or like with Said's Orientalism, the revision and critique of long-established narratives and discourses (Said, 1978, 1981, 1983). There is no, and probably will never be, consensus on one specific and fixed role for the intellectual.

I argue that how attached/detached the intellectual is from the state and/or societal actors is one significant angle to this matter. On one hand, only an autonomous intellectual, one who does not depend/rely, in any form, on the *ruling class*, can genuinely contribute his/her expertise to the public sphere (Bourdieu, 5). On the other hand, an intellectual can act as a functionary to the ruling elite, boosting the hegemonic power of the latter, or may also act as part of a symbolic system, where economic classes seek intellectual representation by trying to augment/justify their respective power/legitimacy[6] via the intellectual (Mayo, 2006, 39–40; Gramsci, 1986, 222–6). Furthermore, when the intellectual is linked to economic classes, he/she might be used to divert attention away from the real source of power (economic wealth and means of production) (Bourdieu, 1984; Gartman, 2013, 104–5).

Out of this dilemma, I choose to define the intellectual in two complimentary manners. First, he/she is someone whose writings are sought for an assumed value that is derived from the intellectual's profile (Foucault, 1969); the intellectual enjoys some cultural asset, such as particular aspects in his/her personal profile that boost this character of an intellectual. Second, he/she is an individual who is interested in debates in the public sphere and is capable of taking part in these debates (Salvatore, 2000, 93–5). The cultural asset aspect will become clear shortly when tackling the personal profiles of al-Banna and al-Bishri, as both enjoyed several traits contributing to their character as intellectuals.

Before proceeding any further, I would like to highlight a key distinction between the Muslim and the Islamic, proposed by Krämer, according to which *Muslim* merely connotes belonging to Islam as a religious community, without associating to political ambition/demand, whereas *Islamic* makes the political demand to turn Islam, as understood by the concerned group or individual, into a program, or a code of conduct. In this way, Muslim scholars are considered *Islamic* when they advocate an Islamic program, or when they work in the field of theocracy, Islamic law or Islamic history (Krämer, 2000a, 32).

Likewise, the scope of interest exhibited by jurists and intellectuals is expectedly different. Whereas it might be argued that the intellectual concerns with issues of his/her time, the jurist is largely concerned with the past (Jāmiʿ, interview, 2010). Yet, there is some room for flexibility between these two categories: jurists can turn into intellectuals, if they decide to address issues of their time and not confine themselves to affairs of the religious (Shūbakī, interview, 2010; Midḥat interview, 2011; Shiḥāta, interview, 2010). Similarly, the task of jurists should not necessarily be to present something new. If they do, they would then be regarded as both jurists and intellectuals (ʾAbū al-Futūḥ, interview, 2011). Certainly, there are more demanding accounts that require clarity of vision or comprehensiveness of one's intellectual project, or even expressing an *intellectual self* in one's writings (Midḥat, interview, 2011; al-Sharqāwī, interview, 2011; al-Munūfī, interview, 2010).

But, once again, the *not-mainstream* stances propagated by intellectuals like Jamal al-Banna, al-ʿAshmawi, Hasan Hanafi and others trigger a huge debate on the character of the Islamic, precisely on the qualification to speak for Islam. One key controversy on the character of the Islamic intellectual pertains to the role of formal education; there are intellectuals with a fair grasp of Islamic heritage (Qur'an, Hadith, history, Islamic philosophy and jurisprudence), but the latter was not necessarily attained through formal education (al-Shūbakī, Interview, 2010; Rā'if, interview 2010; al-Munūfī, interview 2011; ʿAbd al-Majīd, interview 2010; ʿAbd al-Khāliq, interview 2010). Yet, jurisprudential training is considered a prerequisite for contributing on Islam and/or the Islamicate (ʾIbrāhīm, interview 2010; Midḥat, interview 2011; Jāmiʿ, interview 2010). Consequently, it is generally accepted that intellectuals have more freedom because what they present is not regarded as a regulator for social behaviour (Ḥasan, interview 2011; al-Munūfī, interview 2011), and their scope of interests is usually broader than that of jurists (ʿAbd al-Khāliq, interview 2010; Midḥat, interview 2011; al-Sharqāwī, interview 2010). More importantly, unlike jurists, whose claims are relatively binding within time and place, intellectuals' propositions are not (Muṣṭafā, interview 2011).

But this formal education criterion eventually translates into ranking of jurist vis-à-vis intellectual. For those who argue that the intellectual does not necessarily need a formal education in Islamic studies, the jurist enjoys a higher status (ʿAbd al-Majīd, interview 2010). Conversely, for those who find it necessary for the Islamic intellectual to receive such an education, an intellectual has a higher status than a jurist (Midḥat, interview 2011). Hence, the ranking of a jurist and an intellectual based on their formal education or lack thereof signifies the overall respect and appreciation for religious training in contributing to CIPT. Technically, this criterion touches upon the logic of the cultural asset mentioned earlier. For instance, one can claim that when intellectuals with no jurisprudential training debate with jurists, the balance would tilt away from non-jurisprudential backgrounds (ʿAbd al-Majīd, interview 2010).

But, against de-facto exclusionary practices in CIPT, I would stress that opposing long-established stances, or a specific interpretation of the text, is no ground to disqualify an intellectual from his/her Islamic character. Someone can oppose the Islamic state, for instance, and still be an Islamic intellectual, even if, hypothetically, according to established juridical accumulation such a state is part of the faith (Rā'if, interview 2010, Shiḥāta, interview 2011). Today, with the tendency to deflect from mainstream assumptions in writings of intellectuals like Jamal al-Banna, Abu Zaid and al-ʿAshmawi, the term tajdīd (renewal), particularly accepted limits to renewal turned into a wide scholarly debate. This translates into a major challenge in CIPT and is usually addressed within a commonly used duality of authenticity (*'Aṣāla*) on one hand, and contemporaneity (*Muʿāṣara*) on the other; a duality between adherence to methods and positions long acknowledged on Islamic rules and the urge to adapt long-established rules and narratives to today's world (see al-Mīlād, 1999, 90; Sīdā, 1990, 167).

Claims to novelty or to simply present *new* ideas lead up to a more profound inquiry into the scope of constants (*Thawābit*) and variables (*Mutaghaiyyrāt*) in construction of claims and positions in Islamic discourse (Krämer, 2011, 30–2), such as how an intellectual relates to rules for jurisprudential revisions (*Murājaʿāt Fiqhiyya*) (see al-ʿUlwānī, 2008, 23–33). The tension and disagreement on where the limits of renewal are to be found, and how far renewal could go in altering established Islamic rules, capture the core contestation between mainstream/tajdīd CIPT.

Yet, I would particularly emphasize the centrality of two interrelated contributions: first, the aforementioned Islamic, as seeking to develop or apply Islam as a political demand/program or code of conduct (Krämer, 2000a, 32–3); second, an Islamic is also someone who, while tackling the affairs of the nation, the homeland, political and social groups and the like, uses the Islamic heritage/reference, or al-turāth (al-ʿAwwā, interview, 2011). Hereinafter, the *Islamic* would refer to someone who promotes Islam as political demand or code of conduct and relies upon Islamic heritage, including Qur'an, Hadith, Islamic history, jurisprudential and philosophical contributions to Islam, when constructing claims and arguments.

But because contributions of intellectuals, like al-Banna and Abu Zaid, embody the *problematic nature* of tajdīd in Islamic Thought; tajdīd that results in intellectual and/or societal exclusion (see Faḍl 'Allāh, 2004, 213–33), I use the term tajdīd to depict intellectual contributions of those associated with, and resulting in, these forms of exclusion. Yet, as positions on particular CIPT themes do not suffice to distinguish mainstream from tajdīd in the aforementioned sense, with significant overlap in positions between mainstream and tajdīd intellectuals, the key criterion employed in this book to distinguish between both camps is the differing conceptions and employment of the heritage, not merely what is being advocated.

In this regard, the real challenge conducting this research was that I aspired for a systematic investigation of the intellectual production of al-Banna and al-Bishri, that the book wouldn't wholly depend on, or be driven by, their writings per se; that is, their content. This is where contextuality and relativism come into play, realizing that author's (me) knowledge of the subject plays a key role in reading their writings on one hand and the contexts in which they made their contributions shape their content on the other. For this purpose, I use contexts as two aspects: one is a combination of their personal profiles, the times they lived and contributed their writings, when they were written and/or published; the other is the authorities claiming power over the content of these writings.

As much as intellectuals address their readers/audience, they also have to deal with these authorities which define, in more than one way, what they can write and/or how they can write it. Because, normally, Islamic intellectuals are not solely preoccupied with questions on Islam, its history and societies as well as concern for politics, discussed in their public spheres, they end up dealing with two key authorities: one which is religious and another which is political. These authorities don't necessarily take the form of concrete institutions, though in many times they do; a fact that renders the task of reading their writings both interesting and challenging. I was genuinely interested in how their writings *deal with* these authorities; how their ideas are both confined and made possible through them.

In addition, intellectuals present their production in the public sphere; this necessitates some grasp of the latter. The majority of existing scholarly research on the public sphere embarks upon Habermas's notion of deliberative and communicative practices (see Habermas, 1996; Salvatore, 2000, 2007, 5; Karlsson, 2008, 106; Jung, 2011, 83). His perspective of the public sphere as a field of deliberation and communication continues to guide public sphere research till this very day. It's somehow safe to claim his contribution is still valid and even fortified through the internet and new media, as they possess the potential to boost the communicative function of the public sphere (see Balnaves and Willson, 2011, 90–4; Jung, 2011, 83; Lynch, 2006). Similarly, media and press helped stimulate its dialogic nature (Salvatore, 2000, 93–5).

Once again, intellectuals don't exist in vacuum; that part of their contextuality is what I term the *self-imposing themes* they have to deal with or at least react to. So, approaching their writings would require an adequate account on these themes. Towards this pursuit, I borrow Salvatore's notion of *meta-language*, which embarks upon an assumption that in every public sphere, this meta-language defines what to address and how to address it. That is, it kind of sets priorities and draws patterns for public sphere debate(s) (Salvatore, 2000, 93–5). In this respect, I still find great use in Salvatore's depiction of the public sphere as susceptible to practices of power, especially in compliance to the power of ruling elite/regime and inherited norms of conduct, with the effect of guiding the content disseminated in it (see Zaman, 2004, 129; Salvatore, 2011, 9). Yet, one can spot some Faucauldian trace or imprint in this meta-language: the character of discourse/meta-language as compelling, besieging its users, within particular frames, offering guidance to speaking within the discourse, in what Foucault termed *Discourse of constraint* (see Foucault, 1970).

In fact, Foucault made a valuable contribution: his notion of the dichotomy between the *Desire to Know* and the *Desire for Truth* (*la Volonté de Savoir et la Volonté de Vérité*) and the processes of struggle and domination which take place in human societies, as inevitably affecting the content of the knowledge produced and disseminated in them. In his analysis, the interests guiding exclusion practices on the construction of truth are concealed behind the word knowledge/truth and the idea that through institutions and rules, domination could be attained. As knowledge/truth is determined through the various phenomena it presents, it results in endless subjectivity and practices of exclusion, embedded in their production (Foucault, 2008; 2011, 5–6). This subjectivity element will become clear in the construction of the meta-language, as an accumulation achieved through the dominance of particular groups and references in defining self-imposing themes in CIPT in Chapter 1.

Both al-Banna's and al-Bishri's writings, albeit differently, uncover the self-imposing themes of their public sphere and the practices of power over the latter. In a capsule, writings of al-Banna and al-Bishri are grasped in relation to these authorities. More concretely, I was preoccupied, in conducting this research, with answering one major question: *What are the self-imposing themes, and in what ways do they reflect in the intellectual production of al-Banna and al-Bishri?* To answer this question, other queries become indispensable, such as the following: What are the contours, if any, of the field called CIPT and what aspects constitute its power over Islamic intellectuals? How did Realpolitik/real politics[7] affect the content of CIPT themes, towards the state it exists today? What are the areas of contestation associated with these themes? Through which mechanisms do ruling regimes control debates on politics? How does intellectual production uncover/reflect the power of these ruling regimes?

Now, I turn to discuss my case selection. Across tens of books, with a focus on one or more Islamic intellectuals, scholars usually dedicate few lines to make explicit the considerations behind their selection: political affiliation, ideas and stances, influence in society, contribution to intellectual debates and so on. I chose to read the writings of Jamal al-Banna and Tariq al-Bishri, in contexts, for a combination of considerations that I will try to summarize here: each of them offered massive intellectual production and demonstrated exceptional autonomy from ruling regimes and political, social and/or economic actors. Autonomy is, once again, critical towards genuine intellectual contribution (Bourdieu, 5), as it, in principle, diminishes the influence of individuals and/or groups on the production of the intellectual. The abundance of their writings was a factor to their selection; they wrote throughout long decades, mainly under three autocratic regimes of Egypt's modern history. When put in their contexts, their writings do signify the authorities besieging Islamic Intellectuals. But studying them together, in one book, and with a comparative perspective, is driven by the explicit differences in their personal profiles and intellectual orientation.

Both have unique profiles. To elaborate, I offer a brief account on each of them. Al-Banna was born in 1920, the son of a watch mender and a teacher at the local mosque in al-Mahmudiyya. His brother, Imam Hasan al-Banna, was the renowned founder of the Muslim Brotherhood *(al-'Ikhwān al-Muslimūn)* (MB). Jamal al-Banna quit secondary school and resorted to his father's extensive library. During the early days of the MB movement, he participated in the publishing of its newspaper. In 1948, he was jailed with some of its most notable members and as a result clearly distanced himself from the MB (al-Bannā,

2008b, 10–11; al-Bannā, 1997, 7). After a brief and unsuccessful experience with party politics, al-Banna concentrated on the labour movement, something that is reflected in his various publications on syndicates and labour struggle (see al-Bannā, 2010b, 27; also al-Bannā, 1992). By the 1970s, topics relating to Islam also became part of his writings (al-Bannā 1972, 1979a, 1988). He was formerly a devout adherent to Marxism;[8] his adherence translated into active engagement with the labour force.[9] Aside from his brother's profile as the founder of one of the biggest Islamist movements in modern history, the key attraction of al-Banna's intellectual profile is that he defended what he termed *New Jurisprudence*, where he asserted the need to let go of the strict and exclusive commitment to the four schools of jurisprudence in Sunni Islam (see al-Bannā, 1995e, 2005a, 67–70).

His general intellectual orientation could be labelled *liberal*, especially with regard to rights and freedoms in general and rituals in Islam in particular. His character as an intellectual was further boosted through societal interest in his writings, which put him under media spotlights. In 2008, he was hosted by Dream TV, an Egyptian satellite TV station, to speak in a thirty-episode program throughout the month of Ramadan. With the help of a huge financial donation made by his sister Fawziyya al-Banna in 1997,[10] he founded a press house, which was the main avenue to publish tens of his books (Slackman, 2006; al-Bannā, 2008e, 246). He wrote and published around one hundred books in which he addressed Islam and Egyptian politics (al-Bannā, 1987; 1994a; 2003a), and he was often presented in the media as introducing 'progressive and critical interpretations of religious traditions' (Ettmueller, 2008).

Al-Bishri was born in 1933 in Hilmiyyat al-Zatun neighborhood in Cairo; his family was known for specializing in both religious theology and law. His grandfather, Salim al-Bishri, held a high-ranking position at al-Azhar University, and his father, 'Abd al-Fattah al-Bishri, was head of the Egyptian Highest Court of Appeal until his death in 1951. He graduated from the Law School of Cairo University in 1953, where he studied law, jurisprudence and Shari'a. After his graduation, he was appointed to Egypt's State Council (*Majlis al-Dawla*). His shift to Islamic Political Thought evolved after the 1967 defeat, after years of pure devotion to National Socialism, with a secularist overtone.[11] His ideas are widely applauded among both Egyptian and Arab academicians (see Ghānim. (ed.), 1999; Māher, 2019). Like al-Banna, he is an intellectual whose work strongly focused on Islam and Egyptian politics (see al-Bishrī, 1988, 1991a, 2011a).

Although he is largely classified as part of the contemporary reform movement, not only in Egypt but also in the Islamic world,[12] his intellectual production can be justifiably situated within the realm of mainstream CIPT, especially in the sense that he accepted and embarked upon the long-acknowledged rules and tenets of Islamic jurisprudence and didn't question these in his writings.[13] Once again, al-Bishri, like al-Banna, is an independent Islamic intellectual with no political affiliations, although Kifaya,[14] a renowned Egyptian protest movement, urged him to be its presidential candidate in the 2005 elections (see Blaydes, 2011, 184), and he was frequently cited on the MB website.[15]

To sum up on their profiles, both come from families with Islamic roots; while al-Banna is the youngest brother of Hasan al-Banna, al-Bishri's grandfather was an Islamic Sheikh. The judicial educational background of al-Bishri, in addition to his prestigious state occupation, largely contrast with al-Banna's lack of higher education and such a prestigious state position. Al-Banna's engagement with labour cannot be traced, at any time, in al-Bishri's professional life by virtue of being a judge in one of Egypt's most distinguished courts.[16] In addition to their varying relations to the MB, it is the most significant of all Islamist movements in Egypt.[17]

In reading their work, I found great use in Hermeneutics. Although born in the arms of Christianity,[18] it has gone beyond the limits of biblical interpretation (see Puolakka, 2011; Fairfield, 2011; Katsumori, 2011). Notably, the religiously driven/inspired nature of hermeneutic studies spilled over to Islam, with such themes like the hermeneutics of Qur'anic interpretation (*Tafsīr)* (see Vishanoff, 2011; Fudge, 2011; Valkenberg, 2011). The core of hermeneutical interpretation is that there is more than one way to read the interpreted (Faye, 2012, 84–5), and reading an intellectual's work within his/her contexts is what turns the reading into interpretation (see Rogers, 2012). Language itself does not have one single meaning; words are used in language games and involve different meanings according to their different uses (see Wittgenstein, 1958; Lindroos-Hovinheimo, 2012, 32). However, subjectivity in interpretation surpasses the language element and is embedded in the process of interpretation itself. To find a way to interpret texts, the act of interpretation could be deconstructed into two key stages: first is the understanding, a basic grasping of the meaning of the text as a whole; second is comprehension which is a sophisticated way of understanding the text, supported by explanatory procedure. Explanation will then occur between the two stages (see Ricoeur, 1970; see also Faye, 2012, 75). One starts from one's own familiar world knowledge, and any phenomenon is viewed in relation to this knowledge. This is the so-called *hermeneutical circle*; there is no understanding outside this circle of knowledge, although it cannot besiege the interpreter (Stolze, 2010, 61). In the hermenutical process, the intellectual is regarded as *past of the book* (Barthes, 1998).

This is why the two intellectuals' contexts are crucial to read their writings; for, their use of language, which is again subjective and malleable, cannot be fully grasped without adequate knowledge of their contexts. This is the case because hermeneutics simply assumes that the text, virtually any text, falls in the midway between the interpreter and the interpreted, in a cooperative process. It is driven by an attempt of the interpreter to *reach agreement* with the text, exactly like when two humans talk to one another, concerning what the text means (see Gothoni, 2011, 39). It is a double-layered process: the intellectuals' writings depict reality revolving within their hermeneutic circle and in my reading of them, for the purpose of writing this book, I am also besieged by my own prior knowledge, not just of the world but also of the language, the intellectuals and their writings.

In its emphasis on interpretation, hermenutics does concur with other methodologies, such as discourse analysis in the sense that, while seeking to qualitatively investigate texts, it sets assumptions on the effects of language, has a focus on how reality was produced and assumes that context is inseparable from the discourse itself (Burman and Parker, 1993; Hardy, 2001; Hardy, Phillips and Harley, 2004).

Like many scholars, I am aware of the limitations entrenched in the act of interpretation, due to the fact that assessments of truth-claims do not function irrespective of how we view the world under dispute (Margolis 1995, 41; Puolakka, 2011, 14). Prejudgements are inevitable and initially constitute our ability to experience and become aware of our own hermeneutical position. The act of understanding is not an *occurrence* that can be fully controlled and tested (Gothoni, 2011, 25–6). Yet, perception in the sense of both background knowledge (Chilton, 2004) and common cultural background as a tool in the act of interpretation itself (see Gadamer, 1960, 26; Stolze, 2010, 62) were central to my selection of both the book theme and the intellectuals studied.

Towards this end, I began with basic knowledge of their personal profiles and key themes they addressed in their writings. As the research developed into concrete questions and structure, I opted for more in-depth knowledge of their work, their intellectual shifts, the self-imposing themes in their public sphere and the authorities they need to watch out for in their writings. In this manner, the subjective element of the interpreter (me) was counterbalanced, or at least mitigated, through deeper knowledge of the research field.

In collecting data, I depended on both archival research and semi-structured interviews. The archival research was obviously in search for writings of both intellectuals. Through semi-structured interviews, I sought to enhance my knowledge of their profiles and writings, acquiring information not necessarily found in archival material on one hand, and exploring the multiple contexts of their intellectual production on the other. Finally, conducting the field work while both intellectuals were still alive was an opportunity that isn't available to many other authors of similar research interests.

In four related chapters, I present the various aspects of the book theme, highlighted so far. Chapter 1 is largely focused on the religious authority embedded in the key themes of CIPT across time, and the different debates comprised in these themes. Chapter 2 addresses the authority of ruling regimes, under which al-Banna and al-Bishri lived and contributed their writings, and how they dealt with this authority in their work. In this chapter, I demonstrate the interrelatedness between the public sphere where the intellectuals' writings *occurred* and the political sphere, which is typically a field of political rivalry. The red lines, set by ruling regimes, are reflected in their utterances, selection of topics and the content of their different writings. Finally, Chapters 3 and 4 focus on their writings within the contours of CIPT themes that are outlined in Chapter 1. Although I try to present the topic as neatly as possible, the contexts of their writings are multiple, and often overlap, I do my best to unweave how their intellectual production was shaped through these contexts.

1

Contemporary Islamic political thought

Today, because of intellectuals like al-Banna, al-Qimni and al-ʿAshmawi, the character of the Islamic has turned into a huge debate, necessitating a delineation of the contours of Contemporary Islamic Political Thought (CIPT) through its constituent elements, which turns into a prerequisite to properly address the contested character of Islamic intellectuals. Thus, in order to adequately read al-Banna and al-Bishri writings, a discussion of CIPT themes is the focus of this chapter.

As will be evident below, the content of CIPT themes, constituting integral elements of the Islamic meta-language, underwent significant shifts over time. Without these themes and their dynamic debates, I argue, no proper understanding of the intellectual production can be realized. For, the themes and their multiple *sub-debates* represent background information to the act of reading. Moreover, the increasing diversity in positions on them translated into dualities on mainstream-tajdīd (see Kamrava, 2006, 13–23) contesting the *religious truth*. Here, CIPT themes are addressed, at some length, to help define, towards the end of this book, the relative positions of al-Banna and al-Bishri in CIPT and their claims to the *true discourse*.

I depart from Salvatore's notion, outlined in the introduction, that the public sphere has a meta-language, which determines in what manner(s) issues are addressed as well as sets what issues are *worth* addressing. I add to Salvatore's conception, that the formation and shifts in CIPT were mainly guided by the processes of struggle and domination occurring in the history of Islam. In many instances, these processes set and reset priorities within CIPT major themes. This helps, a great deal, with understanding how particular actors/agents, usually labelled mainstream Islamic intellectuals, achieved dominant positions in defining the true discourse in the Foucauldian sense. I, thus, try to briefly delineate the contours of CIPT with an emphasis on Islamic heritage/al-turāth, set out the elements constituting the Islamic meta-language and define the areas of CIPT, over which mainstream/tajdīd camps contest the true discourse.

Unpacking CIPT

In writings on Islamic Political Thought, two key trends prevail. One that presents, more or less, a navigation of its terrain, an amalgamation of contributions and cares to determine key cross-cutting features (al-Bishrī, 1996c), tackles an assumed crisis (Enayat, 1984), or suggests ways to best deal with a crisis (Mitwallī, 1985). Such writings, in most of the cases, pay little or no concern for developing an accurate, or at least overt, contouring of the field, contours that would set the distinction between the Islamic intellectual[1] and others (see al-Shāmī, 2012).

The other trend is zoomed in on the writings of one or two Islamic intellectuals, usually with some reference to their biographies, offering detailed interpretations of their ideas. Under this category, one can list a few leading contributions: Muhammad 'Imara's study of 'Ali 'Abd al-Raziq ('Imāra, 1972); Ibrahim al-Bayumi Ghanim's study of Hasan al-Banna[2] (Ghānim,1992) and 'Abd al-'Ati Ahmed's study of Muhammad 'Abdu ('Aḥmad, 2012). Yet again, most of these writings aim at exhibiting, and often even celebrating,[3] writings of the intellectuals studied (see 'Imāra, 1997, 175–215; al-'Ulwānī, 2010). In many senses, studies of prominent Islamists, like Hasan al-Banna (see Krämer, 2010) or Muhammad 'Abdu ('Imāra, 1985, 309–35) may have contributed to an implicit sense of *agreement* on their character as Islamic, to the effect that being Islamic was not overtly addressed. One way to overcome this bewilderment, here I claim, is through highlighting CIPT constituent elements.

Heritage and Renewal (*Al-turāth wal-tajdīd*)

In scholarship on Islam and Islamic Thought, Islamic heritage, or al-turāth, mainly consists of Qur'an and Sunna[4] ('Arkūn, 1992, 101), history of Islam,[5] juridical, philosophical and intellectual contributions (Jid'ān, 1988, 15) deriving and building on these sources (Krämer, 2013). The tendency to rely on Islamic heritage in the construction of claims and arguments constitutes one major component of CIPT. However, Islamic renewal or al-tajdīd intellectuals take distinct positions towards al-turāth different from those adopted by their mainstream counterparts. In other words, it's not a disagreement, or even a debate about, whether there's an Islamic heritage/al-turāth, or that it is integral to employ it in CIPT writings, to legitimize the intellectual's character as Islamic. Rather, it's about what specifically from within this body of knowledge is constant, binding and relevant across time.

In this sense, al-turāth represents the key arena of contestation among Islamic intellectuals for claims of the true discourse. Within mainstream CIPT, the function of al-turāth is primarily to establish positions and opinions endorsed (see 'Imāra 1989b; Ḥilmī, 2005). Hence, the relation of intellectuals claiming tajdīd to al-turāth is significantly, though not entirely, different. Tajdīd intellectuals largely address it from the perspective of critique and revision as a basis to make different claims which deviate and often contradict those advocated by their mainstream counterparts (see Jid'ān, 1988; Ḥanafī, 1983; 62–9, 78). This, I claim, is a key distinction between mainstream and tajdīd intellectuals, namely, the way in which they relate to al-turāth in their writings.

The term tajdīd in CIPT, here I claim, connotes renewal which transgresses established rules and narratives of mainstream Islam, specially pertaining to Islamic heritage, and subsequently results in societal or intellectual practices of exclusion. It was often used to refer to the Islamic Reform Movement which countered Western domination and sought Islamic revival and reform; the movement emerged in the late nineteenth century and was back then considered tajdīd (Esposito, 2010, 90–2; Ṭabliyya, 2000, 9–24; Faḍl 'Allāh, 2004, 192). But today, this term is mainly used to refer to a wide range of intellectuals who promote *differing* positions and readings of Islamic scriptures, generally deviating from, or at least non-abiding by, the most established juristic contributions in al-turāth (see Kamrava, 2006; see also Krämer, 2011, 182–4). Thus, tajdīd, in its core, regenerates over time (Zaqzūq, 2012, 136).

Al-Banna's liberal stances invoke the Muslim/Islamic dilemma, where not all Muslim-born intellectuals, according to those opposing his writings, qualify as *Islamic*. This trickles down to the aforementioned question on juridical scholarship, as the minimum requirement for fulfilling such a qualification (see El-Hennawy, 2013). Likewise, the study of Islamic Political Thought, when focusing only on Muslim intellectuals who presented their ideas within the framework of juristic formal terminology and claims (see Enayat, 1984, 5), tends to favour mainstream contributions vis-à-vis tajdīd ones, who, in many cases, didn't receive juridical training. In this manner, juridical training actually becomes a blockade/barrier imposed on CIPT.

But blocking specific contributions to Islamic Political Thought isn't a novelty. Both al-Afghani and Muhammad 'Abdu, who were leading figures of the Islamic

Reform and Revival Movement in the nineteenth century, faced contestation to their Islamic character and were accused of not being true Muslims (Ayubi, 1991a, 58). Historically, several orders (*Firaq*) that fell under Theology (*'Ilm al-Kalām*)[6] and offered *differing* perspectives on sacred questions also faced contestation to their Islamic character (see 'Imāra, 1985). For instance, in the second half of the fourth century of Islam, 'Ikhwān al-Ṣafā, a society largely preoccupied with philosophy, became known to the world through the publication of some fifty tracts on both prophetic and philosophic knowledge. In their tracts, they questioned the divine origin of Muslim reason and tried to establish that senses were equal to revelation; the society along with their contributions were utterly rejected and excluded (Tibawi, 1976, 193).

In a similar vein, al-Mu'tazala, who had their emphasis on human intellect and debated the creation of Qur'an and God's features (Krämer, 2013, 101), and al-Murji'a, who did not consider obediences (*Ṭā'āt*) to be a part of the faith,[7] were considered deviants. These schools were also defamed and overtly condemned by ruling elites and established jurists of their times (see 'Arkūn, 1995, 191; Ḥilmī, 2005, 37–52; 'Imāra, 1985, 85). With the *different* content of their Ijtihad, they represented a contestation to mainstream narratives. Furthermore, in Islamic history, true Islam (*al-'Islām al-Ṣaḥīḥ*) was always contested; when Sunnis dominated, the Umayyad and Abbasid dynasties had considered all other communities heretic, or at least deviant. The same happened with Ismai'li Fatimids when they reached power in Tunisia; they treated Sunnis in a similar manner ('Arkūn, 1995, 97).

Today, mainstream and tajdīd camps mainly diverge on the hierarchy of elements of al-turāth. A widely known historical fact is that neither Qur'an nor Hadith were documented, into written texts, during the life of the Prophet. Under the third rightly guided Caliph, 'Uthman, the documenting of Qur'an as a written scripture was initiated (AD 645–652). Once the documenting came to an end, other *incomplete* versions of Qur'anic verses were terminated/annihilated ('Arkūn, 1992, 72–85). Similarly, the Prophet's practice of Sunna stayed largely in the form of tradition and was second to Qur'an (Tibawi, 1976, 87). It long stayed a verbal tradition but as the number of *alleged* Hadith increased by the eighth and ninth centuries AD, a growing need to determine the body of correct Hadith evolved (Krämer, 2013, 95–6).

In addition to Qur'an and Sunna, consensus (*'Ijmā'*) is another source of binding Islamic rules.[8] More precisely, it refers to clerics of the nation (*'Ulamā' al-'Umma*) decisively agreeing on a specific rule regarding one of the matters of religion (al-Qaraḍāwī, 1997a, 14), but the applicability of 'Ijmā' is a matter of intense juridical debate.[9] There is also Qiyās (analogy), where similarities are drawn between text and new situations when no definitive text directly applies ('Iqbāl, 2010, 39).

Whereas 'Ijmā' is totally inconceivable, if not technically impossible,[10] Qiyās is already debated as an independent source of binding rules. It is regarded as falling outside the scope of Origins of Jurisprudence (*'Uṣūl al-Fiqh*) (see al-Azmeh, 1988, 254–6). But the interpretation of rules went through significant shifts regarding the matter of (*Ta'wīl*), one form of exegesis. Originally, it was one way of reading and interpreting Islamic sources (see 'Arkūn, 1995, 192). In practice, it was used by early interpreters (*Mufassirīn*) and meant the mere act of interpreting. Jurists of later generations (*Muta'khkhirīn*) understood Ta'wīl, and treated it, as taking the text away from its original meaning, Ta'wīl is not viewed positively today (al-'Āṣī, 2009, 85–8).

Commonly, there is evident agreement, in CIPT, that Qur'anic text – albeit interpreted differently amongst jurists – is a constant (*Thābit*) and Hadith is *mostly* not questioned (see Faḍl 'Allāh, 1995, 15). Yet, whereas all intellectuals converge on the authenticity of Qur'anic verses (see 'Arkūn, 1995, 193; Krämer, 2013, 93), mainstream and tajdīd camps overtly disagree on Hadith. Tajdīd intellectuals usually argue that some, but not all, Hadith could be used as a reliable source towards understanding Islam, depending on consistency of its content with Qur'anic verses (see al-Banna, 2008c, 2010c).

This is surely not to imply that mainstream intellectuals regard all Sunna as equally credible. In mainstream scholarship, Sunna is generally divided into Sunna (*Mutawātira*), or widely spread tradition, and Sunna (*'Aḥād*), or tradition reported by a single companion. The widely spread Sunna is the sort relied upon in establishing the body of Sunna (al-Fiqī, 1986, 24–30). Sunna al-'Aḥād is viewed as highly influenced and coloured by the conflicts that plagued Islamic history ('Imāra, 1989a, 98–9). Thus, it is generally *not* used as a source for binding rules (Faḍl 'Allāh, 2004, 182). In addition, the juridical effort to maintain a body of credible Sunna was embodied in Hadith-telling (*Riwāyat al-Ḥadīth*), which was systematically launched after AD 750 (see An-Na'im, 2008, 324). There are six major Hadith-tellers in Sunni mainstream Islamic jurisprudence: al-Bukhari, Muslim, Abu Dawood, Ibn Majeh, Tirmithi and al-Nisaa'i (Hashim, n.d). The most credible of which is the convergence between Bukhari (died in AD 870) and Muslim (died in AD 875), the first two in the chain of Hadith-tellers (Krämer, 2013, 96).

The main difference between both camps pertains to the fact that tajdīd intellectuals, who do not necessarily abide by this aforementioned classification of Hadith categories and the ranking of Hadith-tellers in their works, highlight the consistency element as key criterion to accept Hadith content in setting binding rules. They also tend to disagree with their mainstream counterparts on the four Sunni juridical schools: Imam Ibn Hanbal, Abi Hanifa, Malik and al-Shafei (Bassiouni, 2012). Mainstream intellectuals generally accept the binding and/or exclusive nature of these schools (see Hūwaidī, 1987, 111; Faḍl 'Allāh, 2004, 61, 188). They do not end up establishing their own jurisprudence independent and apart from them (see al-Sharīf, 1984; al-Zuḥīlī, 2006), but tajdīd intellectuals usually do (see 'Arkūn, 1995, 117). Accordingly, the departure point is quite similar, the relative weight and centrality of these four schools are different among mainstream and tajdīd contributions.

Yet, then and now, the blockades imposed on the Islamic concur with Foucault's desire for truth, as embedded in struggles and domination practices. Those who present mainstream jurisprudence in Sunni Islam play the role of guardians of the faith; *producers* of the true discourse. Thus, they have the *authority* to set the contours of this discourse and can reject contributions which contradict their understandings. In fact, the domination aspect holds clear political implications, as mainstream clerics/intellectuals were accused of promoting ideas of obedience to the ruler under the claim that an unjust ruler is better than political unrest. Many of them traditionally enjoyed strong ties to ruling monarchs, kings, sultans and the like,[11] who used them to bestow religious legitimacy on their rule[12] (see Ayubi, 1991a, 61, 4–5, respectively).

This is not to suggest that *all* mainstream jurists and intellectuals are culprits that conspire against freedoms and rights. Adhering to the understandings above on the heritage and the exclusive role of the four Sunni jurisprudential schools doesn't automatically translate into serving repressive political rule. Yet, it's a fact that a significant part of the dominance of mainstream interpretations of Islam was achieved through such alliances between Islamic clerics and ruling emperors/monarchs/sultans. Meanwhile, as will be discussed shortly, the heritage isn't a static constellation and this resonated in changes in what mainstream stands for across time.

Hence, if the field of intellectual production is a market, where suppliers compete for demand (see Bourdieu, 1984; Gartman, 2013, 104–5), when new Ijtihad is presented, there is the danger of sharing, eating up or diminishing the power of the mainstream, which, again, traditionally allied with the state/ruling elite (see Ayubi, 1995, 84). Put differently, positions advocated by tajdīd intellectuals and their revisiting of the heritage inevitably splits the public sphere, once dominated by mainstream intellectuals, to comprise diverse intellectual products. The intellectual market would, subsequently, witness more competition among these different *suppliers* divided along the line of mainstream and tajdīd. The formers would not, thus, enjoy the kind of hegemonic status they had before the latters started *sharing* the public sphere. Subsequently, the struggle against tajdīd is not just a struggle for the religious truth, it is also a contestation to the power attained by the mainstream.

In Egypt, the homeland of both al-Banna and al-Bishri, this contestation actualized more than once. Nasr Hamid Abu Zaid, an Egyptian professor of Arabic literature, who suggested a different hermeneutic interpretation of Qur'anic text, in one of his research papers, expectedly collided with mainstream jurisprudence. He was tried and sentenced to legal separation from his wife (see al-ʿAwwā, 2003, 7, 23–6, 71). Hasan Hanafi, Egyptian professor of philosophy, also faced legal charges when he was accused of apostasy in 1997 (al-Azm, 2011, 4). Although Hanafi was acquitted of the charges, his accusation and trial fell perfectly within the same contestation on the true discourse. Hanafi overtly criticized blind adherence to turāth,[13] including the four major Sunni juristic schools (Ḥanafī, 1983, 56; 78), a critique that is typical in tajdīd writings.

The body of turāth itself went through refinements and filtrations, which related, in most cases, directly to real politics. One key example, in this respect, is of excluding Jaʿfarism (*al-Jaʿfariyya*),[14] a school of Shiite jurisprudence, from the body of Sunni juridical scholarship (see Zulkifli, 2013, 95–7), or the refinements to the body of Hadith tradition above. Thus, though it might seem that the body of Sunni heritage is a consented *whole* from which mainstream derives, and tajdīd critically revises, the widely acknowledged turāth in Sunni Islam, today, was already contested and *filtered* more than once in Islamic history. Accordingly, turāth itself, which is a basic ingredient of the Islamic meta-language and the positioning of both mainstream and tajdīd, does not connote the same exact *thing* across time.

Nonetheless, there has always been an aspect of turāth to react to and a dimension of accumulation, as every generation of intellectuals claiming a contribution to Islamic Political Thought viewed and treated, not necessarily all, writings of earlier generations as turāth. The writings of nineteenth-century intellectuals, like ʿAbdu and al-Afghani, quoted and cited earlier contributions to Islamic Thought that preceded their own writings (see ʿImāra, 2006, 443–5; ʿImāra, 1988, 55). Likewise, writings of b. Taimiyya and b. Khaldun dealt with earlier contributions of their time as turāth (see 'Ibn Taiymiyya, 1951; Ṣāliḥ, 1983, 73–84). Practically, turāth turns into a dynamic accumulation of contributions of every *generation*, which then seeks relevance and linkage to earlier ones. This way, older interpretations constitute parts/elements of newer ones, although the latter do not present as replica of the former. Subsequently, different combinations of the old and the new shape the ultimate content of CIPT writings, as we know it today through the works of various Islamic intellectuals.

Contemporary as recent

In multiple sources, the term *contemporary* is used as a synonym for *recent* (see al-Jābrī, 1992, 10; Ḥanafī, 1983; Sardar, 1999, 14; Burgat, 1997, 38; Krämer, 2010, 92). The key criterion of contemporaneity is the ability to witness the phenomenon studied.[15] In this sense, it implies that the author witnessed the studied phenomenon. I use it in a broader sense, though, to include witnesses who can directly describe an event, even if I wasn't yet born or physically there to witness it myself. Al-Banna and al-Bishri started writing and publishing their work before I was born (1981), but both were still alive when the fieldwork for this research was conducted. They provided invaluable details about their writings, their contexts and personal biographies.[16] Because the bulk of their production stretches back to the mid-twentieth century, they do fit into the *contemporary*, which hereafter refers to the Second World War onwards.

Luckily, it has quite similar connotations, in Western as well as non-Western academia (al-Jābrī, 1992, 10; Djaiit, 1978, 7; Krämer, 2010, 92). This convergence overrides the dilemma of Euro-centrism commonly invoked in research on world history, whereby human history is entirely defined and classified in relation to European history and developments:

> The military, political and cultural supremacy of Europe made its ideas, values and ideals prevail over large parts of the globe, so much so that they came to be regarded as the international norm. It is thus no surprise that Europe not only saw itself as the centre of the world, but also considered the prevalence of its ideas, values and ideals to be clear proof of their superiority or naturalness. (Das, 2005, 8)

With contemporaneity defined as recent, CIPT starts neither in the mid-eighteenth century nor in the nineteenth century, as argued by Enayat and al-Bishri, respectively (Enayat 1984; al-Bishrī, 1996c). Subsequently, the works of prominent Islamic intellectuals like ʿAbdu and al-Afghani, though frequently cited and long celebrated in the literature on Islamic Thought (see Ḥanafī, 1983, 101–119; ʿImāra, 2006; al-ʿIrāqī, 1995), do not belong to CIPT. They lived, wrote and published before the start of *contemporaneity* and thus belong to the larger category of Islamic Political Thought.

Here, the relevance of ʿAbdu, al-Afghani (see Ayubi, 1991a, 57) and al-Tahtawi (see Muḥammad, 2007, 89–114), along with many other prominent names from earlier generations, like b. Taimiyya and b. Khaldun, confines to Islamic heritage/al-turāth. The latter falls mainly outside, and earlier than, CIPT and this doesn't negate that a great majority of the writings that today present under the banner of CIPT were inspired by, and built upon, this heritage (see Ḥilmī, 2005; ʿImāra, 1985, 309–35).

The 'Islamic'

As a faith, Islam is the religious creed of over one billion individuals of different racial and national backgrounds around the globe (Nyang et al., 2012, 4; see also Krämer, 2011, 62). Addressing the *Islamic* entails more than the faith in Islam. It is as diverse as its followers and takes on different shapes based on the cultural factors of the latter (al-Bahii, 1991, 51). One can safely claim there are various understandings and presentations of the religious truth (Bayat, 2007, 89).

Accordingly, defining the *Islamic* and its subsequent study entails identifying Islam as a religion with *associated* fields; it is a religion, which reflects, and is relevant to, many other aspects of human life. In addition to the faith, Hodgson's Islamicate, highlighted in the introduction, represents both the multifaceted nature of this scholarly field and the guide to its study. Just for the highlight, Islamicate connotes Islam *itself* as the religion, what could properly be called Islamic, and things *typically* linked to Islam. It, thus, refers to Islam, along with the *social and cultural complex* associated with it and Muslims throughout its history (Hodgson, 1974, 59). In this sense, CIPT qualifies as one of the complexes presented by Hodgson because the heritage element, which was long associated with Islam and its history, is central to the construction of CIPT. I use the Islamicate, here, to emphasize that the Islamic does not have to solely associate with the Religion of Islam and its traditionally consented juridical scholarship. Intellectual production deriving explicitly from Islamic sources can, in principle, be identified as part of the Islamic field.

Several Islamic intellectuals were labelled Islamic; for they *dealt in Islamic subjects* with no emphasis on their personal piety or political preference (Ayubi, 1991a, 67). The Islamic could simply refer to the demand to turn Islam, as understood by the respective group or individuals, into a program, or code of conduct (Krämer, 2000a, 32). Yet again, I argue, using Islamic heritage towards making claims and arguments is a key element in being Islamic.

Languages and places

Speaking of tajdīd, I would like to highlight the role of utterances in CIPT scholarship. Cross-cuttingly, juridical education and/or training usually self-reveal in the terminology used, mainly through the eloquence and depth of the debates presented.[17] For instance, the juridical content and depth exhibited in writings by al-Qaradawi or ʿImara (see al-Qaraḍāwī, 1997c, 89–112; ʿImāra, 1989b), compared to those of Jamal al-Banna or Nasr Hamid Abu Zaid, who come from non-juridical backgrounds and did not receive religious training or education, cannot be overlooked.[18] Still, juridical background does not necessarily set a line of demarcation between mainstream and tajdīd, as might be implied here. Saʿid al-ʿAshmawi, for instance, a prominent tajdīd intellectual, is a former judge, who studied Islamic jurisprudence as part of his legal education at Cairo University. When he addressed turāth, he did it with the purpose of critique and revision, not mainly or solely for seeking legitimacy of deriving rules, in the way the mainstream body of contributions to CIPT normally does (see al-Ashmawy, 1987).

Needless to say, the problem with conceding to the view that juridical education is a prerequisite to CIPT authorship is the inevitable augmenting of the already huge power of religious institution/s (see al-Qimnī, 2006), which would, thus, monopolize the religious truth. Religious institutions that offer this kind of training are generally affiliated with the state and concedes to its exclusive authority; thus, they commonly promote the power and hegemony of the latter.

Likewise, language/s and countries where Islamic intellectuals present their ideas could play some role in moulding the religious truth; particular languages generally associate with specific discourse(s) on Islam. For instance, most writings produced in languages of Muslim-dominated countries,[19] like Arabic, Turkish or Iranian, conform to respective state-acknowledged mainstream jurisprudence, or at least do not easily collide with major tenets of the latter. Likewise, quite often, books on Islam or the larger Islamicate published in Muslim-dominated countries emphasize norms of tolerance, justice, victory and the like as part of Islamic history. They may also reiterate elements from the established turāth of Islamic Political Thought (see al-Khaiyyāṭ, 1989; al-Qaraḍāwī, 1985). This observation might relate to the fact that Arabic, for instance, is not only the language of millions of Muslims but also that of Qur'an and the language of the Muslim community in early history of Islam (see Krämer, 2011, 64).

Conversely, in non-Muslim languages and/or countries, the tendency to deviate, or accept the deviance, from these established narratives is noticeably more salient, even when the intellectual originally comes from a Muslim background. *Satanic Verses*, the widely disputed book by Salman Rushdie, an intellectual of Iranian origins, is one good example in this respect. Though translated into many other languages, the book's widely known version is the English one, which appeared and spread in countries with long-established secular traditions ('Arkūn, 1995, 145). Celebrated in the West, Rushdie's deviance from mainstream conceptions of Islam resulted in the Iranian authorities, in February 1989, issuing a *fatwa* (religious opinion), allowing his murder and one of the book's translators was stabbed to death in his office in 1991.[20] The novel clearly represented contestation to Iranian state authority, which is one of the very few Muslim-dominated countries where moral authority is merged with the state (see Bayat, 2010, 157). Thus, the attack on him and his book was an act of struggle for dominance, not only for the religious truth but also for the hegemony intertwined with religious clergy. Again, this language and country barrier is an area where the exercise of dominance towards the construction of CIPT and the Islamic meta-language could be easily detected. Although CIPT writings do not differentiate between *sub-discourses* based on language, the visible tendency to conform in languages used in Muslim-dominated countries means Islamic intellectuals are besieged, through both language and country in which they contribute their work.

Yet, I would add a grain of salt to the above, as the vast dissemination of knowledge induced by media technological advancements and the internet posed challenges to religious clergy and state-sponsored writings on Islam. It extended the space in the public sphere for *new* interpretations of Islam as faith and practice (see Anderson, 1999, 41; Salvatore and Eickelmann, 2004; Zaman, 2004, 129–31). I argue that these interpretations are eating up the dominant position long enjoyed by mainstream CIPT. Al-Banna, Hanafi and al-Qimni, to name a few, write and speak of tajdīd interpretations of al-turāth, which overtly deflect from their mainstream counterparts, and they do so in Arabic (see Al-Bannā, 2003a, 2005c; Ḥanafī, 1990, 69 and 78). Albeit that many of these intellectuals faced restrictions of different kinds, including public defamation, book confiscations or even court trials, they already use/d new media outlets to promote their ideas, and earlier generations didn't have these outlets to utilize.

To conclude, I define the Islamic within the broad conception of Hodgson above, where the study of the Islamic is not confined to the faith; it comprises the broader cultural and social complex associated with Islam and includes both intellectuals with and without religious training, presenting mainstream or tajdīd interpretations of Islam, as long as they use Islamic heritage to make their claims and promote Islam, as a political demand or code of conduct, in their writings.

Ultimately, CIPT hereafter will be used to connote 'spoken and written language seeking reference from Islamic heritage towards establishing claims and/or arguments, with the ultimate aim of promoting Islam as a political program or code of conduct, on the various manifestations of power, both at the levels of state and society, starting the Second World War onwards'.

CIPT themes

Commonly, writings on Islamic Political Thought, as a scholarly field, address particular themes, in a recurrent manner,[21] and eventually these themes become, in part, constitutive of the Islamic meta-language (see al-Mīlād, 1999; Khalaf 'Allāh, 2010; al-Jābrī, 1992). Although I seek to outline these key themes, I never make a claim, either here or at any other occasion, to present an exclusive account on the latter. It is not the goal to tackle each and every debate comprised in CIPT. Pinpointing these four themes, below, is solely based on their character as *predominantly addressed* in writings falling under CIPT. I do claim that debates comprised under these four themes should be addressed for a proper reading of the latter, especially with the existing contestation between mainstream and tajdīd intellectuals on *the truth* of these themes, translating into claims and counter-claims. These are the state in Islam, *Sharī'a* application, violence as a means of political action (usually under the theme of Jihad) and Islamic identity.

State in Islam or the Islamic state?

How Islam relates to politics attracted scholarly attention for long decades (Fattah, 2006; Salvatore and Eickelman, 2004). *Political Islam* is, in its core, one of the manifestations of the interplay between Islam and politics (Ayubi, 1991a). Historically, the caliphate was the *consented* form of government in Islam, both de facto and de jure. But the convergence between scholarship and real politics has its roots in early history of Islam, particularly starting after the death of the Prophet. The Muslim community was suddenly faced by a leadership crisis after

Muhammad passed away ('Imāra, 1989a, 88–9); thus, Islam was from the outset associated with politics (see Arnason et al., 2006, 11–12). This consensus stayed largely intact ever since the death of the prophet and until the early decades of the twentieth century.

The first serious blow to the caliphate, as a political order, came with the renowned book *al-Islam wa Usul al-Hukm* (Islam and the Origins of Rule), first published in 1925, by 'Ali 'Abd al-Raziq, who, back then, served as an Azhari Sheikh and through this book represented a contestation to the long-established theory and practice of Islamic politics. 'Abd al-Raziq was chastised and eventually fired from his rank in al-Azhar, stripped of his acknowledged juridical authority[22] (Hūwaidī, 1987, 81; 'Imāra, 1972; Faḍl 'Allāh, 1995, 71–2). He was eventually acquitted, the verdict against him overturned and the prohibition on his recruitment to government posts lifted (Hatina, 2000, 38–41). But his daring thesis and subsequent exclusion embodied Foucault's desire for truth, which signified practices of domination, as the group achieving dominance in defining true discourse excluded and marginalized his ideas from CIPT. His case showed clear competition in the intellectual market and the use of mainstream power in it, which is granted by the state, to maintain its position as setting the religious truth.

Yet, the political context of both 'Abd al-Raziq's position and the subsequent attack on him could not be overlooked. As stated above, the book was published in 1925; it was not long after the Ottoman Empire collapsed (Brunner, 2004, 82–7) and a few months after Mustafa Kemal Ataturk formally abolished the caliphate in March 1924 (see al-Ashmawy, 1994, 16). In the Arab world, this was a strong blow to the very political existence of Islam, which was, again, for centuries embodied in this particular political order (see Ṭabliyya, 2000, 18). Accordingly, 'Abd al-Raziq's book, in a way, fortified the position of this nascent state, as according to his thesis, the collapse of the Ottoman Empire, and its caliphate rule, didn't represent a violation to stipulations of Islam.

Yet, the debate on the caliphate as an Islamic rule (*Ḥukm 'Islāmī*) (al-Kinānī, 1998, 25) gradually became part of al-turāth, regarded largely as belonging to history of Islam, not imminently coming into question when politics in Islam is debated (see al-Jābrī, 1992, 91–5; al-'Arawī, 1984, 169). Simultaneously, other questions became central, such as the state in Islam in terms of structure, prerogatives and guiding principles. These debates could be brought under a key theme: the *Islamic state* (al-*Dawla al-'Islāmiyya*) (see Mashhūr, 2004, 9–12).

Very often, this invokes/d the differentiation between an Islamic state and a theocratic one, that derives from *revelation laws* that can neither be modified nor challenged through popular majorities or a ruling monarch[23] (see 'Iqbāl, 2010, 35). Today, the theocratic state, which Islamic intellectuals usually link to the medieval church-state history in Europe, is largely detested (see Hūwaidī, 1987, 102). But the general trend in writings of mainstream contributions revolves around Islam as both a religion and politics; that state, regardless of divergence on details, is part of the faith of Islam (see al-Qaraḍāwī, 1997c, 89; 'Imāra, 1988; 1989b). The underlying rationale is that, at some point in Islamic history, it existed and Islam does, allegedly, offer a theory on/of the state (see Ayubi, 1991a, 1).

Within the tajdīd camp, the Islamic state existed only briefly (al-'Arawī, 1984, 123); intellectuals like al-Jabri and al-'Ashmawi maintain that political rule is not an intrinsic part of the faith of Islam. Muslim societies should not, subsequently, be restricted by preset patterns of rule that were applied throughout Islamic history and may freely adopt Western structures and practices of rule, whenever they see them fit (al-Jābrī, 1990a, 49; al-Ashmawy, 1987).

Yet, with the Islamic state usually conceptualized as an alternative to the secular one (Krämer, 2011, 58), tajdīd stances that reject the notion of the Islamic state trigger tense mainstream/tajdīd contestations, which directly relate to a common intellectual and societal juxtaposition between the Islamic and the secular, especially in the Arab Middle East, depicting the secular as encroaching on the Islamic (see al-Ghazālī, 1987, 133–6; al-Qaraḍāwī, 1997b). Today, media plays a huge role in highlighting such contestations. When 'Abd al-Raziq wrote his aforementioned book, media was not diversified or massive in its production and dissemination.[24] This has changed in the last two decades; as stated earlier, when tajdīd intellectuals present their renewal schemes, they have more than one avenue to present their ideas; to get read and heard and to elaborate on their stances in public.[25] In other words, media allowed them to thrive,[26] and hence added to the contestation facing the religious authority of mainstream intellectuals, including religious clergy who typically promote mainstream CIPT (see Esposito, 2010, 8).

Yet, particular themes are not so clearly cut along the mainstream/tajdīd demarcation; the binding nature of the *Shura* practice is an example, where CIPT intellectuals disagree on the matter (al-Hibri, 1999a, 75). The Islamic state, today, entails a key debate on Shura as a way of governance, that is mainly preoccupied with what the word Shura means and how central it is to Islam's conception of the state/political rule.[27] It expectedly touches upon whether Shura could/couldn't be applied, and if yes, how it is/should be applied (see Ḥawwā, 1994, 125–9; Ramaḍān, 1987, 74–6). Although it is based on definitive text (*Naṣ Qaṭ'ī*) of Qur'an,[28] Shura, in linguistic terms, does *not* oblige the ruler to abide by its content (al-Jābrī, 1992, 126). Mainstream contributions do not exclude Western practices, as contemporary societies pose challenges to the application of Shura and the way it was endorsed during early years of Islam. They commonly consider the juridical term of the General Good (*al-Maṣlaḥa al-'Āmma*)[29] (Zaman, 2004, 131–5), reaching the conclusion that Islamic Shura does not contradict, in fact requires, organs/structures that are associated today with Western democracy. They use terms like collective Shura (*al-Shūrā al-Jamā'iyya*), which should be based on organized opposition, such as associations and parties ('Imāra, 1989a, 96–106; see also al-Mīlād, 1999, 148).

Interestingly, the juxtaposition of democracy and Shura was sometimes situated within a wider juxtaposition between democracy and Islam (see al-Jabri, 2009, 122–6 and al-Zuḥīlī, 2006, 450–69), where the debate on Shura and democracy takes one of two directions: either Shura is presented as *better* than democracy (al-Turābī, 1988), or that Shura is the Islamic version of, and/or is *comparable to*, democratic settings such as parliamentary politics or separation of powers (see Sharaf, 1982; al-Hibri, 1999a, 77; al-Jābrī, 1992, 120). But the inclusion of elements from Western political structures and arrangements as conducive to applying Shura is not a line of division between mainstream/tajdīd intellectuals.

The discussion on Shura and the call for democratic politics cannot, however, be grasped in disconnect with political realities of the largest part of Islamic history (see Faḍl 'Allāh, 1995, 115), commonly discussed under terms like the Just Despot (*al-Mustabid al-'Ādil*) (see al-Jābrī, 1992, 130–1). The continuity of the Shura debate in CIPT might well be a by-product of continued autocratic regimes in most Muslim-dominated countries (see al-Hibri, 1999b, 523). Plus, there is an undeniable element of real politics to the relative centrality of the debate on Shura because of the strong appeal of democracy in many Arab countries (al-Jābrī, 1992, 119–20), a system of rule which originated and developed in the West (al-Mīlād, 1999, 48). After the fall of the Soviet Block and the subsequent end of the Cold War, democracy was coined as the only plausible alternative. *The End of History and the Last Man* (Fukuyama, 1992) gave a new impetus to democratic settings; one key question took centre stage: Can the Islamic state be democratic? (see Krämer, 2011, 117; see also Sisk, 2000, 15–32).

Shari'a: Orientalism in focus

> The place of Islamic law in the modern world is part and parcel of the fate of the Religion that gave birth to and nourished the law. (Arabi, 2001, 189)

These words encapsulate the core of Shari'a as a key CIPT theme: the association between Islamic law, derived from Shari'a, and the faith as a sacred revelation, the angle from which Shari'a is mostly discussed in writings of Islamic intellectuals (al-Qaraḍāwī, 1985, 11–14). It is perceived to cover both rules regulating beliefs and rituals (*al-Mu'taqadāt wa-l-Ṭuqūs*), and that of transactions among people (*Mu'āmalāt*),[30] through legal and moral principles (see al-Shirbīnī, 1999, 10).

In early days of Islam, theft, adultery and murder, among other crimes, were penalized with specific punishments drawn from Qur'anic text, and could be presented as a rule according to God's revelation (*al-Ḥukm bi-mā 'Anzal 'Allāh*[31]). These were largely known as God's penalties (*Ḥudūd 'Allāh*) (see al-Qaraḍāwī, 1985, 102–4). Though these penalties were based on the text of Qur'an, the most binding of all texts and the most respected component of all the heritage (Krämer, 2011, 184), there was no unified codified Shari'a until the nineteenth century (Griffel, 2007). After the death of the Prophet, both Abi Bakr and 'Umar adopted variations of *Ḥudūd*, as applied during the life of the Prophet. Abi Bakr fought those who refrained from paying the Islamic almsgiving (*Zakāt*), in what is known in the literature as Wars of Apostasy (*Ḥurūb al-Ridda*), and named 'Umar as his successor. But the Prophet did neither in his life (see Faḍl 'Allāh, 1995, 87). Likewise, 'Umar tagged prices to commodities and stopped giving part of the Zakāt to those whose hearts were inclined towards Islam (al-*Mu'allafati Qulūbuhum*),[32] but the Prophet prohibited price tagging and gave part of Zakāt to this category (Hūwaidī, 1987, 74).

Jurisprudence (Fiqh), a word commonly used in Shari'a debates, is not identical to Shari'a (see Griffel, 2007). It is the intellectual and systematic attempt to interpret principles of the latter and is carried out by jurists (see Ajijola, 2007, 15). Jurisprudence, particularly through schools of juridical scholarship, came much later in Islamic history, under the Abbasid Caliph al-Ma'mun (rule 813–33). Al-Ma'mun was a relatively tolerant caliph, and the four Sunni juridical schools, named after their founders, represented alternative methods of deriving rules (*'Istikhrāj al-'Aḥkām*). Still, Shari'a continued to be neither unified nor codified (Krämer, 2013, 87; 97; see also An-Na'im, 2008, 324).

The point I am trying to highlight here is that de facto Shari'a was applied much earlier than the de jure one, and that political context played a dual role: it paved the way for juridical scholarship on Shari'a under al-Ma'mun on one hand, and suppressed further Ijtihad under autocratic rulers in later phases of Islamic history on the other (see Krämer, 2013). Accordingly, de facto Shari'a varied under different caliphs, before it was codified into laws in the nineteenth century (see Griffel, 2007, 15). The de jure Shari'a, that the four schools significantly established, inevitably embodied hermeneutic interpretation and relativism. This is clearest in the case of Imam al-Shafi'i, founder of the Shafi'i juridical school, who modified his jurisprudence after he moved from Iraq to Egypt (al-Hibri, 1999b, 509; Hūwaidī, 1987, 74–5).

Unsurprisingly, tajdīd intellectuals often highlight this dimension, namely the impact of history and hermeneutics on the body of al-turāth in two parallel ways. First, as an argument towards promoting tolerance for various interpretations of Qur'an and Hadith, the primary sources of Islam (see Ḥanafi, 1983, 69; 78; 'Arkūn, 1995, 117). Second, as another argument that relativism and contexts did shape established Islamic rules (Ḥanafi, 1990, 45; 'Arkūn, 1992, 43; 114; Ayubi, 1995, 84). In other words, reading text, any text, must be done within its hermeneutic circle (see Stolze, 2010, 61; Katsumori, 2011, 94) and invokes the role of the interpreter in the act of interpretation (Davidson, 2001, 14).

In addition, serious contestation is associated with whether Ḥudūd, as a component of Shari'a, should/could be applied today (see Ḥanafi, 1990, 44). This dimension of the debate, in its current form, was greatly shaped by developments Muslim-dominated societies incurred as consequences of both modernization and direct colonization. The modernization scheme was actually intended as a defensive measure against European encroachment (Ayubi, 1995, 86–7). Muhammad II (ruled 1451–81), the Ottoman, was probably the first Muslim ruler to endorse a collection of laws, known as (Qanun-name) in the fifteenth century, to be used, side by side, with the written but not codified Shari'a. The collections covered areas of rule and administration and parts of the penal code. Yet, in the seventeenth century, European intervention was augmented under the auspices of, for instance, protection of Catholic and Orthodox communities. In Egypt, Muhammad 'Ali, the Ottoman ruler who arrived in 1801, endorsed European-inspired modernization of the army, the economy and civil service. Nonetheless, European-inspired reforms were applied via new institutions, without removing traditional settings (Krämer, 2013, 198; 217; 252–6).

In the nineteenth century, the traditional state resorted to legal codes and procedures inspired by positive law, without consulting Islamic jurists or using their hermeneutics. The practice was further intensified under the nation-state, before gradually and steadily giving up on Shari'a as the sole source for legislation (Ghuliyūn, 2007, 431). Such contestations to Islamic codes of conduct gave rise to many reform movements, including the renowned Wahhabi *reform* movement (Krämer, 2013, 247–8). Thus, after Islamic history witnessed both the establishment of the four juridical schools and the assumed application of Shari'a under different Islamic dynasties, modernization and colonization incited a strong shift in the nature of the debate. The primary goal was focused on answering the more imminent question of whether Shari'a (here mainly ḥudūd) could be applied after these developments altered the landscape of Muslim states and societies and how to relate to positive law as a manifestation of the infringement on the Muslim self.

> For those who think that applying Shari'a is just changing laws, especially those regarding crimes and penalties (al-ḥudūd), are also wrong, because they think that applying Shari'a is through whipping the one drinking wine and cutting off the hand of the thief, stoning or whipping the adulterer and other penalties, and this is a huge misconception. ('Abd al-'Azīz, 2001, 61)

Nowadays, within the debate on ḥudūd as a component of Shari'a theme in CIPT, two major trends could be traced. The first is an overt calling for a Shari'a/ḥudūd revival, especially where definitive and explicit text (*Naṣ Qaṭ'ī wa Ṣarīḥ*) exists (Faḍl 'Allāh, 2004, 195; 213–33; al-Khaṭīb, 1982). This is the position frequently propagated in mainstream writings (see al-Ghazālī, 1987). The second seeks *compromises*; it claims that applying Shari'a does not necessarily mean radically uprooting positive law, as applied today in many Muslim-dominated countries. Most tajdīd intellectuals fall under this category.

On this particular point, the latter employ Islamic jurisprudence to support their position, emphasizing the cause (*'Illa*), which, according to them, in many cases does not exist anymore. To them, when 'illa ceases to exist, there should be no obligation to apply ḥudūd (al-Jābrī, 1992, 63). As evident from this divergence on its application, the dichotomy is actually one of text (*Naṣ*) versus benefit (*Maṣlaḥa*),[33] that is, of the room for hermeneutic interpretation vis-à-vis the wording of explicit text (*Naṣ Ṣarīḥ*) (see Hūwaidī, 1987, 79–88; Faḍl 'Allāh, 1995, 91).

They also argue for the non-replicable nature of the early history (see al-Ashmawy, 1994, 12). In this regard, contemporaneity turns out to be an essential ingredient of the tajdīd proposition. The virtuous nature of early Islamic society, under the Prophet and the rightly guided caliphs ('Uwaiys, 2002, 144), is often highlighted as one obstacle to the application of ḥudūd in the contemporary world. According to this line of argument, they were applied in early history of Islam, which is the non-replicable part of the heritage, where authority did not merely revolve around coercion (al-Ashmawy, 1994, 12). Additionally, they assert these penalties are originally meant for deterrence, rather than application (see Hakeem et al., 2012, 7–23). For mainstream counterparts, the fact that ḥudūd are overtly mentioned in Qur'an and were applied during the early days of Islam largely known as the golden age[34] (*al-'Aṣr al-Dhahabī*) establishes the argument to apply ḥudūd (see al-Qaraḍāwī, 1985). The disagreement could be situated, I argue, within the larger debate on tajdīd and specifically on its limits (Krämer, 2011). While mainstream intellectuals usually confine tajdīd to Mu'āmalāt (Farrūkh, 1986, 9–10), tajdīd counterparts expand its scope to rituals, like praying and fasting (see al-Bannā, 2002a; 2005a).

To capture the variation, the debate on ḥudūd pertains to details and does not dispute the wider theme of Shari'a. Both camps do not defy the concept itself as an integral component of Islam that should, or could, be applied (see Hūwaidī, 1987, 55–78). Additionally, both depart from, and converge on, traditional Islamic theology: that God laid rules that must be followed/abided by (see Krämer, 2011, 29). Likewise, the hermeneutic interpretation produced by the four juridical schools may be disputed, but never the sacredness of the text itself, especially of Qur'an, upon which their scholarship is based (Krämer, 2011, 184–5). Thus, the different positions on the matter emanate from different hermeneutic interpretations of an almost identical body of heritage and, unsurprisingly, yield very different positions on the matter of Shari'a in its ḥudūd dimension.

Violence: Debating the 'subjective'

Islamic troops conquered vast territories in the thirteenth and fourteenth centuries (Said, 1978, 59); early Islamic history witnessed vast military conquests, which are known as *Futūḥāt*. In the writings of Islamic intellectuals, these conquests are generally depicted as not only righteous but also glorious; a source of pride and a sign of strength in the heritage (see 'Ibn Taiymiyya, 1993, 124–5; al-Shihābī, 1992, 29). Yet, whether these conquests were launched in assumed abidance to the dictations of Islam (Tibawi, 1976, 53; Farrūkh, 1986, 79–80) or the mere calculations of real politics, as part of a larger perspective that politics shaped the history of Islam (see Lambton, 1981, 13; Bielfeldt, 2004, 158), is a huge debate in Islamic Political Thought that is seemingly still relevant today (see al-Jābrī, 1992, 87–90). As widely documented, the Muslim community, right after the Prophet's death, was faced with the issue of government, upon which it had to establish some rules for political authority and conduct[35] (Ayubi, 1991a, 1–34; see Bielfeldt, 2004, 158). Thus, history of Islam was neither wholly nor exclusively guided by stipulations of the faith. Such a perspective gives some room for debating the nature of these conquests.

When futūḥāt are presented as a dictation of religious scriptures, this is mainly done through citing Jihad verses in Qur'an (Kuraiyyma, 2003, 293–338), and they are presented as part of the Islamic faith, which is by virtue of Qur'anic text sent to all humanity (Tibawi, 1976, 53). In these writings, conquests were instigated by the faith of Islam; such were necessary to spread God's word, Islam and/or protecting the Islamic nation (Tibawi, 1976; 'Ayūb, 2005, 35–46). But even in writings that disagree with this conception, Islamic intellectuals vehemently challenge an offensive character of futūḥāt (see al-Quaraḍāwī, 2004, 167–72) and converge on that Islam knows no religious war (*Ḥarb Dīniyya*) (see 'Imāra, 1988, 117, 136). This *non-aggression* feature of the conquests is eloquently summarized in this quote:

> What we need to assert is that Islam did not take up the sword, fight and struggle through its long history, not to occupy a land, not to humiliate a people, nor to make a fortune, nor even to force anyone to enter Islam. ('Abd al-'Azīz, 2003, 132)

Almost the entire body of literature on Jihad is guided, on defining this particular concept, with two parallel mutually non-exclusive directions: *One*, the prospect of employing violence towards the application and/or the fulfilment of the duty of Jihad, thus, arguing Jihad does entail the carrying of arms or the use of other sorts of coercive force (see Maḥmūd, 1994, 42–4). *Two*, non-violent forms of Jihad, like delving into one's own soul and freeing oneself of materialistic pursuits (al-Misīrī, 2002, 176), working on bettering one's manners, dedication in work, resisting human weaknesses of greed or sexual desire and the like. This definition of Jihad is wider and more comprehensive than committing violence or armed struggle (*Qitāl*) (al-Juhaiynī and Muṣṭafā, 2005, 76–81).

In a similar vein, CIPT writings frequently reiterate the descent treatment of populations, especially towards people of the book (*'Ahl al-Kitāb*)[36] in conquered lands[37] ('Arkūn, 1992, 115; 'Anān, 1969, 78–83). Generally referred to as conquerors (*Fātiḥīn*), Muslim rulers did not, for instance, impose the Arabic language on inhabitants of these lands (see al-Khaiyyāṭ, 2006, 101). Both the language and the faith were gradually adopted by populations in the Near East (Tibawi, 1976, 53). Commonly, Islamic intellectuals depict the faith of Islam as promoting mercy and tolerance[38] (see Fāyid, 1976, 115–16).

In fact, such appraisals of the conquests that Muslims treated people of the book in a fairly decent manner (*'Ahl al-Kitāb*) ('Arkūn, 1992, 170; 'Anān, 1969, 78–82) are corroborated through similar records available in Western scholarship. Records of Islamic history, at least for the first two centuries, assert that Muslims left administrative practices of conquered lands intact and their imposition of Jiziya was relatively less burdening compared to the Byzantines (Cleveland, 2000, 14–15). Likewise, Western records on Muslim rule under the Fatimids assert that Muslims, Christians and Jews peacefully coexisted, a coexistence also evinced under the Ottomans, where graveyards and shrines of Muslim, Christian and Jewish saints (*Heiliger*) were visited by all social strata and religious communities, surpassing the boundaries of individual creeds (Krämer, 2013, 124, 207).

Nonetheless, these conquests eventually came to be linked to a critical debate on the general profile of Islam as a *violent religion* (see Lane and Redissi, 2004, 18, 32), mainly in the West. This linkage and the revisiting of the military conquests were incited by key developments pertaining to Islamist militancy. The 11 September attacks induced a general image of Muslims as violent, and of Islam as supposedly promoting violence (see Esposito and Mogahed, 2007). Even earlier, the violence orchestrated and carried out by several militant movements working under the banner of Islam promoted the reputation of Islam as a violence-promoting creed. In 1943, MB in Egypt employed its secret apparatus (*al-Nizam al-Khas*) to *shield* the movement against Egyptian police and government through the use of violence, even though this apparatus was initially created to support the Palestinian cause against Israel (Mitchell, 1993, 31–4). Years later, several militant groups,[39] such as al-Jamaʿa al-Islamiyya and al-Jihad, were established.[40] Around 90 per cent of the limited disturbance incidents committed in Egypt between 1976 and 1990 were executed by extremist Islamist militant groups (Zarnūqa, 2002, 84), and these groups mostly exhibited their acts as a practice of Islamic Jihad.

But the entire debate on the permissibility of using violence in Islam coincided with a claim that the West searched for a new enemy. After the former USSR collapsed, the new enemy became Islam, usually labelled *the green enemy* (see ʿAbd al-Fattāḥ, 2008, 30; al-Mīlād, 1999, 120). There was also an assumed bias in the West against Islam, with an alleged overemphasis on Islamist extremism and terror in Western media (see ʾArkūn, 1992, 37; al-Mīlād, 1999, 120). Esposito and Mogahed represent this line of argument:

> With few exceptions, when the Western media speaks about Islam and Muslim culture, discussion tends to center on religious extremism and global terrorism: How many Muslims support extremism and terror? What is about the Religion of Islam and Muslims that produced extremism and terror? What can be done to counter and eliminate religious extremism and global terrorism? Is there hope for Islamic reform? (Esposito and Mogahed, 2007, 1)

The main rationale behind this alleged defaming of Islam is a hostile consensus, evolving amongst media professionals, politicians, political analysts and ordinary citizens (see Esposito, 2010, 25). Such consensus posits Europe's Muslims, who generally came to Europe as craftsmen and hand workers, but turned into an integral part of the functioning of European societies,[41] as an incoherent constellation irreconcilable with European/democratic norms (see Said, 1981, 51). Central to this point of view is the term *Eurabia*, connoting a blend of Islamophobic sentiments and conspiracy theory, portraying a European future culturally colonized by Islam (Carr, 2011, 13–14). In this sense, Eurabia is the fear of counter-colonization by Islam, and it is, almost at the same breath, an identity-based depiction drawn along the lines of demarcation set by Said in his Orientalism thesis (see Said, 1994, 186).

But unlike the case with Shariʿa, one can't trace a clear line of demarcation between mainstream and tajdīd on the theme of Jihad. Islamic intellectuals mostly converge on condemning sporadic violence against civilians (al-Ghazālī, 1987, 103) but insist on the right to use Jihad against occupation (see Helfont, 2009, 43–4).

Identity: Self-image with repercussions

> In the search of the satisfying feeling of 'us', those to be put in the position of 'them' must be found. (Shaker, 2010, 87)

Identity has always been a question of deciding on the *we* and the *they*, which could be drawn along religious, ethnic, racial, national or other lines. As presented in the quote above, identity is not simply about the question of who the *we* is, it is also about what the *they* represents, and this duality was/still is central to the identity theme in CIPT. In Islam, the individual belongs to the community of believers (*'Umma*), which is a supra-national bond; it is stronger than the allegiances between social and economic classes (Lane and Redissi, 2004, 137–8). Yet, some identities seem to concur for historical reasons; Islam isn't easily juxtaposed to Arab identity in CIPT writings. Although some nationalist projects were intertwined with secularist ideological counterparts in the 1960s and the 1970s (see Esposito, 1999, 567), history of Islam as a revelation in Arabic, first appearing in the Arabian peninsula, led to some considerable convergence on Islamic and Arab histories and identities in CIPT. Subsequently, *Arab* is typically presented as a source of unity, rather than a rival identity to Islam (see al-Ḥafiyān, 2006, 69; al-Jābrī, 1992; 15–31, 124).

Yet, there is presently a strong tendency to address what might be termed intra-identity aspects. As illustrated in the introduction, there is the differentiation between the Muslim and the Islamic (Krämer; 2000a, 32). In parallel, there is the differentiation between Muslim and religiously devout Muslim (Ayubi, 1991a, 67) and between ordinary Muslims and clerics (*'Ulamā'*) (Zaman, 2002, 85). Although the general position in the 'Umma is that everyone is equal and distinctions are of function, not of rank (Lambton, 1981, 13), some differentiations have serious ramifications. For instance, the religiously devout, historically, were part of the morality enforcement and practiced *Ḥisba*[42] over the larger Muslim society (Krämer, 2013, 96; Bayat, 2010, 145). Clerics, unlike ordinary Muslims, had the right to hold sessions (*Majālis*) to educate the masses on juridical matters (Kilpatrick, 2006, 762).

As highlighted earlier, Sunnis and Shiites are the two largest Muslim communities. As the history of Islam witnessed brutal struggles between these two key communities (Krämer, 2013, 39–42), both communal and juridical differences among Sunnis and Shiites (see 'Imāra, 1989b) became part of the identity theme in CIPT (see Ayubi, 1991a, 4–5; 'Arkūn, 1995, 192–3). But, except for the historical developments which led later on to the establishment of the Shiite creed, known as the first *Fitna* (see Krämer, 2013, 39; see also, 'Imāra, 1989b, 95–102), no particular aspect of Sunni/Shiite relations tends to persist in discussions on the identity theme today.[43]

Instead, Jurists were, and are still, largely preoccupied with how Muslims relate/should relate to non-Muslims (al-Qaraḍāwī, 2004, 102–4; al-Ghazālī, 1987, 29–40). Terms like *Dār al-'Islām/Dār al-Ḥarb*,[44] *'Ahl al-Dhimma* and *Jiziya* traditionally associated with jurisprudence on identity. As with other aspects of CIPT themes which were altered through real politics, the duality of Dār al-'Islām/Dār al-Ḥarb was coined at a time when Muslims were conquerors (see Krämer, 2011, 69). As Muslims are not leading human civilization anymore, this duality is largely set aside or at least re-questioned (see al-Qaraḍāwī, 2001). When invoked, it is mostly for the purposes of displaying the juridical history (see al-Ghazālī, 1987, 108; 'Imāra, 1985, 36).

Likewise, as Muslims were strong and conquerors of other lands during early days of Islam, conversions from other religions to Islam were significantly higher than conversions in the opposite direction, especially with the economic benefits associated with converting to Islam during early history of futūḥāt (see Ayubi, 1991a, 4–5; Krämer, 2013, 91). The mainstream juristic position on conversions from Islam to other religions was to follow specific procedures of repentance (*'Istitāba*), and if that did not work, the convert/apostate (*Murtad*) would be executed (see Esposito, 2010, 98; Peters, 2005, 27). However, with the territorial boundaries between states drawn without regard for religious/racial/ethnic divisions by colonizers (al-Jābrī, 1990b, 94), most Arab states today, largely dominated by Muslim populations, include one or more religious minority/ies. In addition, after modernization and colonization brought about institutional and legal settings from the West, terms like *'Ahl al-Dhimma* and *Jiziya* ceased to embody the realities of Muslim societies (see Wood, 2013, 162–4). Nowadays, constitutional and legal provisions in Muslim-dominated countries, historically applying Jiziya, like Egypt, do not use this terminology in legal texts at all; instead, notions of citizenship and equality prevail.

Conversely, media contributed to bring the particular issue of apostasy to the spotlight; cases of conversions and subsequent state and communal harassment of converts (see Human Rights Watch, 1994; Al-Arabiya News, 2009) pushed it to the surface. Questions like, 'under what conditions do conversions constitute no violation to Islam?' turned central in this regard (al-ʿAwwā, 2003). Yet, whether the convert should be executed or not, in line with the classical position of Islamic jurisprudence, became a division between those who insist on the procedure, and those who maintain reality is different today. The latter think there is no basis anymore for the penalty stipulated in the body of jurisprudence (see Saeed and Saeed, 2004). Among mainstream and tajdīd intellectuals, the lines of demarcation are still blurred on this topic. Although the general position of mainstream supports, even if with some qualification, the juridical procedure of repentance (*'Istitāba*) established in the Sunni body of jurisprudence (al-ʿAwwā, 2003, 23–8), which precedes the penalty, both mainstream and tajdīd often advocate freedom of faith (al-ʿUlwānī, 2006; al-Bannā, 1995b). It's common to find mainstream CIPT intellectuals who insist that conversions from Islam, as individual faith and practice, should not be penalized as long as the person does not try to spread apostasy among Muslims (al-ʿUlwānī, 2006, 15; al-ʿAwwā, 2003).

Similarly, across the mainstream/tajdīd divide, most CIPT intellectuals agree that Jiziya is a historical practice. When non-Muslims weren't enrolled in militaries of Muslim-dominated countries/empires, there was an underlying rationale for imposing Jiziya, which was paid, in their view, in exchange for protection offered by Muslims, when the latter conquered and ruled non-Muslim territories (see ʿImāra, 1985, 63). In a similar vein, with the growing phenomenon of Muslims living as minorities in non-Muslim societies today, through labour immigration to the West (see Esposito, 2010, 25), other themes and juridical contributions became more central to CIPT and represented the need for a re-definition of the juridical terms of Dār-al-Ḥarb (Land of War) and Dār-al-Ṣulḥ (Land of Peace) (Krämer, 2011, 69). Minority Jurisprudence (*Fiqh al-'Aqalliyyāt*), largely pioneered by al-Qaradawi and al-ʿUlwani, is one good instance of the alteration and manifestation of the role of real politics in shaping CIPT debates (al-Qaraḍāwī, 2001; al-'Ulwānī, 2002).

Additionally, demarcation lines between mainstream and tajdīd are evidently vague when it comes to non-Muslims' right to hold state top positions, known as (*Wilāiya*). Such positions were historically confined to Muslims, both in jurisprudence and practice. Unlike mainstream intellectuals, who disagree on that matter, tajdīd counterparts are more unified in this regard; they typically maintain excluding non-Muslims from these positions is part of a historical reality, arguing that several considerations[45] no longer apply, even if majority of the population is Muslim (al-Hilālī, 2014). Some mainstream intellectuals concur with this position though (see 'Imāra, 1985, 36; Hūwaidī, 1999).

In fact, the debate on identity has always intersected with that of Shari'a, in its Mu'āmalāt aspect, as it was/is predominantly occupied with the rights and obligations of Muslims/non-Muslims. Whereas, in the past, legal and political rights of non-Muslims were different from that of their Muslim counterparts, regarding taxation and holding of state positions; today, the identity debate intersects with Shari'a on the religious duties Muslims are expected to fulfil under non-Muslim/secular rule (al-Qaraḍāwī, 2001).

To sum up, CIPT, in this book, refers to spoken and written language seeking reference from Islamic heritage towards establishing claims and/or arguments, with the ultimate aim of promoting Islam as a political program or code of conduct, on the various manifestations of power, both at the levels of state and society, starting the Second World War onwards. Four main themes tend to dominate CIPT writings: (1) State in Islam, (2) Shari'a, (3) violence as Jihad (4) and identity. Each one of them comprises debates signifying what elements are most relevant/central today. Highly guided by historical events and struggles for power, these elements changed and/or fluctuated in significance over time. This is most salient in the fact that the caliphate became a part of the heritage, which is not invoked anymore as a viable alternative for political rule. Meanwhile, Islamic intellectuals evidently address CIPT themes in their writings, and those who defy established *knowledge* are usually subjected to practices of exclusion, but their ideas are not necessarily eliminated.

Under the wide appeal of democracy, as well as the growing juxtaposition between the West and Islam, democracy came to be juxtaposed to Islam and Shura. Yet, many Islamic intellectuals don't reject democratic arrangements. Mainstream CIPT doesn't by default reject Western settings such as political parties and parliamentary elections, often considering them contemporary equivalents of Shura in Islamic history, but mainstream/tajdīd camps are divided over the concept of the Islamic state. The tajdīd camp would maintain that the practice of the early history of Islam was exceptional, and that the largest part of the historical practice is not an essential part of the faith.

On Shari'a application, mainstream/tajdīd converge on the general principle of Shari'a application and diverge mainly on the need to apply ḥudūd. Particularly, there is disagreement on how the text in general and the text on ḥudūd in particular should be applied today. In this respect, tajdīd insists on 'Illa as a decisive factor for ḥudūd application, whereas mainstream generally asserts that they are applicable today as much as they were during early Islamic history.

The theme of violence in Islam is mainly dominated by three aspects: (1) Islamic conquests, (2) the notion of Jihad and (3) contemporary Islamist militancy. Although these conquests are commonly propagated as a sign of strength and glory, portraying Muslim conquerors as fair and even merciful to populations of conquered lands in CIPT writings, they are commonly depicted, in the West, as part the accusation of Islam as a religion promoting violence. Meanwhile, such conquests as part of the faith is a matter of disagreement among Islamic intellectuals, regarding if practices of early Islamic history were based on real politics, or the faith.

The question of identity is not solely occupied with Muslim/non-Muslim relations; *intra-identity* classifications are also part of the debate, between the Islamic/Muslim, the Muslim/religiously-devout and the ordinary Muslims/'Ulama, which have substantial societal ramifications. Still, the more immediate question in the history of Islamic Political Thought, and today under CIPT, concerns Muslim/non-Muslim relations. There is no clear-cut division between mainstream and tajdīd on the particular point of non-Muslims paying taxes in Muslim-dominated countries. Meanwhile, as millions of Muslims live today in non-Muslim Western countries, an emerging theme in jurisprudence, and CIPT, has turned central to identity debates, concerning how Muslims are to guard their faith and peacefully co-exist under secular rule. Likewise, conversions, highlighted in the media, re-posed the question of repentance in Islam. The historical economic and political privileges associated with converting to Islam don't exist anymore and the lines of demarcation between mainstream and tajdīd intellectuals are not clear-cut on this debate.

2

Egypt: Surviving autocratic regimes

Authoritarian regimes may endorse tactical, or even strategic, openness; they don't necessarily maintain the same level or intensity of oppression across time (Wickham, 2002, 64). The public sphere can, thus, witness varying degrees of freedom. Al-Banna and al-Bishri's intellectual productions were written and published in Egypt throughout long decades of autocratic rule, mainly under three presidents: Nasser, Sadat and Mubarak, with few publications after the ouster of the latter in 2011. In order for them to contribute their writings and avoid persecution, they necessarily had to watch out for regime red lines, especially that being Islamic intellectuals doesn't necessarily mean they were only vocal on matters of religion. Like many of their counterparts, they engaged with, and contributed on, politics.

To be sure, al-Banna and al-Bishri often discussed both simultaneously, sometimes in one publication and other times in more than one publication using different perspectives. This chapter is, thus, focused on the tools employed by successive ruling regimes to achieve control over the public sphere and how both intellectuals dealt with this confinement in their writings. More precisely, how did they maintain their inclusion in the public sphere and avoid regime repression?

From a theoretical standpoint, I address the Egyptian public sphere based on the assumption, above, that spaces *allowed* for political mobilization do not remain constant all the time. Thus, I argue the regimes' strong hold on the public sphere fluctuated, and it can be safely assumed that this fluctuation would mirror in the intellectual production of al-Banna and al-Bishri. In other words, the work of al-Banna and al-Bishri as two intellectuals who lived, wrote and published mainly under the three regimes of Nasser, Sadat and Mubarak are expected to embody their control over the public sphere.

Tens of scholarly sources, local as well as international, expressed sheer interest in, and concern for, the functioning of Egypt's autocratic regimes, particularly on the various dynamics these regimes employed in order to achieve/maintain their dominance and control (see Ḥasan, 2012; Kienle, 2000; Hartmann, 2011). Within this focus, two major trends prevailed: one that assumes the centrality of, and thus pays much attention to, the head of the state, that is Nasser; Sadat and Mubarak (see Beattie, 1994, 2000; Lippman, 1989; ʿAbd al-Ghanii, 1993; ʿĪsā, 2008), and another that casts light on central actors/groups contesting these regimes' power and dominant position, that is the MB or Copts (see Alt, 1980; Ibrahim et al., 1996; Zahid, 2010). In this book, Authoritarian State is used to denote one with limited political pluralism, a low-level of political mobilization and a few safeguards for individual rights (Spector, 2007, 40). They are generally juxtaposed to democratic ones (see Timm, 2010, 98) based on a common belief that, within Western democracies, public involvement in politics should be encouraged (Dalton, 1988, 35), while in authoritarian states, politics may be reserved for the ruling elite (Bealey, 1999, 254).

Unsurprisingly, due to al-Banna's self-acclaimed *liberal* non-mainstream profile, which conflicts with established juridical and intellectual production regarding what Islam is and how it should be practiced (El-Hennawy, 2013), two of his books were confiscated (see ʿAbd al-Ḥalīm, 2008). That is, the pressure on al-Banna would expectedly emanate not only from the ruling regime/s but also from the religious institution, al-Azhar. In order to assume intellectuals watch out for regime controls over the public sphere, I claim one must concede to the Gramscian proposition that the very basic aim of any individual is to secure his/her physical and moral safety (Gramsci, 1986, 17). Put differently, the intellectual is generally expected to evade red lines set by an autocratic regime, which are associated with potential jeopardy to liberty, as freedom from control. Yet, as will be evident here, the intellectual could still find ways to criticize the regime and touch upon red lines, without directly colliding with it.

The three regimes, above, *managed* to jeopardize the individual autonomy of intellectuals in very similar ways, and this resulted in similar patterns of writing under each and every one of them. In this regard, several incidents of the state harassing intellectuals will be highlighted, not for the factual details of these incidents per se, rather, for their anticipated impact on the writings of the intellectuals studied. More precisely, it is the role of these incidents in delineating particular *red lines* in Egypt's public sphere, namely incidents associated with large-scale persecution and harassment of prominent intellectual figures in Egypt rather than minor incidents, that might go unnoticed by al-Banna and al-Bishri.

Last but not least, when it comes to the authority of al-Azhar over the public sphere, the notion of contestation as presented by Casper is particularly relevant. According to him, authoritarian regimes may face contestation from the religious institution, which enjoys a strong popular appeal because of the repressive measures the regime endorses (see Casper, 1995, 17). Thus, Egypt's successive regimes subordinated and co-opted al-Azhar to maintain its Islamic profile among the populace on one hand, and to avoid Casper's scenario of the religious institution opposing and mobilizing against its repressive rule on the other. But in return, al-Azhar could, more than once, *dictate* specific limitations and/or controls over ideas disseminated in the country's public sphere.

Nasser: Politics after the 1952 coup

Nasser's rule came after a military coup[1] in 1952, widely known as the 1952 Revolution (Muḥī al-Dīn, 1995), which ousted the monarch and established the republic. In its core, it was orchestrated towards ousting the Ottoman monarch and was, thus, arguably a means to both independence and democratic rule (see Johnson, 2004, 163). Along the same lines and in concordance with popular aspirations, the Revolution Command Council (RCC) (*Majlis Qiyadat al-Thawra*) utterly pledged a *sound* democratic system (see Gordon, 1992, 6). Nonetheless, shortly after the coup, in December 1952, the constitution was annulled (see Moustafa, 2008, 133) and freedom was confiscated by authority. It simply meant freedom of rulers to do whatever they like (Ḥasan, 2012, 244).

Intelligence and charisma

Nasser's regime constituted a sharp turn in the country's political path; the country's intelligence service grew unprecedentedly bigger under his rule and was largely plagued with corruption.[2] The presidency itself has developed and continued to be the most dominant force in Egyptian politics, since he ascended to the executive branch in 1956 (Kassem, 2004, 11). With early signs of political opposition such as the February 1968 demonstrations,[3] he established Central Security Forces (CSF) (*Quwwat al-Amn al-Markazi*) for the purpose of achieving internal suppression, and citizens of modest backgrounds were deliberately recruited, using them as tools towards absolute suppression (al-'Umrī, 2009, 433). It might be useful to stop at Woodward's words on Nasser:
He had been such a dominant and personal ruler, and had left so little by way of viable political institutions that scarcely any serious thought had been given to presidential government as a system. (Woodward, 1992, 130)

Nonetheless, he possessed an undeniable charisma (Podeh and Winckler, 2004, 18). This was partly promoted through his Arab socialism, which was the regime's formal ideology, declared in the National Charter published in May 1962 (see Rejwan, 1974, 94–5). Adopting large-scale socio-economic revisions and reforms, he promoted social mobility, which was intended to boost his popularity (Ibrahim, 2021).

> There is no question that Egypt exercised a profound regional influence during the Nasser years. Not all of the domestic turmoil in the Middle East can be attributed to Nasser, yet it seems clear that his example inspired imitators and attracted followers throughout the Arab world. His attempts to break away from the Western embrace and its imperial connotations found a responsive echo in Baghdad and Damascus, in Tripoli and Algiers, and the promise of social and political reform associated with his policies became the ideal for reformers elsewhere. (Cleveland, 2000, 333–4)

In this quote, Cleveland highlights Nasser's regional weight, which cannot be grasped away from his domestic achievements; standing up against the tri-lateral aggression of France, Britain and Israel, the nationalization policies (known as *Tamsir*), the unity with Syria and the collapse of the despotic royal regime in Iraq in 1958 (see ʿAbd al-Fattāḥ, 1975, 11) served him well. In particular, the Suez Canal nationalization[4] was a strong base for Nasser's popularity (see Hussein, T., 2012); his achievements translated into regional power for Egypt, which was also an attribute to his charisma.

The 1967 defeat but continued charisma

In 1967, Egypt was bitterly defeated after a scandalous military performance in the war against Israel, in what is widely known as *al-Naksa* or The Crisis (see Shlaim and Louis, 2012). But Nasser's charisma survived this defeat; Egyptians rejected his voluntary withdrawal from politics (see Hofstadter, 1973, 39). Masses of Arab citizens in Cairo, Damascus and Beirut demanded that he stay in power (see both Abdel-Malek, 1971, 10, and Bilāl, 1974, 56).

When the grave societal damage that surpassed the military humiliation is taken into account, Nasser's strong popular base becomes even clearer and more evident. The defeat uncovered false heroism and brought the public morale to severe frustration (ʾAmīn, 2009, 54; Shama, 2010). The war also burdened the country's overloaded economy. Rutherford points this out:

> As the population expanded, and as economic growth remained modest at best, the viability of the statist system came into question. Its underlying

> weaknesses were made even more apparent after the 1967 war and the ensuing reconstruction of the military, which diverted vast amounts of capital from productive economic investment. (2008, 135)

By the early 1960s, Egypt's bureaucracy became inefficient and it exhausted the budget (Dekmejian, 1972, 229); salaries were inadequate and most civil servants were involved in bribery and corruption (Waterbury, 1983, 347). Corruption was used to augment Nasser's powers and to enlarge his circle of influence (*Da'irat al-Nufudh*) ('Amīn, 2009, 51). The economy was technically on the brink of a massive collapse by the end of his time and was weighed down by defence costs, weak foreign investments and a swollen public sector (Mcdermott, 1988, 44). Surprisingly, his charisma and popularity were largely left intact, as McDermott eloquently puts it:

> Nasser left Egypt defeated, economically weak and unconvinced that it had been a *thawra* (revolution) which had been carried out in 1952, but he remained and remains Egypt's hero, as indicated by the massive outpouring of grief and the throngs in their millions at his funeral in Cairo. (1988, 39)

Taken together, economic difficulties, the 1967 defeat and the sectors which were damaged must have created dissent on the part of those who suffered. However, the socio-economic and nationalist achievements and the strong grip on the country through intelligence and security forces inhibited popular dissent from growing big enough to jeopardize his rule. Moreover, his personal control over press content, as will be shown below, meant the press was not an outlet for *rival* ideas to surface.

Political oppression and the 'Islamic'

Under Nasser, political detention was a common practice and prison officers brutally tortured detainees (see ʿAbd al-Fattāḥ, 1975, 85–92). Related and coupled with this practice was the enormous intelligence activity:

> The inflation of internal (state security) and external (general intelligence) security agencies were supplied with unknown and un-knowable financial capacities, with absolute authority limited by nothing other than the self-defined requirements of state security, with fanciful tools that could bring any citizen, without seeing it, under the microscope, with the power to carry out its tasks secretly, watch secretly, follow on matters secretly and implements secretly, like depressed ghosts. (Saif al-Dawla, 1977, 90)

He was also suspected to have planned the physical attack on ʿAbd al-Razzaq al-Sanhuri,[5] who was head of the State Council at that time (see Jāmiʿ, 1998,

111–16). Strongly controlling the political terrain through intelligence and arbitrary detentions, he opted to strike a fragile balance between cracking down on Islamist activists, especially from the MB (Gordon, 2006, 56) and, at the same time, promoting the profile of a president who does not oppose Islam (see 'Abd al-Ghanii, 1993, 272).

As part of his Islam-friendly profile, he went on pilgrimage; his photos with the modest (*Ḥaj*) dress were widely circulated. He also sent his vice president, Sadat, to attend Islamic congresses (Gordon, 2006, 56). Religion became obligatory in school curricula in 1957. Under al-Wafd government before the 1952 coup, religion was not taught in schools (Labīb, 2012, 23). Nasser was himself a practising Muslim and rejected specific tenets of Marxian socialism because of its affiliation with atheism and philosophical materialism (see Muzikar, 1989, 105–6).

Meanwhile, he sought control over religious institutions; al-Azhar and all its endowments (*'Awqāf*),[6] through the law 103 for 1961, were put under the jurisdiction of the Ministry of Religious Endowments (Morsy and Brown, 2013). He cancelled religious courts (*Shar'iyya*) in 1955; later in the 1960s, he also controlled religious education (Bayat, 2007, 36–7). These decisions were not random; they reflected an attempt to partly control the *Islamic reference*, to make it at the service of the ruling regime (Ḥabīb, 2012, 19). His approach to Islam is best illustrated by Dekmejian:

> His socialism was tempered with religious belief. Abd al-Nasir was born a Muslim Egyptian; he propounded a secular and fierce nationalist doctrine; he died a Muslim Arab and was laid to rest in his neighborhood mosque. (1972, 310)

As stated above, Islamists' political engagement wasn't tolerated; he clamped down on Islamist activists[7] and banned the MB in 1954. Many of its members were imprisoned and tortured, including their leading ideologue Sayyid Qutb, who was eventually executed in 1966 (James, 2006, 177). But he made some effort to keep the MB ban from sabotaging his Islam-friendly profile. In January 1954, students from the Liberation Front (*Haiy'at al-Tahrir*) attacked students from the MB and the latter responded violently. These clashes were then used as a justification to ban the movement (see Yūnis, 2012, 67). Furthermore, in his struggle with Islamists, Nasser used religion and religious clergy (Gordon, 2006, 56), but his attack on Islamists was counterbalanced by a public profile of a president who does not antagonize religion. Not trying to secularize the society, or drive it away from its religious character, he not only spared himself the potential challenge of the religious institution, here al-Azhar, as with the aforementioned pattern of autocracies co-opting the church (see Casper, 1995, 3–17) but also diminished the chances of Islamist activists contesting his rule.

Intellectual life circumscribed

Within the context of the highly controlled political sphere, Egypt's intellectual life was strictly regulated under Nasser. The regime deliberately opted for recruiting leading members affiliated with varying intellectual streams to become members of government committees and institutions in order to contain them (see ʿAbd al-Ghanii, 1993, 217). Moreover, his close supervision of the public sphere was partly facilitated through state employment of intellectuals; most of the latter were dependent on government jobs. In result, the voicing of dissent was a rare practice; for those living in Egypt, criticism was only possible through implication or advice intended for the betterment of the state of affairs (Dekmejian, 1972, 63).

The press was subjected to extensive oversight from 1953 onwards, both through personal contacts with chief editors of big newspapers and direct editing of papers' content (Muḥī al-Dīn, 1995, 228–9). He also coordinated with the Ministry of Information, which housed the bureau for censorship that was responsible for blocking articles and publications addressing government corruption (see Beattie, 1994, 137). In 1953, Nasser let the masses believe they had decided on the country's party system through an orchestrated magazine poll, while he planned the matter from above (see ʿAbd al-Ghanii, 1993, 217, 236–8). This way, he not only *played* the public sphere towards his preset political preferences but also used it to fortify his grip on the political terrain, as the single-party system circumvented the prospect to institutionalize political opposition. In this regard, he posited the image of a president who cared for people's preferences, without adopting democratic reform.

As pointed out earlier, when intellectual's autonomy is jeopardized, the act of writing most likely signifies *cautious* attitudes towards *particular* issues, which are believed to incite regime harassment. Nasser overtly infringed on the individual autonomy of intellectuals, who presented *unwelcomed* critique of his rule. Fikri Abaza, a prominent Egyptian journalist of his time[8] was forced to write an apology to him in *al-Ahram* newspaper in 1961. In a similar vein, he did not like an article by Hilmi Sallam commenting on him; so Sallam was informed that he was on an open leave. For several years, no publisher could publish his work because of Nasser's *informal* ban on him (see Fawzī, 2001, 89, 43, respectively).

Moreover, intellectuals could get *collaterally* harassed when political activists were the actual targets. In 1959, sixteen writers were detained in a massive campaign against the Left *(al-Yasar)*. Detained writers included prominent names like Lutfi al-Khuli, Mahmud al-Sa'dani and Louis 'Awad (see Stagh, 1993, 70–1). Neither al-Banna nor al-Bishri was detained in this campaign, but it became clear to intellectuals in general that they were not immune to regime persecution and should watch out for its red lines to avoid direct collision with it. Luckily, the two studied intellectuals, in particular, did not have to watch out for this collateral harassment, by virtue of their deliberate distance from any political stream. Al-Banna's imprisonment in the late 1940s was due to his family and professional association with the MB and was a case of collateral harassment, but did not occur under Nasser (al-Bannā, 1997, 7). Al-Bishri's judicial status obliged him to stay away from political activism, so there was no prospect of collateral persecution in his case.

Yet, Egypt's public sphere, under Nasser, though heavily controlled, was not solely besieged by the ruling regime; al-Azhar, at least once, exerted pressure and managed to impose its own *ideas*. Youngsters of our Slum (*Awlad Haritna*), by Nobel Prize winner Najib Mahfuz, was the subject of al-Azhar's pressure to ban the novel on allegations of blasphemy. The novel was first published in *al-Ahram* newspaper in 1959. After filing petitions, al-Azhar incited its followers to protest and the novel consequently was never published into a book inside Egypt under Nasser (see Stagh, 1993, 157).

In a similar vein, when Sheikh al-Ghazali, a renowned Egyptian Islamic cleric, was personally offended in public by Nasser and the insult was highlighted in several newspapers, the popular Sheikh firmly objected and *al-Ahram*, under the pressure of the overwhelming Islamic outrage, had to publish an apology to him (see 'Abd al-Ghanii, 1993, 477). In fact, the case with the novel manifests how al-Azhar exercised direct pressure on the Nasser regime to accommodate its power over the public sphere, although, as shown earlier, he legally and structurally subordinated al-Azhar and religious endowments in 1961.

This meant those involved in intellectual production, like al-Bishri and al-Banna, had to watch out for two potential authorities: the Nasser regime and/or al-Azhar. Naturally, the ideas Nasser *blocked* were, as shown above, about government and politics, whereas those blocked, or sought to be blocked, by al-Azhar pertained to its definition of the religious truth.

Al-Banna and al-Bishri under Nasser

The fact that al-Azhar co-defined spaces allowed in the public sphere did not represent direct confinement on Jamal al-Banna's tajdīd intellectual production simply because he, back then, had a clear focus on socialism as an ideology and a labour struggle. His accounts on religious and juristic matters evolved under Sadat, and his renewal scheme was strongly presented later under Mubarak. But his interest in socialism cannot be adequately grasped in separation from the regime's socialist ideology. Although al-Banna expressed genuine interest in labour struggle, Nasser's endorsement of socialism, propagated by the Soviet Bloc (Ferris, 2012), and the regime's generally unfriendly relations to the capitalist West (Springborg, 2013) meant writing on socialism was a safe terrain well tolerated by the regime. In fact, the array of ideas al-Banna published under Nasser fell in line with the regime's preferences in two parallel ways. On one hand, he addressed the comparative syndical history (al-Bannā, 1967). On the other, he criticized capitalism, which, in his writings, was intertwined with unemployment and promoted unleashed freedom that could result in chaos (al-Bannā, 1957). This way, his profile did not pose a risk of collision with the regime's strong control of the public sphere. But this doesn't negate that before the 1952 coup, he expressed discontent with communism. In 1946, during the liberal phase of Egypt's modern history and before the Republican era, he published his first book New Democracy (*Dimuqratiyya Jadida*), where he not only criticized socialist society's oppressive measures curbing freedom of speech but also detested certain aspects of communism, arguing that there is no trace of the human being as an end in itself (al-Bannā, 1946, 140–2).

Perhaps it's worth noting that he was harassed after the 1952 coup. Years after Nasser passed away, al-Banna uncovered direct harassment he experienced during the early months of the republican regime. Shortly after the coup, al-Banna wrote his book Rationalizing Renaissance (*Tarshid al-Nahda*), where he maintained the 1952 overthrowing of the king was technically a coup d'etat. Authorities immediately confiscated the book while it was still in press; he kept it unpublished for long decades (see al-Bannā, 2011, 6–8). Accordingly, the salient focus on socialism that he largely propagated under Nasser may not have entirely been driven by his personal profile as a labour activist. It could well also be a by-product of the aversion instigated by his direct harassment above, when discussing topics the regime overtly barred from the country's public sphere.

Meanwhile, when al-Banna criticized political oppression in his book Law and the Judiciary in the Socialist Society (*al-Qanun wa-l-Qadaa' fi-l-Mujtama' al-Ishtiraki*) (1963, 115–26), published under Nasser, he did so with no reference whatsoever to Nasser or his regime. The few instances of legal and political critiques towards Egyptian politics, in this book, dealt with *the past*, highlighting the corruption plaguing Egypt under the monarchy. In fact, criticizing the monarchy promoted the cause of the 1952 coup because the latter ousted the monarch. It was published in 1963, that is, after the regime's repressive character towards its political rivals became evident in the 1950s[9] (see Springborg, 2013). Therefore, the general profile of al-Banna under Nasser complies with Baker's idea that the intellectual is suppressed under autocratic regimes, where they either support it or simply keep silent (Baker, 1990, 193).

The first thing to be noted on al-Bishri's writings is that it is relatively difficult to determine when exactly, and under which regime, his publications were written.[10] For instance, the available edition of Muslims and Copts within the Frame of the National Community (*al-Muslimun wa-l-Aqbat fi Itar al-Jama'a al-Wataniyya*) ([1980] 2004) is the fourth (refined) one, and in the introduction, he made it clear that his interest and writing on the topic started with the defeat of 1967. He mentioned that he wrote small pieces on it in the years 1970 and 1973 before he decided he should present a more profound and comprehensive account on the matter, asserting that writing this book was done many years before it was published in 1980 (2004, 5–8).

Likewise, Contemporary Personalities and Issues (*Shakhsiyyat wa Qadaiyya Mu'assira*) (2002b) is a collection of separate articles he published in *al-Hilal* magazine. Although the book was published in 2002, there is no way to tell which part of the book was written first, or under which regime (2002b, 5–14). Similarly, although original publishing dates of different articles in his book Studies in Egyptian Democracy (Dirasat fi-l-Dimuqratiyya al-Misriyya) (1987a) are listed, the book cross-cuts through the two regimes of Nasser and Sadat. Published in 1987, the book contained a selection of articles that he wrote between 1967 and 1977 and another article published in April 1981 (1987a, 5).

Under Nasser, al-Bishri's key contribution was his huge book The Political Movement in Egypt 1945–1953 (*al-Haraka al-Siyasiyya fi Misr 1945–1953*). As evident from the title, he does not collide with the regime, as he discussed political movement(s) in the period directly preceding the 1952 coup and before Nasser officially seized power in 1954 (2002a). The coup itself is addressed under Sadat (2004, 738–40, 795–800) and again under Mubarak in his book Democracy and the 23rd of July System, 1952–1970 (*al-Dimuqratiyya wa Nizam 23 Yuliyu 1952–1970*). Again, his book did not hold a potential for collision with the ruling regime (1991a). Similarly, he offered historical accounts of the 1919 revolution and the power struggle back then between the king, al-Wafd Party and the British mandate (1987a, 77–106).

Interestingly, his account on the MB under Nasser[11] is one that indirectly promoted the regime. Commenting on the founding principles announced by Hasan al-Banna, the MB founder, he maintained the movement *confiscated* religion for its own interests and at the same time made anyone who was not a member in the group fall outside the religion of Islam. Similarly, he labelled the secret apparatus as *the terrorist organization in the MB* and depicted the movement's decision-making as highly dominated by the person of its supreme guide (2002a, 117–19, 127).

In his own assessment, the MB was relatively less exposed to the national cause and took a very blurred stance towards it (2002a, 121). Needless to say, this was a strong critique of the movement; the national cause is of huge importance to al-Bishri, as seen in his frequent accounts on the damage inflicted by colonialism on Egypt (2007b, 97; 2007a, 37), and his assertion that the nation's collective identity is formed through its struggle against colonialism (1978, 27–42). As shown earlier, Nasser opted for cracking down on the movement starting 1954 as he perceived it as a counter-force that might diminish his own power. Subsequently, al-Bishri's account on the MB, where he numerated MB pitfalls, indirectly served Nasser's rule, his strong grip on the political sphere and did not constitute any risk of harassment.

Sadat: The premises of pluripartidism

After almost two decades of totalitarian politics, indoctrination, mobilization, control over press content, security agencies with vast prerogatives and a military defeat, Sadat faced the challenge of breaking away from Nasser's charisma and improving an ailing economy burdened by an oversized bureaucracy and costs of the 1967 defeat. Shifting his foreign policy towards approaching the West after the 1973 war, Sadat was confronted with growing popular dissent under his economic Infitah[12] policy and peace treaty with Israel (see Harders, 1998). Unwilling to reverse his economic and foreign policies, he quelled dissidents and restricted pluripartidism towards the end of his rule.

Incremental towards political dominance

Since he came to power, Sadat was perceived as a temporary substitute for Nasser (Bar-Joseph, 2005, 46), an interim successor to him (McDermott, 1988, 56). Relations with Israel, which later on took a sharp turn with the signing of the Camp David Accords (see Caso, 2008, 79) started out in the Nasserist coat:

> At first it seemed that nothing had changed as in his first months in power, Sadat followed his predecessor's policy. Like Nasser, Sadat, too, demanded that Israel return every last inch of occupied Arab land. Nor was he willing to negotiate or sign a separate peace treaty with Israel. And, Sadat insisted, there would be a single, comprehensive peace treaty between Israel and the Arab world, or no treaty at all. (Gat, 2012, 5)

The first move towards breaking away from Nasser's legacy was his move against his predecessor's men. Sadat first sought widening the cleavage between them, the army and the people. Then, he pulled al-Laithi Nasif, back-then head of the Republican Guard (*al-Haras al-Jumhuri*), close and eventually put them all on trial over accusations of conspiracy and spying (Jāmi', 1998, 128–41). At the same time, he sought defaming the former regime through a campaign of movies, highlighting the human rights violations committed under Nasser's rule (see 'Allām, 2012, 149). Sadat's incremental approach towards establishing his own power and breaking away from the Nasser legacy was best summarized by Lippman:

> He began to dismantle the Nasser legend within months of his accession, but in the beginning his position was delicate. Sadat had to move boldly to establish his own authority, but he could not simply repudiate Nasser all at once. (1989, 28)

The 1973 October war, however, established Sadat's legitimacy as a leader of Egypt, and thus his need to follow the steps of his predecessor receded. Due to this war, he forced concessions on Israelis, and the potential for renewed armed combat was drastically diminished (see McDermott, 1988, 50). As Egypt's financial needs could only be met through external financing, he capitalized on his new international profile with foreign parties (Barnett, 1992, 137). The incremental approach with the West led up to peace with Israel, which Sadat opted for in 1977. He launched the peace process, which earned him the Nobel Peace Prize and supporters in the United States and Israel (Pace, 1981).

In result, politics, under Sadat, was torn between two conflicting tides. One, approaching the West, mainly the United States and Israel, throughout the post-1973 war period, created the pressure to open up the political sphere (Harders,

1998, 268). This pressure naturally did not exist before this war, when Egypt was closer to the Soviet Bloc, heavily dominated by autocratic regimes (see Kenez, 2006, 103–32; 243–78). As stated earlier, Nasser's charisma was never based on democratic practices, so Sadat was not urged to open up the political sphere when he initially pretended to follow his steps. Two, the rise of domestic Islamist opposition, and Sadat's harshening of controls and limits on political expression and activism towards the end of his rule (Beattie, 2000, 273–4; Hassan, 2010, 321).

Economic Infitah and alleged political liberalization

In addition to the political opposition resulting from the peace treaty with Israel, economic upheaval troubled Sadat's rule. In the 1970s, economic performance deteriorated and the class gap widened enormously ('Amīn, 2009, 49–50). Sadat's Infitah strongly impeded productivity and led to heavy consumerist behaviour (Ayubi, 1991b, 25); non-interference with individual economic activity and the private sector, even if forbidden or illegal, also characterized his Infitah (see Ramaḍān, 1986, 159–60).

Under Nasser, Egypt produced around 250,000 graduates, all of whom were employed, albeit at the expense of overstaffing the public sector. Starting the end of the 1960s and for a whole decade, the country produced about half a million new graduates, while organizational and industrial activities declined due to the changing role of the state under Sadat (see Ayubi, 1991b, 111). All this accumulated into political dissent, which ended up with the infamous bread riots of 1977 which were the by-products of his massive subsidization of commodities. He partly contributed to the development of dissent, as he introduced the subsidies so massively and initially provided them without qualification, with the effect that all economic strata accessed them (McDermott, 1988, 80–1).

Hence, compared to Nasser, economic performance was declining, and economically inspired political dissent was on the rise. However, Sadat's political liberalization, largely motivated by approaching the West after the 1973 war, decisively took the country further towards opening up the political sphere. The Committee of the Future of Political Action (Lajnat Mustaqbal al-ʿAmal al-Siyasi) was founded in 1976. It established three formations representing the right, the centre and the left, which turned, upon Sadat's decision, into political parties. This was the basis for the law on regulating political parties, passed in July 1977 (see Ramaḍān, 1986, 376).

Nonetheless, in the 1971 Constitution,[13] drafted and enacted under Sadat, president of the republic was also head of the government and supreme commander of the armed forces (Baker, 1990, 59). This way, the concentration of power in the hands of the president, which prevailed under Nasser, was legally left intact. Sadat used the Parliament, when he deemed necessary, to rewrite laws to legalize whatever he wanted done, including the establishment of special courts for political detainees. Decisions of these courts were not subject to review by the conventional judiciary (Lippman, 1989, 37). This way, the executive, legislative, and also partly the judiciary were technically under his command.

Particularly, through his control of Parliament and laws, the country's political sphere was besieged, even when it was supposedly opening up in other directions. The promulgation of laws no. 33 of 1978, concerning the Protection of Internal Front and Social Peace (*Qanun Bi-sha'n Himaiyat al-Jabha al-Dakhiliyya wa-l-Salam al-Ijtima'i*), and no. 95 of 1980, concerning the Protection of Values from Shame (*Qanun Himaiyat al-Qiyam min al-'Aib*) – known as the *Law of Shame* – were landmarks of Sadat's regime. They ironically concurred with the dissolution of the former single party, the Arab Socialist Union (al-Itihad al-'Arabi al-Ishtiraki, ASU) in 1977, and the first multi-party parliamentary elections in 1979 (Kienle, 2000, 19).

Furthermore, Sadat pushed for a constitutional amendment of Article 77 in 1980 to allow himself indefinite renewals of presidential terms (see 'Allām, 2012, 40). Although political parties were allowed, participation was confined to a small, and rather artificial, set of parties, and their freedom of expression was restricted (Wickham, 2002, 65). Opposition was allowed but its capacity to compete for political power, and constitute substantial rivalry to Sadat's rule, was circumvented (see Harders, 1998, 274). It was by no means a state of institutions, and the personal character of Sadat's rule was growingly salient (Lippmann, 1989, 189).

> Sadat was at ease with pulling men closer, then pushing them away, changing cabinets, expelling some parliament deputies from parliament after stripping them of their membership. (al-Bāz,1998, 89)

Faced with popular dissent, Sadat issued a series of decrees that curtailed freedoms and liberties (see Hassan, 2010, 321). This was the case during the aforementioned bread riots of 1977 and after signing the peace treaty with Israel. Following the signing of this treaty, precisely on 2 September 1981, he took unanticipated measures to arrest 1,536 individuals, including intellectuals, among others (Beattie, 2000, 273–4; Ayubi, 1991b, 94). Activism against the treaty was contained through declaring the state of emergency, which allowed the regime to arrest and detain citizens with no regard to normal legal procedures and regulations (Harders, 1998, 273).

Nonetheless, Sadat's regime wasn't the same as that of Nasser. Although major parties were politically excluded, such as the New al-Wafd Party, or deprived of publication rights, such as al-Tajjammuʿ al-Taqqadumi Party, political parties did not entirely vanish under Sadat (see Ayubi, 1991b, 53–4). In addition, average Egyptians enjoyed larger personal freedoms compared to Nasser's time (Lippman, 1989, 189). This distinction is crucial in establishing that the writings of al-Banna and al-Bishri, under Sadat, were expected to reflect this widening scope of freedom, the nascent, though restricted, political plurality[14] which was missing under Nasser.

The 'Islamic': Between the regime and the MB

Sadat, similar to Nasser, cared to posit the public image of a president who didn't antagonize Islam. One could get reductions on construction costs if a room was set for prayers (see McDermott, 1988, 51). In many photos, Sadat is seen practising Islamic rituals (Kogelmann, 1994, 87). He deliberately augmented his character as a president who *cared for* Islam when he included a provision in the 1971 Constitution stipulating that Islam was a key source of legislation. This provision was amended a few years later to the following: 'Islam is the key source of legislation.' Such provisions did not exist in the constitutions drafted and ratified under Nasser, namely those of 1956 and 1958 (see Muzikar, 1989, 109).

In the early 1970s, he initiated an *Islamic* debate, through al-Azhar, about the Islamic economy (*al-Iqtisad al-Islami*) and its compatibility with key propositions of capitalism (see Zahid, 2010, 82). Strongly co-opting al-Azhar, Sadat used the clergy in his rivalry with Islamist opposition, which, as stated earlier, grew fiercely after the signing of the peace treaty. He had top-ranking religious clergy propagating the treaty. It was announced, in a communiqué, that both the Camp David agreement and the peace treaty were in complete concordance with Islam (see Görgün, 1997, 61).

Initially, Sadat released members of the MB who were imprisoned by his predecessor (Makari, 2007, 55), but his approach to Islamists was generally utilitarian. He played them against the left and viewed them as a counterweight to leftist opposition (see McDermott, 1988, 51; Zahid, 2010, 82). It was also his approach towards other Islamist groups, like al-Jamaʿa al-Islamiyya, which grew in power and gained influence due to Sadat's initial use of Islamists against the left (see Bayat, 2013b, 186–7). Therefore, *promoting Islam* in the political sphere came from Sadat himself (McDermott, 1988, 188; Karūm, 2012, 35).

Sadat succeeded in controlling the country's political landscape, excluding groups capable of attesting his rule before and after pluriparty politics, through *flexible* legal provisions defining legitimate and illegitimate political forces within 'controllable routes' (Harders, 1998, 274). Thus, although the regime opened up, the peace treaty and the widening social inequality resulting from Infitah brought Sadat wider opposition and less popularity than Nasser.

Towards outlining regime red lines in the public sphere, he persecuted several public figures. Fu'ad Siraj al-Din, al-Wafd Party leader of the time, described the Free Officer's Movement (*Harakat al-Dubbat al-Ahrar*), to which Sadat belonged, as a mere 'coup d'etat'. In retaliation, Sadat drafted a legislation for political isolation in order to politically exclude Siraj al-Din (see Gordon, 1992, 7). The harassment of Siraj al-Din became known due to his relatively prominent position in Egypt as a top-ranking politician, who survived blockage imposed on al-Wafd Party and his founding of the *revived* al-Wafd Party in 1977 (see Goldschmidt, 2013, 435).

Similarly, when Ihsan 'Abd al-Qudus, the renowned Egyptian novelist, disagreed in 1976 about a statement that Sadat made in public relating to his intention to get the army to protect the constitution and upon Sadat's own advice published an article expressing his view, he was directly removed from his position in *al-Ahram*, as head of its executive board (see Fawzī, 2001, 150). These two incidents meant Sadat's public statements and the 1952 coup were red lines he set through direct harassment of prominent public figures. Evidently, the common ground of Nasser's and Sadat's regimes is setting a red line on criticizing the head of the state, as established through the cases of Hilmi Sallam and Ihsan 'Abd al-Qudus.

Meanwhile, under Sadat, journalists *criticizing Egypt* were stripped of their nationality, even when they resided abroad (al-Bāz, 1998, 89). The press syndicate fell under government influence. Authorities employed regime resources to guide the outcome of syndicate elections; some candidates who criticized the regime faced difficulties or were simply blocked (see Beattie, 2000, 242).

Al-Banna and al-Bishri under Sadat

Compared to his writings under Nasser, al-Banna's Islamic profile was evolving; he wrote overtly about Islam, especially about syndicalism from an Islamic perspective and Islamic calls (al-Bannā. 1978; al-Bannā 1981b). Yet, he largely maintained two features. First, he posited a very positive understanding of the religion and the practice in early Islamic history. Second, his writings visibly conformed to mainstream claims; he maintained there is a state in Islam, that Islam entails politics, not just the religion (1978, 139; 1979a, 53). Although there is a faint trace to his renewal scheme in his claim that Islam is Qur'an and Sunna and that juridical efforts should be seen within their respective contexts (al-Bannā, 1979a, 24; 1981b, 106), controversial elements of his intellectual record, colliding with mainstream propositions, appeared later under Mubarak. Accordingly, there was no ground for al-Banna to get persecuted by al-Azhar, which appeared, as pointed out earlier, to be a co-player in the country's public sphere.

Otherwise, he stayed largely concerned with syndicalism and labour struggle (1973; 1979c; 1981b); he also wrote on Egyptian politics. As shown earlier, the multi-party system in Egypt was enacted in July 1977. In his book The Intellectual Origins of the Islamic State (*al-Usul al-Fikriyya li-l-Dawla al-Islamiyya*), he maintained that one reason for the totalitarian nature of fascist and Nazi states was their endorsement of the single-party system (1979a, 95). His view on party politics as *acceptable* was clear when he discussed the prospect of adopting it in the Islamic state, where he argued that there is no ground to reject multi-partism (1978, 253).

While strongly avoiding direct critique of Sadat's policies, al-Banna wrote overtly on the vices of corruption that plagued Egypt under King Faruq's and Nasser's oppressive politics. He associated the 1967 defeat to political ignorance (*Jahala Siyasiyya*), which, according to him, became a feature of both leaders and masses in Egypt (al-Bannā, 1977, 7). Likewise, while criticizing the subordination of Egyptian Press, he referred to incidents and practices which took place under Nasser and Faruq and portrayed the former as 'the man who conspired against the MB and did not commit himself and his rule to the path set for the 1952 revolution' (al-Bannā, 1978, 10–11).

As pointed out earlier, Sadat not only promoted a public image of himself and his rule as caring for Islam but also used the MB, with many of its members allowed back from neighbouring Gulf countries, against the left and other political forces. Only towards the end of his rule did Sadat antagonize the MB, especially after the signing of the peace treaty in 1979 (see Beattie, 2000, 273–4; Ayubi, 1991b, 94; Hassan, 2010, 321). Put differently, before the peace treaty, Sadat's policy vis-à-vis the MB was not only more tolerant compared to Nasser but also largely utilitarian. Accordingly, writing about the MB was for the largest part of Sadat's rule quite *safe* and this resonated in al-Banna's writings under Sadat. On one hand, he blamed Nasser for oppressing the movement, while on the other hand, he highlighted the various strengths of the MB compared to other contemporary Islamist movements like *al-Jama'a* in India (1978, 10; 186–95). More generally, his books on syndicalism constituted no ground to collide with Sadat, as his interest and involvement in syndicalism started years before Sadat's rule, and his works contained long historical narrations, heavily occupied with theoretical aspects (1973) and Western syndical history (1979c).

Expectedly, writing about the 1952 coup under Sadat meant greater space to freely assess and criticize it, except for calling it a coup d'etat, which was reason to persecute Siraj al-Din above, and it was equally all right to criticize the Nasser regime. This was traceable in al-Bishri's writings when he asserted the regime was despotic and did not abide by democratic procedures, be these parliamentary or party politics, and when he addressed the political harassment committed against the MB under Nasser (al-Bishrī, 2004, 796–8). In a similar vein, he wrote on the pre-1952 history, offering a very positive account on the provisions of the 1923 Constitution. He also displayed the history of parliamentary opposition in Egypt starting the mid-nineteenth century up till Nasser's rule, which, in his account, suppressed this opposition (1987a, 55–74; 107–23, respectively). Through these ex-regime accounts, there was no ground for collision with the Sadat regime, as no red lines were crossed. In fact, depicting the Nasser regime as repressive served Sadat's presidency, which, as shown above, was keen to shed negative light on his predecessor's time through movies.

Once again, after the peace arrangements with Israel, Egypt's Islamists opposed Sadat's foreign policy, which culminated into one of the strongest cracks on freedoms in 1981. Writing on Israel as *the enemy*, the Arab-Israeli conflict and/or Arab unity must have become part of the public debate but, by the same token, must have fallen under this pressure towards the late 1970s. Al-Bishri's article, first published in July 1978 – the year of the Camp David Accords – signified this pressure. His account on Arab unity maintained that advocating the Palestinian cause against *Zionism*, which he defined in the interviews as a movement based on the call to immigrate to Palestinian lands and the establishment of a state there (Interview, 2 June 2011), was integral to the rhetoric of any wide-appealing political movement at the time the state of Israel was created in 1948. He also asserted that the 1952 *revolution* was carried out by the military, partly because of the centrality of Palestine and its cause to Egyptians (1978, 37–41). Although published in 1978, the article stopped in its account on the Arab-Israeli conflict at the mid-1950s. Thus, while exhibiting the centrality of the Palestinian cause to Egyptian politics, al-Bishri *silenced* on Sadat's policy towards Israel, which was a main source of Sadat's political opposition.

Not addressing the accord and the larger shift of Sadat's policy towards Israel could arguably be associated with the intended focus of al-Bishri's paper, and not with the Sadat regime/opposition contestation over peace with Israel. But his position on the accord is expressed under Mubarak; he mocked Sadat's visit to Israel as *amazing* and presented the Camp David Accords as an effort orchestrated by Zionists and Americans who failed to end the conflict and rather shifted it from conventional armed combat to liberation movements from within the masses (2006c, 20–1). With such an opposing tone, this account might have directly collided with Sadat, especially at a time when the political landscape was heating up with dissent and the regime overtly suppressed the opposition. Publishing it under Mubarak, thus, spared him potential collision with the Sadat regime.

Mubarak: New media under control

Mubarak inherited the peace with Israel as well as the large-scale detentions of opposition forces that Sadat initiated towards the end of his rule. Shielded with the vast presidential prerogatives in the 1971 Constitution and control over Parliament via sweeping majorities, the restricted multi-partism, which was launched under Sadat, could not shake his regime's strong grip on power. The upheaval resulting from inflation and corruption found expression through the public sphere, which enlarged starting the 1990s. Yet, the regime could still control disseminated material through irregular acts of harassment and setting its own red lines.

Controlling the legislature

Already entitled to constitutional vast presidential prerogatives[15] (Ḥasan, 2012, 344) like Nasser and Sadat, Mubarak sought to extend his control over the legislature. Towards that goal, forging elections became a common practice to secure two-thirds of the seats required for passing bills into laws (see Farrūkh, 2011, 24). The regime had *easy* access to electoral registers and could manipulate elections through impeding access to polling stations and tampering ballot boxes (Kienle, 2000, 27). At the advent of the first parliamentary elections in 1984, Mubarak amended the electoral law to add impediments on political competition and secure his ultimate dominant position so that only candidates of legalized political parties could run for Parliament (Zahid, 2010, 97). These were parties licensed by the Committee for Political Parties Affairs, which was, on its turn, seen as part of the regime and serving its interests (Stacher, 2004, 220).

One infamous incident, in this respect, was that of the Centrist Party (*al-Wasat*), which first appeared in January 1996. It was denied permission by the Committee. A later appeal in May 1999 was also rejected on the suspicion that Abu al-'Ila Madi, founder of the party, was member of the MB, although he denied links between the party and the MB. There was also no clear evidence linking the two (see Makari, 2007, 130–5). In a similar vein, the Alliance of People's Working Forces' (*Tahaluf Quwa al-Sha'b al-'Amila*) application to establish a political party was declined, on the allegation that party program, inter alia, indicated commitment to totalitarianism. Similarly, socialists/Nasserists were denied legal existence. Blocked from the political sphere, they resorted to conspiracies, and subsequently were arrested and ill-treated in prison (Baker, 1990, 111).

Moreover, the state of emergency allowed the regime to obstruct opposition parties from organizing electoral meetings in public places and arrest party activists or candidates at polling stations (Kienle, 2000, 27). The regime could smoothly block undesired candidates (Hartmann, 2011, 108), and voter buying (*Shiraa al-Nakhib*) was a common practice during elections (see Blaydes, 2011, 104). Therefore, the multi-party system, initiated by Sadat, was maintained under Mubarak, who had a similar drive to concentrate power.

To sustain the grip on vital state organs and the political sphere, rivals were frequently called in by state security (*Amn al-Dawlah*); its headquarters in Cairo were used as centres for torturing detainees[16] (Farrūkh, 2011, 41). Meanwhile, emergency laws maximized state's authority to detain those suspected to represent a threat to National Security (Wickham, 2002, 71). The renewal of emergency laws expanded the autonomous authority of the president in decision-making (Harders, 2009, 305). Many inside-prison suicide cases, incited by cruel treatment, were reported and there was an escalating level of food strikes on the part of prisoners (see Shammākh, 2012, 66). Under the broad banner of combating extremism and terrorism, innocent civilians were detained along with actual terrorists, and massive detentions did not end acts of violence (see 'Īsā, 2008, 89). Even worse, the regime, through its intelligence service, resorted to recruiting agents through direct blackmail (Sirrs, 2010, 171–2).

Worth noting, the military courts used under Mubarak, and the harsh trial conditions associated with them, have roots under Nasser and Sadat (see Brown and Dunne, 2014). The aforementioned 1971 Constitution, still in force under Mubarak, allowed the law to establish courts, define their powers and set criteria governing the appointment and transfer of their members.[17] Moreover, state security courts, which are used mainly against political activists and the larger opposition, along with their powers, were determined through laws[18] (Kienle, 2000, 42). Authoritarian practices were, thus, an accumulation of successive autocratic regimes.

Mubarak, like Sadat, passed laws to secure political dominance and his regime capitalized on these laws in its adversity with the MB. This started after the MB electoral rise in many professional syndicates; a law was passed in 1993 to reorganize syndical elections, so that at least half the members should cast their vote, as a threshold for the first round, and a third of them for the second one. The underlying rationale was that the MB could make it to top syndical positions due to apathy amongst the majority of syndicate members ('Abd al-Majīd, 2010, 135). Likewise, through law No. 84/2002 on regulating the establishment of non-governmental organizations (NGOs), all associations with at least ten members must register in the Ministry of Insurance and Social Affairs. In case of non-compliance, members would face imprisonment. While the law allowed NGOs to work in the field of human rights activism, the respective organizations had to get permission from the ministry. Hence, there were limitations on their freedom to organize, especially since Article 11 of the law included broad themes of *not pursuing goals violating national unity, public order and morals.*[19]

Put together, the regime maintained political control through tailor-made laws, forging elections and emergency laws. Nonetheless, under Mubarak, this tendency to control or manipulate the political sphere faced two *counter-effects*; namely, the economy and the media.

Economic upheaval and controlled 'new' media

Unemployment, especially among the educated, was on the rise, and prices soared rapidly compared to income, the gap between living standards widened, housing prices sky-rocketed and squatter settlements spread enormously ('Amīn, 2009, 247). Launched in 1991, privatization included some profitable companies, in sectors like tourism and construction material, but Egyptian decision-makers did not have a specific plan or strategy for applying the privatization scheme (see Zahid, 2010, 53; see also Kassab, 2018).

Corruption was another challenge to add to deteriorating economic conditions and increasing popular dissent. Starting 2005 onwards, several top-ranking state officials and big businessmen were involved in corruption scandals but were not held responsible for their misconduct (see 'Īsā, 2008, 180–2; Blaydes, 2011, 134). With roots under Nasser and Sadat, corruption of the Mubarak regime was deeper than just the listing of a few incidents:

> The phenomenon of political corruption in Egypt is characterized by several traits. At the core is the fact that corruption has become an integral part of the working mechanisms in a number of state institutions, due to the inability of the Central Auditing Organization to audit the lower echelons of the administrative structure. Another reason is the involvement of some of the higher political and administrative officials in corrupt practices. (Hassan, 2010, 324)

Thus, under Mubarak, the economy performed poorly and popular dissent boiled. This was clearest towards 2005, when economic demands of textile factories in al-*Mahala al-Kubra*, an Egyptian governorate, escalated into a huge strike in 2006 and exerted serious pressure towards economic reform (see Iskandar, 2014, 121–32). Mubarak did not endorse a national ideology (ʾAmīn, 2009, 30) that might have helped counterbalance economic hardships, and with the regime unwilling to offer economic or political concessions in order to mitigate dissent, restrictions were severed. More than once, journalists, criticizing the regime in party and independent newspapers, were physically attacked; it was widely believed that State Security orchestrated and carried out these attacks. Jamal Badawi, back-then editor-in-chief of *al-Wafd* newspaper, and ʿAbd al-Halim Qandil, back-then chief editor of *al-ʿArabi* newspaper, were both brutalized (ʿAllām, 2012, 144).

Likewise, when Nawal al-Saʿdawi, a renowned Egyptian intellectual, published a play titled God Resigns at the Summit Conference, she spent three years in exile until her lawyer convinced the judge that Mubarak was not *the God* in the play (see el Saadawi, 2011, 6). Besieging the public sphere, Egypt turned into a jail of opinion prisoners (*Sujanaʾ Al-Raʾy*) without trials, and based on no legal grounds, other than the aforementioned emergency law (ʿĪsā, 2008, 89). All these constraints culminated towards jeopardizing individual autonomy of those involved in intellectual production, who dared transgress specific red lines, regarding Mubarak and his family.

Media and the internet were potentially a counter-effect to the regime control in this regard; both could potentially serve as means towards uncovering state violations and highlighting economic suffering and the subsequent popular dissatisfaction (see El Tantawy and Wiest, 2011). In Egypt, starting the 1990s, the regime granted licenses to several non-state-owned media channels. Thus, the public sphere was expected to partly break away from the regime's strong grip. However, using articles from the penal code and the state of emergency, the regime continued *guiding* content of the material disseminated through non-state-owned channels (Abdulla, 2014). Even non-Egyptian media were exposed to state harassment; after pointing out the economic activities of ʿAlaa Mubarak, the president's son, in a Saudi magazine called *Saiyadati* (My Lady) in 1997, the Cairo office of the magazine was closed and employees were laid off ('Allām, 2012, 146).

Despite being strongly restricted, developments in the field of media partly contributed to relative vividness of the country's public sphere. Since 2005, official newspapers and the opposition/independent rivals contested government performance, where the first portrayed the second as selfish and unpatriotic agents with false information, damaging the country's security, and the second claimed they reported on government corruption and social injustice and accused national press of speaking for the regime (el-Bendary, 2010, 8).

Opposition parties' newspapers and conferences condemned government performance and policies (Kahmīs and Mukhtār, 2011, 23–4), but this press rivalry was allowed within the ceiling of Mubarak and his family. Jamal Badawi, as pointed out above, was harshly beaten by men who were never identified, after he published an article criticizing one of Mubarak's statements. Similarly, 'Abd al-Halim Qandil referred to Jamal Mubarak's succession scheme, which will be discussed below, before he was physically attacked ('Allām, 2012, 144).

Prohibition of publishing *false news* such as defaming the president and foreign leaders, and the requirement of avoiding defamation were irregularly used to set red lines and control the public sphere. Some of the legal restrictions imposed on press freedom under Mubarak date back to the Nasser era, such as those prohibiting Egyptian journalists to publish about the military without prior permission (Abdel Kouddous, 2011). Commonly, charges of defamation were used as a way to silence critics (Mansour, 2013).

Although the regime managed to set its red lines and generally mould public sphere debates, the growing public sphere, with new media, internet and private newspapers, drove the regime towards *rationalizing* its oppressive apparatus.[20] This put more scrutiny on the content of particular media, like newspapers, compared to others, like printed books. But the Mubarak regime managed to *tame* the internet as a venue for popular dissent. In 2008, using the internet, Israa 'Abd al-Fattah, an Egyptian female activist, supported the cause of the textile factory strike on facebook. She cut across the country's secularist/Islamist spectrum in protest of the regime's corruption and worsening economic conditions of the population in what is known as the 6 April Youth Movement. 'Abd al-Fattah was shortly detained by state security in the aftermath of the protest day (Salvatore, 2011, 9). Under Mubarak, several bloggers were jailed; the regime closely monitored internet content, and when necessary resorted to direct arrests and intimidation (Hussien, 2018). Ultimately, boundaries on freedom of expression seemed as if they were expanding with independent newspapers, non-state-owned media and the internet, though covert censorship was increasing (Mehrez, 2008, 18).

Thus, while economic hardships fed popular dissent, the regime succeeded in controlling the media and internet, through licenses for TV channels and security arrests of political activists who used the internet to mobilize against the regime. Hence, the new avenues that emerged first during Mubarak's rule were, as shown above, largely circumvented by the regime towards suppressing its opponents. In particular, the case of Israa 'Abd al-Fattah demonstrated how the regime realized the potential the internet held for political mobilization, and subsequently penalized those involved.

Likewise, Mubarak's son Jamal's succession scheme instigated fierce opposition, after he assumed high-profile positions as the Assistant Secretary-General of the NDP and Head of the party's Policy Secretariat, and frequently represented his father abroad (Cook, 2007, 138). The corruption scheme, which added to economic challenges, pointed out earlier, and the rise of Jamal in the country's politics were marred by an alliance between those who had money and those who had power, including President Mubarak himself (Farrūkh, 2011, 17). Persons like Muhammad Mansur, Rashid Muhammad Rashid and Ahmed 'Izz,[21] who largely associated with Jamal Mubarak, were granted ministerial and top NDP positions (Roll, 2013, 9). One famous protest movement, called Enough (*Kifaya*) played a key role in drawing public attention to this infamous succession. It began in 2004 and evolved as one by-product of the blockage and political *stiffness* of political parties (see Qandīl, 2010, 187). It started by formulating basic reform demands, such as preventing Mubarak's re-election and Jamal's hereditary succession (Arafat, 2009, 158). Its principal architects of the coalition came from diverse political groups (Oweidat et al., 2008, 11).

The uniqueness of the movement was not in its motto or its distinguished members, rather, in the fact that it was the start of a round of protests (see Ḥasan, 2012, 221), the fabric of *Kifaya*, comprising Islamists and secularists, also meant the poles of the opposition spectrum could work together against the regime. The same was again evident in 2008, with the coalition established by Israa 'Abd al-Fattah above (Ezzeldeen, 2010). Both movements capitalized on the public sphere – the 6th of April, via facebook, and Kifaya, through a focus on bloggers first, then on the general public, then on local and international media (see Oweidat et al., 2008, 22). They technically moved contestations occurring in the political sphere to the public sphere; their key members were, thus, harshly persecuted by the regime.

Yet, except for Mubarak and his family, red lines were shifting all the time, creating a duality of *must/may be penalized* pool of topics. Opposition often tested the shifting red lines (Brown and Hamzawy, 2010, 13–14); they mainly shifted on government corruption. Whereas several journalists, reporting on it,[22] were persecuted by the regime, many others were not.[23]

This was different from the state of the public sphere under Nasser and Sadat where red lines were, for the most part, fixed. While direct critique of Nasser's rule and writing on democracy and freedom were singled out as red lines which should be evaded, through the cases of Sallam and Abaza, defaming the 1952 coup resulted in repressive measures against Siraj al-Din under Sadat. Still, shifting red lines do not necessarily induce the potential for a freer public sphere with fewer controls. In fact, it ends up with intellectuals spending more time and effort to *keep themselves informed* about these shifts; maintaining a sense of caution and disguise in the public sphere does not, thus, decrease.

In a similar vein, openly persecuting activists who used the internet for mobilization sent wider signals to similar initiatives of the potential harassment by the Mubarak regime. Detentions and arrests of tens of journalists and bloggers, carried out under Mubarak, due to defamation charges meant those involved in the public sphere fell under similar pressure of the Nasser and Sadat regimes. Yet, it largely targeted journalists, newspapers and media TV channels rather than intellectuals and books,[24] like the ones published by al-Banna and al-Bishri. This feature will become visible in the profile of al-Bishri, who despite tense relations with the Mubarak regime, wrote on government corruption and the need for more frequent alternation in positions of power in Egyptian Judiciary between Autonomy and Co-optation (2006b), but was never persecuted and his book was never confiscated.

The regime-Azhar duality

Like its predecessors, the Mubarak regime tried to establish some degree of Islamic legitimacy (Ḥabīb, 2012, 36), and regime's relation to al-Azhar was largely cooperative. Al-Azhar's Grand Sheikh/Imam is appointed by the government and approved by the president – Mubarak – himself (Bayoumy, 2010). Their cooperation was strongly embodied in the bank interest rates scheme; Muhammad Sayyid Tantawi, al-Azhar Grand Sheikh at that time, insisted that interest rates offered by state banks are in full compliance with Islamic rules (Mostyn, 2010). Later on, he endorsed a ban on the face veil in public schools, which is part of Islamic law, according to some established religious clergy. He also supported France's decision to ban the hair veil in public schools (Hardy, 2010).

But this support must be read in context; under Mubarak, namely in the 1980s, several Islamic businesses were on the rise and this resulted in serious competition to state banks. The emerging businesses attracted millions of dollars, which were partly invested by remittance companies and offered relatively higher rates compared with those offered by state counterparts. As some of these companies faced economic difficulties, the Egyptian Central Bank did not cover the deposits and entertained that the public might link these businesses to Islamist militancy in the 1980s. The country's public sphere was, thus, heavily employed to foster and propagate the position of both Islamic businesses, mainly through al-Qaradawi[25] – a renowned Egyptian Jurist – and the state, through al-Azhar Sheikh Tantawi (see Wilson, 2003, 147–8).

Likewise, during the 2011 uprising, at the time of drastic and escalating upheaval against the Mubarak regime, al-Azhar support was still echoed through Ahmad al-Tayyib, Grand Sheikh of al-Azhar, who called the protests *civil strife* (Maʿhad al-ʿArabiyya lil-Dirāsāt, 2012). All this reflected the co-optation of al-Azhar by the regime. But this resembles Sadat's relation to al-Azhar regarding the peace treaty, and it is not really different from Nasser's general profile of using religious clergy against Islamist activists. The three regimes practically spared themselves potential contestation from the religious institution and *used* the latter to combat rivals and gain ground. Without exaggeration, regime's relation to al-Azhar did not break away from the legacy established under Nasser to subordinate al-Azhar and rely on its cooperation against political/economic rivalry, a relation largely guided by the typical logic of al-Sheikh/al-Sultan or the clergy/the ruler in Islamic history (see al-Qimnī, 2022).

Largely cooperative, al-Azhar co-defined content circulated in the public sphere under Mubarak. A Banquet for Sea Weeds (*Walima li-Aʿshab al-Bahr*), a novel written by Haydar Haydar, was harshly attacked by *Al-Shaʿb* newspaper, of the Socialist Labor Party (hizb al'amal al-ishtiraki), as blasphemous to Islam. Though published under the supervision of the Ministry of Culture – the government – Tantawi, Sheikh al-Azhar at the time, condemned the novel and its author. He held the ministry responsible for its content and demanded that al-Azhar censored its publications (Mehrez, 2008, 19).

Adding to this, *societal* Islam was visibly present. By the early 1990s, private – Ahli – mosques were around 40,000 in number; this was more than a 100 per cent increase in less than two decades, even though government-controlled mosques also increased at about 40 per cent from 1975 till the late 1980s. But religious welfare associations and Islamic activism among the younger generations proliferated. Several Muslim intellectuals, like Muhammad Salim al-ʿAwa and Muhammed ʿImara, promoted their own religious call (*Daʿwa*) (Bayat, 2007, 32–5,137).

Furthermore, with the rise of privately owned media, Muslim televangelists addressed youngsters mainly from the middle and lower classes. They attracted a huge audience and had their preaching on DVDs and audiotapes, private media and the internet (Salvatore and Eickelmann, 2004). This media offered alternative views to the ones propagated by state-sponsored religious institutions. Meanwhile, the Iranian revolution indirectly resulted in the Gulf states issuing larger financing to Islamist groups around the globe, including the MB and al-Jamaʿa al-Islamiyya – groups which were mainly part of the opposition of the Mubarak regime – to combat the Shiite tide represented by the Iranian system (Esposito, 2010, 8; 76). Thus, under Mubarak, societal Islam was growing across the country and the regime-Azahr alliance did not translate into the regime having a full monopoly of Islamic preaching.

Al-Banna and al-Bishri under Mubarak

Due to the fact that al-Bishri's writings do not deviate from the general tenets of mainstream Islam,[26] technically, al-Azahr did not constitute a threat to his intellectual path at large. Nonetheless, al-Banna, especially under Mubarak, posited a clearly liberal profile (see al-Bannā, 1995e, 2002a, 2005a). The content of his books contradicts, and even collides, with the juristic profile and intellectual production propagated by al-Azahr (see Slackman, 2006), especially when it comes to the Hadith filtration he so whole-heartedly advocated (see El-Hennawy, 2013). So, the potential role of al-Azhar as a co-definer of ideas *permitted* in the public sphere was more relevant to the work of al-Banna under Mubarak compared to his writings under Nasser and Sadat. Al-Azhar banned two of his books, namely The Responsibility for Failure of the Islamic State and Other Research (*Masʾuliyyat Fashal al-Dawla al-Islamiyya wa-Buḥūth ʾUkhrā)* (1994a) and The Muslim Woman between Emancipation of Qur'an and Jurists' Restrictions (*al-Marʾa al-Muslima baiyn Taqiyyid al-Fuqahaʾ wa Tahrir al-Qurʾan)* (2002c) under Mubarak (see ʿAbd al-Ḥalīm, 2008).

Still, al-Banna mostly presented al-Azhar in negative light, criticizing its lack of autonomy from the state (see al-Ḥirānī, 2014) and wasn't penalized for it. This meant the Mubarak regime was focused on itself. In other words, as much as government critique was occasionally tolerated, criticizing the religious institution was also overlooked. In fact, the Mubarak regime had an implicit secularist orientation that was heavily symbolized through his Ministry of Culture, under Faruq Husni (see Mehrez, 2008, 19). It was also exemplified through his awarding of al-Qimni, who strongly deviated from the mainstream body of jurisprudence.[27]

But as two of his books were actually banned under Mubarak, the duality of censorship, under Nasser, continued to dominate the country's public sphere, where the regime censored the political and al-Azhar censored the religious. The attack on al-Banna was not just about the content of his Ijtihad per se. It touched upon the larger question of 'who speaks for Islam' (see Kamrava, 2006; Krämer and Schmidtke, 2006), who qualifies for an Islamic intellectual and ultimately who defines the religious truth. In the same breath, it is the contested *benchmark* of jurisprudential background, presented in the introduction, which got al-Banna's intellectual production scrutinized.

Aside from his Islamic renewal scheme, syndical interest was still traceable in his writings (1981b, 1987b, 1990, 1992, 1995d, 1993, 1994b). A significant bulk of his contributions on syndicalism and labour movements in general were published under Mubarak, such as Syndical Freedom *(al-Hurriyya al-Niqabiyya)* (1989) and Professional Syndicates in Egypt in the Survival Battle (*al-Niqabat al-Mihaniyya al-Misriyya fi Ma'rakat al-*Baqaa) (1995d). His critique of the Egyptian syndical movement in the first book is a clear embodiment of the kind of control the Mubarak regime imposed on the public sphere; intellectuals might criticize a law or government performance but not the president, his policies or his family. Even when he referred to the linkage between autocratic regimes and a strong grip over syndicates (1992, 617), he presented it from a theoretical angle, without naming the regime or syndicalism under Mubarak. When assessing the history of syndicalism, al-Banna kept the critique very general. He did not specifically attribute the negative sides he addressed to Mubarak or his regime (1992, 617–41), although the regime was known to control syndicates mainly through legal frameworks (see Hassan, 2011).

Once again, the Islamic renewal profile of al-Banna was visible mainly under Mubarak (1991b, 1994a, 1995e, 2000, 2008c, 2010c), where he openly argued against abidance to the four schools of Sunni jurisprudence and maintained committing to Hadith is to be evaluated according to its consistency with Qur'anic text (1983, 8; 2005c, 239–56; 2008c, 7–9; 2010c, 3–6). Although al-Banna's press house, established towards the end of the 1990s, meant larger autonomy in publishing his renewal stances, there is reason to believe the regime was *not* offended by the content of his writings. Regime harassment of intellectuals and public figures was heavily induced by political critique of Mubarak, his policies and family. Al-Banna was never jailed or even reprised by state security during Mubarak's thirty years in power, even with al-Azhar confiscating two of his books as pointed out earlier (2002c, 1994a; see ʿAbd al-Ḥalīm, 2008).

Apart from these two main themes of syndicalism and Islamic renewal, there is no one particular theme that was characteristic of al-Banna's writings under Mubarak. Generally, he maintained the habit of criticizing former regimes and presidents like in his writings under Nasser and Sadat. Under Mubarak, he defamed Nasser for resisting the MB and torturing prisoners, which he claimed instigated Islamic radicalism. He also blamed the corruption leading up to the 1967 defeat and maintained Nasser should have been penalized for it (1996b, 93; 1997, 104–18). Likewise, he blamed regime corruption under Sadat for the growing tensions between Muslims and Copts, and highlighted the instrumental nature of Sadat's approach to the MB, stating that using them against the left was part of Sadat's strong hold on power (2006b, 280; 1996b, 80–1). Al-Banna's tendency to generalize his critique, when he linked autocratic rule to strong controls on syndicates, was also visible when he addressed electoral fraud. In spite of the fact that all three regimes resorted to forging election/referendum results, al-Banna's account was rather *abstract* in nature. He wrote of how democratic practices, like elections, could be abused and result in fortifying autocratic rule (1986a, 11). This way, he negotiated red lines. On one hand, he highlighted the practice of forging elections, which was characteristic of the Mubarak regime; on the other, he evaded direct collision with the regime through avoiding addressing the issue in an overt manner.

Whereas al-Banna contested al-Azhar on the religious truth, al-Bishri contested the Mubarak regime control over the political sphere. In 1992, serving back then as head of the administrative court, he ruled against a presidential decision to transfer a number of civilians with an Islamist background to military courts. Al-Bishri was, in result, deprived of his potential promotion to preside the State Council (Muṣṭafā and Raḥīm, 2011). As pointed out earlier, emergency laws and military courts were employed by the regime as part of intimidating and excluding political opponents. Hence, al-Bishri's decision served as a counter-blow to the regime blockage on Islamists in the political sphere.

Moreover, authoritarian regimes, like that of Mubarak, usually resort to subtle means of controlling judges, who are legally autonomous. Physical attacks on judges were quite rare, and mechanisms like institutional incentives or limiting access to justice in order to contain judges are usually employed (see

Moustafa and Ginsburg, 2008, 14). From this perspective, al-Bishri's writings on the judiciary (2006b) cannot be solely read as the by-product of his background as a judge apart from this particular incident, above, and the subsequent regime *retaliation* on his judicial career. His strong emphasis on judicial independence in his writings could be well grasped in light of his personal encounter with the regime. Although al-Bishri's decision was based on objective and substantial legal grounds, this incident of nullifying military trials of Islamists and his focus on judicial autonomy in his books signify how the political sphere instigated *debates* in the public sphere. Seen from a different angle, it is an element of silence in al-Bishri's intellectual production; the book does not tell the whole story. It addressed a critical issue in the country's political sphere, but his own experience was not brought up, although the book was published long after this incident.

Still, he overtly addressed a physical assault in the 1950s, on the Egyptian judge and head of the State Council of the time, ʿAbd al-Razzaq al-Sanhuri, amid regime-orchestrated demonstrations. He presented the incident as a sign of government encroachment on state authorities, including that of the judiciary (al-Bishrī, 2006b, 14–18). This open criticism of the Nasser regime falls well within the aforementioned trend of *safely* criticizing ex-regimes and late presidents, as one way of avoiding direct collision with ruling ones. More than once, al-Bishri invoked democracy (2007a, 28–30) and judicial independence (2006b), without referring to the Mubarak regime, which was evidently authoritarian. The key feature of his writings, under Mubarak, was tackling abstract debates which do not represent, in principle, a transgression on regime red lines, such as Islamic Thought (1996c), Arab and Islamic unity (1998) and the concept of contemporaneity, (2007b) on one hand, and his overt Islamic profile (2001, 2005a, 2007a) on the other. Under Mubarak, his fascination with Islamic Shariʿa could be spotted more than once; he praised its capacity to renew its branches while preserving its origins (*'Uṣūl*) (2005a, 102) and asserted Shariʿa enjoyed sacredness among Muslims (2008, 63).

As pointed out earlier, the Mubarak regime maintained a public image conforming to mainstream Islam. This was partly due to its cooperative relation to al-Azhar, which was evident during the interest rate debate in the 1980s, above, and the general Islamic-friendly profile of the regime. Thus, praising Shariʿa did not cause collision with the regime, which introduced itself and its legal provisions as based on, and conforming to, Shariʿa.

The closest he ever came to crossing regime red lines under Mubarak was in his book Egypt between Disobedience and Disintegration (*Misr baiyn al-'Isiyan wa-l-Tafakkuk*), where he addressed the succession scheme as being *under preparation* (2006a, 41). Although the succession scheme was one of the *fixed* red lines that could not be publicly transgressed under Mubarak, his statement was still broad and brief enough not to incite regime harassment. In addition, as shown earlier, books under Mubarak were not the key targets of regime persecution, rather the press, media and the internet, in the last decade of his rule. This way, al-Bishri managed to express his views without colliding with the repressive regime of Mubarak's rule.

Post-uprising politics: Positions reshuffled

As the regime managed to keep control over internet content, top government figures such as Mubarak's own son Jamal, made fun of notions like change through facebook (al-Hawwārī, 2012, 85), which became fatal to the entire regime in 2011. The resistance that started out with Kifaya ended up with ousting Mubarak (Oweidat et al., 2008, 22). Along with economic upheaval, Jamal's succession, the money-power alliance and its association with economic corruption led the Mubarak regime down a spiral (see Hussien, 2018). Egyptian politics under Mubarak was turning into an interwoven, multi-layered set of political and economic trouble:

> More political openness and participation alone can not legitimize the system – esp. if they are confined to the loyal forces, the majority of which belong to the middle and upper class, as long as the basic problems of population explosion, economic weakness, over-bureaucratization and corruption are not seriously addressed. The socially, economically and politically motivated dissatisfactions, namely the academic youth and the under paid and underemployed public officials grow and through democratization of political institutions alone will not be contained. (Krämer, 1986, 126)

After Mubarak's ouster on 11 February 2011, al-Banna and al-Bishri wrote and published very few books, compared to their relatively large accumulation of writings throughout their intellectual paths.[28] In addition, al-Banna passed away in January 2013 and this ended the fieldwork period, which took roughly two years. Therefore, I here present relatively brief accounts on alterations in the political sphere after the uprising; the focus is on the shift from the typical Mubarak regime to the Supreme Council of Armed forces (SCAF), then to the MB-led government, then to SCAF again till Sisi's 2014 election as president.

After Mubarak, the opposition went through serious alterations, mainly through including new elements and forces, which were politically blocked under the three regimes but were allowed legal and institutional existence after the uprising, then at the advent of Mursi's ouster in 2013, relapsed into pre-2011 repressive practices and re-excluding the MB along with Islamist parties which supported the latter (Dunne and Hamzawy, 2017). Themes of political and economic corruption largely remained in the scope of contesting the new regime, with the succession scheme put decidedly aside. These shifts in regime/opposition composition are the key alterations that I expected to resonate in the works of al-Banna and al-Bishri, regarding themes addressed in their writings after Mubarak's ouster.

Regime and opposition re-constructed

> On the 25th of January, all agreed to one of the demands of the revolution, which is that of preventing succession and the transfer of power from a man to his son in a gloomy and stormy climate. (Rizq, 2012, 32)

Though quite central, Jamal's succession was, by no means, the sole reason why Egyptians revolted. The day of police force in Egypt, 25 January, was chosen for the protest, signifying political oppression, not just Jamal's succession (al-Anani, 2014). Symbolically, name of the Egyptian young man who was brutally beaten to death in public in 2010 was used by the group (*Kulluna Khalid Sa'id*) We Are All Khalid Sa'id; its call triggered the Egyptian uprising,[29] resentment and combat of police brutality in Egypt was *one* reason why police stations were burned down in many Egyptian governorates (see Raiyyān, 2011, 110).

In addition, the Mubarak regime avoided the sudden-change policy that resulted in incidents like that of the 18th and 19th of January 1977 under Sadat, at the assumption that Egyptians would not mind compromising freedom, democracy and human rights as long as they can sustain their living, and applied gradual price increases (see Ḥasan, 2012, 220). Yet, the escalating poverty and unemployment, inflation and the power-business alliance accumulated to severe economic upheaval and overall dissatisfaction (Abdel Meguid et al., 2011; Essam El-Din, 2011). This could be seen in the slogans demanding social justice and basic economic rights from 25 January onwards.[30] While the succession scheme was technically over when Mubarak withdrew from power, the political oppression and economic upheaval *elements* continued to represent the central and common profile of contesting SCAF, and under the MB-led government.

Centrality of the military to the regime breakdown was clear during Mubarak's alleged withdrawal from power on 11 February. ʿUmar Suleiman, one of Mubarak's top figures, gave a short speech announcing the president's withdrawal from office (see Muntaṣir, 2011, 15). With this speech, Mubarak and his close associates like Zakariyya ʿAzmi, Kamal al-Shazli and others representing the regime, were ousted. SCAF took over in a transitional period, which ended in August 2012 after eighteen months of rule (Rashwan, 2012).

The MB presidential runner, Muhammad Mursi, won the presidency in June 2012 in a close race (Weaver, 2012) and became the first Egyptian president from a civilian background (Tarek, 2012). Even that the MB didn't play a decisive role in the initial break out of the uprising (Ben Jelloun, 2011, 56), it had strong access to the political sphere by virtue of its better organization and mobilization skills, compared to other opposition groups (Shenker, 2011a). Therefore, the regime, after the uprising, was dominated first by the military, and then by the MB.

During the eighteen days of the uprising, the opposition was largely amalgamated under the term The Revolutionaries (*al-Thuwwar*). These included all politicized and many of the de-politicized segments of the populace under Mubarak. The MB, which established the Freedom and Justice Party in June 2011 (Morshedy, 2014), as well as other opposition political parties, like al-Wafd and al-Tajammuʿ, were among the politicized groups (Zahran 2013; Ali, 2011). The new elements included Salafis, who did not express clear interest in political engagement before the uprising (Hussein, E., 2012) and established several parties including al-Nour Party after it (Morshedy, 2014). Other parties were also established, with no clear pre-uprising political record, like Free Egypt Party (*Misr al-Hurra*).[31]

At the advent of the first parliamentary elections in November 2011, both the MB and Salafis shifted from opposition to Parliament (Shenker, 2011b). Even that the National Assembly was dissolved upon a court order in 2012, the election of Muhammad Mursi as president, in June 2012, fortified the MB power status as presiding the executive branch (see Hussein, A., 2012; Nordland and El Sheikh, 2012). Yet, after less than a year in office, he was faced with the Tamarrod call in April 2013 to impeach him and was, upon the military's intervention, ousted in July of the same year. A second interim period followed where SCAF was back running civilian politics, until Abd el Fahttah al-Sisi, who served as defence minister under Mursi, was elected president in 2014.

Contested themes intact

Although the regime/opposition composition was largely altered, main grounds for contesting the post-2011 regime technically remained the same as those under Mubarak; political oppression and economic upheaval remained key elements of contestation. During the first military-led transitional period, the repressive character of SCAF rule was the focus of the contestation. Large-scale arrests, military trials of civilians, controversial virginity tests (*Kushuf al-'Udhriyya*) (see Grant, 2011) and reported political torture of detainees (see Soueif, 2011) kept the profile of an authoritarian regime intact. Meanwhile, the overall economic performance of the country was not improving and thus the economy was still a source of popular dissent. Strikes all over the country reflected the continued economic frustration of large segments of the population (Beinin, 2013).

Nonetheless, the ousted regime of Mubarak and his peers became part of the corruption scheme, highlighted earlier, during the first interim period. As the trials of Mubarak's top regime officials went relatively slow, protestors gathered in Tahrir Square, in April 2011, demanding the trials should proceed at a faster pace (Khamīs and Mukhtār, 2011, 77). The election of Mursi, again coming from a civilian background, raised hopes for more open political and public spheres compared to the general authoritarian practices that had prevailed in pre-uprising Egypt (see Abdel-Rahman, 2013). Nonetheless, three main incidents helped maintain the profile of an authoritarian regime under Mursi: dismissing the Egyptian Public Attorney 'Abd al Majid Mahmud, who cannot be dismissed, from a legal point of view (Gamal El-Din, 2013), monopolizing the process of writing the 2012 Constitution[32] and the issuance of an infamous presidential decree, on 22 November 2012, which declared presidential decisions immune from judicial supervision (Sayah and Ahmed, 2012).

Across both the first interim period and MB-led government later, the public sphere suffered serious infringements, particularly targeting verbal expression. During the first interim period, Dina 'Abd al-Rahman, an Egyptian female TV moderator, was allegedly fired from Dream TV channels because of her comments and/or way of addressing military generals (Awad, 2013). Likewise, Rim Majid, another female TV moderator, was called in by SCAF because of her comments on SCAF rule (Khazbak, 2011). Similarly, under Mursi, TV moderator Basim Yusuf was legally prosecuted for insulting the president; the case drew international attention.[33] Likewise, Egyptian Television and Radio Union forced Dream TV, an Egyptian satellite TV channel, to stop broadcasting on similar grounds (Abou Bakr, 2013). After Mursi's ouster, freedom in both the political and public spheres was drastically restrained (Dunne and Hamzawy, 2017) and many citizens were allegedly persecuted and defamed on the basis of their political standings (Dunne and Hamzawy, 2019). Thus, criticizing the military and/or its role in civilian politics became the key, and most visible, red line since the 2013 ouster. Meanwhile, floating the Egyptian pound in 2016 led to significant inflation rates and thus economic hardships stayed a key challenge (Saleh, 2017).

In this manner, political oppression and economic upheaval remained in the scope of contestation after the uprising, with direct criticism of the regime instigating open harassment and persecution. There were only two minor alterations compared to Mubarak's time: Jamal's succession scheme had already vanished as Mubarak was ousted, and publicly criticizing the country's military became a strong source of persecution.

Writing under a re-shuffled political sphere

The regime/opposition reconstruction reflected in al-Banna's first book after the 2011 uprising. It addressed the revolutionaries which, as shown above, were the masses of Egyptians who protested and toppled the Mubarak regime and the one representing the amalgamation of the opposition, which later on organized into parties and movements. This book was published in March 2011, at an early stage of the opposition transformation. The direct and overt manner in which he criticized the Mubarak regime demonstrated the drastic alteration in the regime depicted above, where Mubarak and his associates were no longer in power positions. This way, he maintained the *habit* of criticizing former regimes, in the same manner he did when criticizing Nasser under Sadat and then Sadat under Mubarak.

Al-Bishri's first book after the uprising, The State and the Church (*al-Dawla wa-l-Kanisa*) (2011a), was similarly an embodiment of the alteration in the regime/opposition structure. Compared to his two other books addressing Muslim-Coptic relations in Egypt (al-Bishrī, 2004,[34] 2005d), this one had a stronger tone. It also took a more overt approach to *chastising* the church and Shenouda III, the late Coptic Patriarch in Egypt, for allegedly fostering the withdrawal of the Coptic community (al-Bishrī, 2011a, 24–5, 51).

Under Mubarak, discussing Coptic-Muslim relations in general was directly influenced by external pressure exercised by the Coptic diaspora. This translated into congressional debates in the United States about the possibility of imposing conditionality on US assistance to the government.[35] Likewise, the debate on family law in 2007/2008, when the church insisted that only clerical laws apply to Coptic community marriages, culminated into sensitivity on the Coptic theme in the public sphere (see Iskander, 2012, 140; see also Bayyoumi, 2011). Thus, ousting Mubarak meant greater freedom and less restraint in expressing one's stances on the Coptic issue. In fact, in the case of al-Bishri in particular, with his outspoken mainstream Islamic profile and the 1992 judicial incident, such a critique would have surely triggered a collision with the Mubarak regime.

Thus, like al-Banna, he maintained the tradition of criticizing former regimes, which was evident in his earlier publications. After 2011, he argued that the Mubarak regime destroyed the state apparatus towards attaining the control of a *parasitic* group and weakened the state to better Israeli security (al-Bishrī, 2012b, 19–20), that his rule was exclusionary and political power was concentrated in the hands of a few people who had access to decision-making processes (al-Bishrī, 2013, 84). Though not directly addressing military rule during the interim period, one of his first books published after the uprising included a *smart* gesture to the old National Democratic Party program of 1911, where he praised, inter alia, that it maintained the concept of *temporary military intervention* which would come to an end once the rights of the nation were guarded (al-Bishrī, 2011a, 78). This way, he conveyed his message, which combined both his long-proclaimed respect for the role of the military in the country's national history (1991a) on one hand and his support for democratic rule (al-Bishrī, 2003a, 177) on the other, without directly colliding with SCAF.

Yet, he took some *daring* positions on Egypt's political arrangements including overt critique of the military which was, again, a key red line, especially after Mursi's ouster. For instance, in his book The 25th of January Revolution and The Struggle for Authority (*Thawrat 25 Yanāyir wa-l-Ṣirāʿ ḥawl al-Sulṭa*), he maintained that the 2013 ouster was a coup and not a popular revolution (2014, 175) and blamed SCAF for much of the legislative trouble Egypt suffered after the 2011 uprising. The harsh tone and explicit critique to SCAF and the military were only mitigated through his reference to the latter as part of the country's state institutions and as a key stream in post-2011 Egypt (al-Bishrī, 2014).

There are other factors that might have helped him *get away* with this appraisal though. At the time the book was published, al-Bishri, a former renowned judge in the Egyptian State Council, was already in his early eighties; persecuting an old and reputable judge wouldn't surely serve any ruling regime. Adding to this, he didn't have any prior hostilities with the country's military under Mubarak. Note also, he was a key judicial figure in post-2011 Egypt as he served as head of the Committee/Panel drafting the March 2011 constitutional amendments (Kirkpatrick and Fahim, 2011). Plus, he made very harsh comments on the MB political engagement, in the same book above and elsewhere, especially regarding the November 2012 declaration where Mursi shielded his decisions from judicial review and asserted the pivotal role played by the military in the historic 2011 uprising. Finally, the book was published before Sisi's election in June 2014, so it couldn't be taken as critique of the latter.

In 2015, after the second interim period was over, a new constitution (2014) was founded and Sisi was elected, al-Bishri published a recollection of introductions he contributed to about thirty books and thus can't be taken to address Egyptian developments at the time of publication. Yet, what's remarkable about this collection is that it signifies the range of themes he showed interest in throughout his intellectual path, such as Islamic Thought, colonialism and its impact on Arab countries, the interrelatedness between national liberation movements and Islam, democracy, emphasis on unity and the rootedness of laws and societal practices in human societies and the like (al-Bishrī, 2015).

To sum up, Nasser's rule was repressive; he banned political parties, made opposition illegal and barred the MB when their political ambitions rivalled his power dominance. Through augmented intelligence and security apparatus, his grip on the country's political terrain was tightened. Although largely autocratic, his socio-economic revisions, charisma and nationalist ideology cemented a strong legitimacy that helped him survive the 1967 defeat. His personal and institutional monitoring over press content, state ownership of radio and TV broadcasts and the recruitment of intellectuals to government jobs boosted his control over the public sphere. He set red lines through cases of direct harassment of prominent journalists. Still, sponsoring the public sphere was shared by al-Azhar, which co-defined its contours. The regime allowed it this role in order to maintain its Islamic profile and avoid the risk of al-Azhar representing a source of contestation to it.

Both al-Banna and al-Bishri's writings largely evaded the red lines set by the regime; they were not subject to direct harassment, which was a common result of any direct critique of Nasser or advocating democracy and freedoms. Al-Banna's focus on syndical struggle and al-Bishri's pre-occupation with the history of pre-republican political movements were practically *safe zones*. The confiscation of al-Banna's book using the term Coup to refer to the 1952 ouster of the king didn't take place under Nasser who took over in 1954.

Sadat's reconciling the West after the 1973 war moved the country towards opening up the political sphere; he allowed political parties in 1977. Still, through legal frameworks, he kept the public sphere under control, especially through laws on social safety and protecting society from shame. Like Nasser, he co-opted al-Azhar and used it against his opposition, especially after Islamists turned against him following the Camp David Accords in 1978 and the peace treaty with Israel in 1979.

Al-Banna's emerging Islamic profile under Sadat, conforming to mainstream jurisprudence, did not pose a challenge to al-Azhar in the public sphere or to Sadat's strong Islamic public image. Al-Bishri's accounts were also in harmony with regime's political preferences. When tackling the Arab-Israeli conflict, al-Bishri's open and strong critique against Egypt's peace with Israel came under Mubarak. Thus, he avoided possible harassment by a regime that grew slowly impatient towards opposition to his policy regarding the Arab-Israeli conflict.

Mubarak's regime infamously opted for voter intimidation, tampering ballots, buying votes and irregular arrests of political rivals. Growing economic upheaval – caused by inflation, a crescendo of unemployment and privatization – increased the pressure on the regime at a time when private and new media were on the rise. Nonetheless, through laws on press and media broadcast, the regime managed to keep dissent *within desired limits*, arresting tens of journalists and bloggers on accusations of false news dissemination and defaming.

The majority of Mubarak's regime persecution in the public sphere targeted journalists and bloggers. Because al-Banna and al-Bishri mainly presented their work in the form of books, they were less susceptible to regime harassment. Meanwhile, al-Azhar co-defined the contours of the public sphere. The symbiotic regime-Azhar relation, which started from the time of Nasser onwards, affected the intellectual path of Jamal al-Banna, as two of his books were confiscated by al-Azhar. Al-Bishri's tense relations with the Mubarak regime, by virtue of his decision against trying civilians before military courts in 1992, reflected in his strong emphasis on judicial independence in his writings, which did not mention the incident, representing an element of silence in his intellectual production.

Through the 2011 uprising, Egypt's political sphere was drastically altered; both regime/opposition elements were re-shuffled. Mubarak and his peers were ousted and SCAF, then the MB led-government, became the regime. Likewise, political forces which were barred under Mubarak were allowed and de-politicized segments engaged in politics after this uprising. Yet, political oppression and economic upheaval continued and thus the themes for contesting the regime stayed largely constant. Criticizing the country's military or SCAF became one key red line imposed over the Egyptian public sphere though.

Al-Banna's first book on the 2011 uprising embodied the drastic alteration, overtly defaming the Mubarak regime. Likewise, al-Bishri's book on the Coptic Church, published after Mubarak's ouster, comprised a stronger sense of critique of the church and its Pope, compared to his prior accounts of the Copts. After Mursi's ouster, al-Bishri's publications were overtly criticizing former regimes; they also contained some negative accounts on the military's political role but didn't result in his persecution, probably because of his old age, judicial status, role in post-2011 Egypt and still referring to the military as part of Egypt's state institutions.

3

Jamal al-Banna on CIPT

As stated earlier, studies of Islamic Thought, with a focus on particular intellectuals, were preoccupied with the multiplicity of views presented throughout the intellectual's path and mainly with the latter's Islamic profile. Though quite informative with extensive accounts on prominent names, attention to CIPT themes as departure points was mostly missing in these studies, even when these themes strongly shape/d the intellectual's contributions. I claim such an anchor is much needed as to help with conducting a systematic investigation of intellectual production, especially in comparative studies like this one.

In this chapter, the Islamic meta-language, particularly how it is addressed in al-Banna's writings, is examined in two parallel ways. One, the four key themes of state in Islam, Shari'a, violence and identity are the lenses through which his writings are read. Two, the reference to Islamic heritage, which is constituent of his profile as *Islamic*, is detected in order to determine which elements of this body of knowledge he employed towards his own intellectual contribution, and ultimately his relative positioning on the mainstream/tajdīd duality. So far, research on his intellectual path has not presented a thorough account covering all his available publications (see Akouri, 2005; al-Banhāwī, 2009).

But as pointed out more than once, an Islamic intellectual usually contributes on matters of politics; not all what they contribute is solely focused on the religion of Islam as a faith and/or its practice. Hence, it becomes sometimes necessary to offer brief, and often general, accounts of particular aspects of Egyptian politics to fully understand the overlap between his writings on Islam and those on politics on one hand and the intellectual's stances and views on the other. Technically, I seek answering three major questions in this chapter: Where does al-Banna stand on the four key CIPT themes? How does he present his renewal scheme within addressing these themes? And where do his political and Islamic profiles intersect? Finally, al-Banna, like any other intellectual, paid unequal attention to different themes, and some sections require a grasp of specific aspects of Egyptian politics, as stated above. Hence, different sections of this chapter – and the same applies to Chapter 4 – vary in size.

The state: Pluralism as benchmark

With the caliphate regarded as part of the historical practice, CIPT intellectuals tend to address it as part of the turāth, not as a binding/re-applicable pattern of political rule in Islam. As shown in Chapter 1, this shift indicates the dynamic nature of the CIPT themes, particularly when the juridical and societal resistance to ʻAbd al-Raziq's appraisal of the caliphate is considered. Today, Shura and democracy are largely juxtaposed in writings of Islamic intellectuals. Inspired by democracy and Western practices like elections, parliaments and political parties at large, these elements do not represent decisive lines of demarcation between mainstream and tajdīd intellectuals. Rather, it is accepting/rejecting the Islamic state and, in many times, the religious nature of the state in early Islamic history and/or many of its practices that constitute demarcation lines. Contributions on the state, the Shura/democracy juxtaposition and the lines of demarcation between tajdīd and mainstream all contribute to the construction of al-Banna's own writing on the state in Islam.

Dictatorships excluded

Across his many writings, particular forms of political rule are utterly rejected. He overtly rejected dictatorships[1] and despotic[2] (*Istibdadi*) rule. Nonetheless, he frequently, in this rejection, invoked instances from both Islamic history, the modern history of Egypt and other Muslim-dominated countries, to fortify his claims. Through these mixed accounts, his Islamic and political profiles converged.

In his writings on the state, his appraisal of coercive politics is utterly negative. For instance, he was opposed to despotic rule for curbing peoples' freedoms and attributed the backwardness of Muslims to their adherence to interpretations that did not reflect *correct Islam*. Rather, he argued their understanding was within the spirit of their time, 'which was a closed, despotic one'. The result was the suppression of humanistic and civilizational values (al-Bannā, 2004, 5; see also al-Bannā, 1986a, 91). He maintained this critique during interviews, when he asserted that the golden age was the first forty years of Islamic history, after which came hereditary rule to perpetuate practices of domination (Interview, 3 November 2010). Here, Islam, or correct Islam, is used as the argument against this rule; he sought legitimacy from Islam and Islamic heritage, which is *the* criterion for defining the Islamic character of the intellectual. At the same time, it is an attempt to scrutinize CIPT by raising doubt about, and directing critique to, the established body of jurisprudence – one integral part of the heritage.

Likewise, he argued that despotic regimes were among the factors shaping Islamic jurisprudence. In his analysis, this started with the time of Muʿawiya b. Abi Sufiyan (al-, 141, 187) and continued until the time of the Abbasids. These regimes, to him, besieged the freedom of jurists which resulted in clashes with rulers, with the effect that the four leading jurists of Sunni Islam – mentioned in Chapter 1 – were subjected to massive oppression at the hands of Abbasid caliphs from Abi Jaʿfar al-Mansur to al-Maʾmun. This, according to him, undermined the meanings of freedom and justice in Islamic jurisprudence (al-Bannā, 2004, 113; see also al-Bannā, 1994a). His position on despotic rule in particular drove him away from the logic of the just despot, which prevailed in Islamic authorship on history of Islam after the death of ʿUthman onwards (see al-Jābrī, 1992, 130–1), and closer to the tajdīd CIPT authorship, highlighting the role of real politics in constructing the body of Islamic heritage.

In his view, the political, economic and social conditions – referring to the same time period he called despotic – negatively affected the jurisprudential position on freedom of belief, which, to him, was heavily restrained and mandated that those who convert from Islam should be asked to repent. If not, then they should be killed (al-Bannā, 2004, 116). He maintained a link between autocratic rule and lack of autonomous jurisprudence, and he claimed that, under authoritarian rule, jurists were restrained. The latter focused their efforts on the jurisprudential perspective of rituals that neither addressed nor collided with rulers, while deliberately ignoring matters of politics and the state (al-Bannā, 1994a, 21–2). Here, he indirectly invoked the hegemonic role of the religious institution, which again was frequently emphasized in authorship on Islamic history, especially in tajdīd authorship (see Ayubi, 1995, 84).

Yet, al-Banna added some qualification to the Sheikh/Sultan phenomenon (al-Qimnī, 2022), when he distinguished between two different impacts of this despotic rule on jurisprudence: lack of resistance versus cooperation. To him, the jurisprudential stance was avoiding dissension (*Fitna*) (see al-Bannā, 2005c, 216), which resulted in the jurists promoting the power of unjust rulers. He depicted jurists who collaborated with despotic regimes as follows:

> These jurists did not merely accept the despotism of kings as a hateful necessity, they rather called on the masses to give in to these kings and not to resist them, they have abhorring sayings in this regard, esp. those of Hanbalites who claimed rule cannot be ousted because of ruler's tyranny ('Aṣf al-Ḥākim), his injustice of taking away money, torturing people, wasting rights and suspending penalties (ḥudūd).[3] (al-'Bannā, 2004, 121)

This despotic rule, which was backed by juridical notions of obedience and avoiding dissension, in his appraisal, prevailed throughout Islamic history after the first forty years (al-Bannā, Interview, 3 November 2010). So far, the despotic regimes he rejected affected the content of jurisprudence, which later became part of the Islamic heritage. He depicted these regimes as influencing content of the heritage, which is integral to knowledge on Islam. The ultimate effect of which was eliminating aspects of freedom and justice from the jurisprudence, which are, for him, intrinsic to Islam. Thus, in his attempt to establish his renewal scheme, he claimed there had been *wrongful* influence exercised on Islamic heritage in the past.

In fact, he didn't stop there; the accounts he presented on the damaging effect of ruling regimes on jurisprudence are actually, as will be evident in the Shari'a section below, constitutive of his ultimate positions on the question of its application. He utilized specific instances from Islamic history towards making his argument against autocratic rule:

> At the time when Islamic society flourished, before despotism killed freedom spirit, the companions and the followers used to deal with those who differed (*Mukhālifin*), like *Mu'atazala*, *Murji'a* or *Qadariyya*, with kindness and good faith, exchange discussions, not resent them, not confiscate their ideas or call for penalizing them, though their ideas represented a denial of the fundamental essence of Islamic law (*Ma'lūm min al-Dīn bi-l-Ḍarūra*). (al-Bannā, 2004, 133)

As stated earlier, al-Banna cited in his rejection of dictatorial rule both instances in Islamic history and in the contemporary world where dictatorships promoted terror and drained developmental efforts. He quoted a speech of Ziad b. Umaiyya, known in Islamic history as the Amputation (*al-Batrā'*), as part of his argument that political rule took a sharp turn towards despotic rule when Mu'awiyya b. Abi Sufiyan reached power. He described the speech as a potential *terror manifesto* for any dictatorial rule, not only because it numerated severe penalties, but also because its overall spirit targeted the spread of terror and oppression as well as favouring indifference and apathy (al-Bannā, 2005c, 45, see also 206). As an Islamic intellectual who sought reference mainly in Islamic heritage to legitimize his stances, the critique is naturally not to the faith of Islam; al-Banna traced political apathy down to ruling regimes. This is a commonly used strategy for making claims about Islam: to distinguish between Islam and the practice of Islam (see Faḍl 'Allāh, 2004, 105; Black, 2008, 31).

Summarizing the forms of political rule al-Banna presented as contradicting Islam, he wrote:

> The Islamic state should not be that of the individual dictator (*al-Fard al-Diktatur*) or the single party or the class state, or the military elite state. (al-Bannā, 2004, 143)

However, the categories he detested are not clearly separable from one another in his writing. This was evident when he referred to Nasser's rule as both military and individual rule. Therefore, the lines of demarcation between these forms are not as clear-cut as it may seem at first glance.[4] His rejection of these categories directly relates to his concern for freedom as an Islamic value. On this, al-Banna wrote three books (al-Bannā, 1985; 1995b; 1999a), where the main line of argument was that Islam, in divergence from the bulk of Islamic political history, is a religion that promotes freedom. He relied heavily on heritage, Qur'an, Hadith and historical examples, mainly derived from early Islamic history, as support for this conviction of his. The early history is, as shown in Chapter 1, the most highly regarded period in Islamic history for its acclaimed *virtuous* nature and is thus invoked throughout his writings to validate his arguments on freedom.[5] He asserted its centrality,[6] regardless of what one gets in exchange for it (al-Bannā, 2003b, 114).

> Freedom is the mother of plurality, if freedom does not exist any more, there is no plurality. (al-Bannā, 2001a, 53)

Even before he gave up on his claim that there is a state in Islam, freedom was, to him, one basic foundation of the Islamic state. In the latter, freedom of thought, belief, and publication, among other things, should be guarded and not subjected to any sort of censorship (al-Bannā, 1991a, 35). In his book Five Criteria for the Credibility of Islamic Rule (*Khamsat Ma'ayyir li–Misdaqiyat al-Hukm al-Islami*) published in 1996, he pinpointed *the atmosphere of freedom* as one of these criteria. He argued that, unlike the common conceptions of Islamic rule as one that is anti-freedom, Islam is based on thought and belief in freedom (34–5). He again reiterated this view on freedom as one of the pillars of the Islamic state in his book The Responsibility for Failure of the Islamic State and Other Research (*Mas'uliyat Fashal al-Dawla al-Islamiyya fi al-'Asr al-Hadith wa Buhuth Ukhra*) (1994a, 33).

No taste for military rule

As pointed out above, al-Banna doesn't admire military rule. Yet, some account on the Egyptian military in politics is due, in order to be able to depict his overall stance on this topic. Egypt's modern history witnessed a strong military presence in the country's political sphere from 1952 onwards. Nasser came from within the ranks of the military, but so did Sadat and Mubarak (see Ayubi, 1991b, 260) and even Naguib, who ruled only briefly and in a mostly symbolic manner before he was put to compulsory house arrest by Nasser (Mitchell, 1993, 129).

The assumption that the presidents' military background might have contributed to the repressive nature of the three regimes can't be fully discarded. In fact, a wide-ranging pool of literature does link authoritarian practices to military involvement in political rule (see Svolik, 2012, 32–3; Ching, 2014). Still, to assume that the military, as an institution, dominated decision-making processes in Egypt is basically a reductionist portrayal of the country's political terrain.

> The political system of Egypt is multi-layered. At the center, there is actually a seemingly neo-patrimonial president. However, the military, the most important pillar of the regime, is by no means his Marionette. It has it own institutional interests. (Hartmann, 2011, 113)

Successive pre-2011 regimes were highly personalized, with laws and regulations set through the executive dominating the legislature and law-based restrictions on the political sphere. Even when the military interfered, it was called upon by heads of the state, and not on its own independent initiative. Sadat called upon the military to *restore security* after the 1977 bread riots. It was similarly called upon in 1986 by Mubarak to deal with the crisis of the Central Security Forces' disobedience, known as the Central Security Coup (*Inqliab al-Amn al-Markazi*)[7] (see Rizq, 2012, 99). Furthermore, particularly under Sadat, there was a strong tendency to restrain the political role of the military through civilian cabinets. It was excluded from the Alliance of Forces of the Working People, which was established by Nasser. Its role was only re-established when Sadat resorted to the military to suppress the bread riots (Ayubi, 1991b, 260).

Nonetheless, before the 2011 uprising, as shown in Chapter 2, military courts were employed towards blocking regime opponents (see Brownlee, 2002, 6). In the rivalry between the Mubarak regime and the MB, emergency laws were employed as a basis to justify the referral of civilians to military courts. Originally intended to provide a swift sentencing in cases related to terrorism, military tribunals were increasingly used to try civilians, who were not involved in violence against the regime (see Cook, 2007, 72).

Expectedly, the military was privileged in many senses. The Central Agency for Mobilization and Statistics (al-Jiahz al-Markazi li-l-Ta'bi'a wa-l-Ihsaa) was presided by a former military general for many years. The agency is not only the source of vital information for any project, but it has also a *control* role, as any large-scale statistical study must be approved by this agency, which reports directly to the president (see Ayubi, 1991b, 90). Many influential top state positions were also occupied by army personnel, such as governors, city mayors or managers of state-owned firms (Abdel-Rahman, 2013). Plus, military budget was always presented as a single-item document to Parliament, and the size of its business capital was kept secret (see Abul-Magd, 2011; Kirkpatrick, 2011; Bradley, 2012; Abdelhadi, 2012). Thus, regime-military relations remained cooperative in nature, as there was no rivalry with the military, as an institution, and the latter did not contest ruling regimes till the 2011 uprising.

However, a military-regime cleavage was evident during the late years of Mubarak's rule, at least within close political circles, when the military stood against the Jamal succession scheme and expressed this rejection through direct and indirect messages (al-Bāz, 2011, 147–8). After Mubarak's ouster, the military became the regime until the end of the transitional period in August 2012 (Rashwan, 2012). The confidentiality of government military expenditure items, which was characteristic of the pre-uprising regimes, continued (see Bradley, 2012).

Thus, the military politically survived Mubarak's ouster and came to represent the post-uprising regime through SCAF during the first interim period; in addition, the privileged status of the military in pre-uprising Egypt was significantly left intact. Yet, associating the military with autocratic practices, common in the literature (see Svolik, 2012; Ching, 2014) was fortified after the 2011 uprising. Increasingly repressive tactics against popular dissent, including the trial of hundreds of civilians before military tribunals and massive violence against young protestors in Tahrir Square, were part of the political scene (see Elgindy, 2011). As mentioned in Chapter 2, after Mursi's ouster in July 2013, SCAF took over for a second interim period, and Sisi, who served as defence minister under Mursi, was elected president in June 2014.

After Mursi was ousted, a strong limitation to the benefit of the country's military was installed in the 2014 Constitution; namely, that the president would need SCAF's approval of his/her selection of a defence minister (Brooks, 2021). Meanwhile, significant public attention was drawn to the military's political and economic privileges after Sisi's election in 2014 (Salama, 2018; Mandour, 2018; Sayigh, 2019). The return to the pre-2011 pattern of presidents from a military background shed light on his election as shielding, or even augmenting, privileges of the armed forces from both drastic structural change and public scrutiny. Yet, after a foreign currency crisis peaking in 2022–3, there was some pressure on the military's role in the economy. The IMF bailed out the country with a multi-billion-dollar package but requested to *level the field* between the public and private sectors, openly referring to military-owned enterprises (England, 2023).

In discussing military rule in Egypt, al-Banna's account covers the time from Muhammad 'Ali to Nasser. During this time, he argued authority aimed to completely control and subdue the personality of the individual, making him/her a subordinate to the state (*tabi'an li-l-dawla*) and suppressing his/her freedom (al-Bannā, 1996b, 61; al-Bannā, interview, 22 May 2011). As shown in Chapter 2, in his writings, Nasser was singled out as an oppressive ruler. Al-Banna attributed the rule of the individual (*Hukm al-Fard*) to autocratic practices of Nasser (al-Bannā, 1995a, 27; see also 28–9).

Excluded from that general trend was, to him, the time stretching from 1923 to 1952, largely known as the liberal phase,[8] when ruling with bayonets (*Hirab*) and the military was the exception, not the rule (al-Bannā, 1995a, 36). Al-Banna showed clear interest in this period of Egypt's history before the 1952 coup, the elections, party politics and government decision-making. Ironically, this was the period of time when his brother was assassinated in 1948 (al-Bannā, 1988, 19–25) and he himself was jailed in the 1940s.

Remarkably, al-Banna used the word *coup* rather than *revolution* to refer to the Free Officers' ousting of King Faruq on 23 July 1952[9] (see al-Bannā, 1988, 275; 2000, 20). This usage resulted in his book (*Tarshid al-Nahda*), originally written to comment on the 1952 coup, being confiscated in September 1952, and a ban was imposed on its publishing (1952/1999b, 5–6; 2011, 6–8). The confiscation meant al-Banna, in person, experienced regime restrictions on the public sphere, decades before the Siraj al-Din incident under Sadat, which is discussed in Chapter 2. Accordingly, al-Banna's accounts of the 1952 coup were guided by his own personal experience.

More generally, there is no one *huge* account on the military in al-Banna's intellectual path. This feature should not be taken to infer that he feared addressing the topic as to avoid collision with the regime, which had its heads of state coming from the military, as there are several aspects to be considered in this regard. One, before al-Banna introduced his Islamic renewal scheme, he was largely occupied with syndicalism and labour movement, as highlighted earlier. Two, the military, as an institution, was largely out of political rivalry and only interfered upon command of the head of state. Its economic and institutional interests were realized through occupying strategic positions. It had a military budget that was held confidential, thus, keeping it away from public scrutiny. His relatively small focus on the country's military might be largely induced by these considerations, which translated into very little public knowledge about its actual political weight.

Before 2011, al-Banna's key account on the military was focused on the 1952 period, which he discussed at some length in his book Islam Is the Solution (*al-Islam huwa al-Hal*) (1988, 66–200). Highly concerned with freedoms and plurality which dictate, in his view, alternation of power allows opposition and restrains power of the ruler (2001a, 77; 2008d); he firmly stands against military rule. Furthermore, in his frequent defaming of the Nasser regime, he usually referred to the military background of the latter (1988, 202). He even blamed the *despotic military regimes*, in his own words, for alienating the Egyptian society from Islam (1983, 148). The strong defaming of military rule (see 2005c, 100; 2004, 7) in his writings can't be read apart from his negative experience with the confiscation of his book, highlighted in Chapter 2.

In a similar vein, to him, the post-colonial democratic/liberal experience in Muslim-dominated countries – including Egypt – did not survive because of the emergence of military rule. Such rule had a 'decisive, disciplined and strict' pattern and opposed free thinking and pure conscience.[10] In al-Banna's words, 'its rule exacerbated the situation and got the region into a chain of adventures that ate up what was left of these states' (al-Bannā, 2005c, 5). Noteworthy is that he used examples for autocratic rule from neighbouring countries, he referred to al-Turabi as a tyrant military ruler in Sudan, while asserting his rejection of military rule (al-Bannā, 2005c, 142).

Democracy

Al-Banna presented a huge account on democracy as being congruent with Islam, and it is frequently positively depicted in his books, albeit with reservations which will be highlighted below. He argued that alternation of power, freedom of opposition and limits on rulers' prerogatives through the will of the people as relating to pluralism in the political sphere (al-Bannā, 2001a, 77). Likewise, he praised activism in all forms, including writing articles to newspapers, or using the internet. In fact, he opted for a broad definition of activism. To him, it may take the direct form of participating in political activity, through membership in political parties, or through campaigning or voting in elections (Interview, Cairo, 18 October 2010).

Throughout his intellectual path, there is a strong trace of these forms he put under activism. For instance, in his book What after the Muslim Brotherhood??? (*Ma Ba'd al-Ikhwan al-Muslimin???*), where he addressed MB's history, three main instances of activism were spotted. One, fund raising and booklet publication carried out by the movement in support of Palestinians during their first revolution in 1936.[11] Two, the participation of Sa'id Ramadan, the cousin of Hasan al-Banna, in a demonstration in Cairo. Three, the movement's electoral engagement and subsequent parliamentary participation in 1987 (1996b, 49–50, 87).[12]

As an intellectual strongly focused on liberalism, he firmly stood for freedom of thought and belief; publication of books and newspapers; establishing political parties, syndicates, associations and clubs; freedom of public meetings and political opposition, and voiced his support for a participating populace (al-Bannā, 1994a, 35, 7 respectively). Conversely, he viewed syndicates' unwillingness to engage in activism as a failure. In 1920 Germany, when syndicates had a great chance to lay the foundations for the society they desired, in his analysis, this should have initiated a general strike but did not (al-Bannā, 1981, 147–8). Through these accounts, an indirect call for engagement in politics could be induced from his writings.

To be precise, this call conforms to his distaste towards the aforementioned call for obedience among Sunni jurists, which was, according to tajdīd accounts, employed towards boosting the hegemonic power of the ruling elite (Ayubi, 1995, 84). Meanwhile, his extensive accounts, in the interviews, on the role of strikes and boycotts as forms of political engagement (Interview, 18 October 2010) relate to his own personal profile as an intellectual who worked for long years on labour struggle. He often bluntly praised democracy:

> Democracy was an openness (*Fatḥan*) in the political sphere, as was capitalism in the economic sphere, it gave the world a strong push forward. It is useless to deny this. The salience of the individual's character (*Shakhsiyyat al-Fard*) and reaching freedom of thought, spread of newspapers, media, establishing parties and entities with all multiplicity and variations, the flourishing of popular calls and syndical movement and socialism itself, arts and literature, leisure time entertainment. All of these would not have appeared, weren't it for democracy. (al-Banna,1984a, 112–33)

> Democracy has undeniable virtues; the phases of progress[13] humanity reached can be attributed to it, esp. that of freedom of thought. (al-Bannā, 1986b, 17)

Furthermore, comparing democracy to several ideologies, he showed preference to the former vis-à-vis the latter:

> It is without a doubt that democracy is better than the three systems we exposed [that is, of secularism, nationalism and socialism]. It is even the best what is currently there. (al-Bannā, 2003b, 124)

In this regard, Bhaba's critique of Said's Orientalism – where he maintained the Orient voluntarily internalized notions of progress and development and used them in their discourse (1996) – applies strongly to al-Banna's accounts of democracy. As evident in the quotes above, even that he recognized the Western character of democracy, he both praised it and indirectly promoted it through positive accounts of its constituent elements of alternation of power, pluralism and the like.

Historically, the West came to mean all that is Christian, and the East connoted all that is Muslim (Kalmar, 2012, 30). This dichotomy was partly surpassed in the late nineteenth century as intellectuals from the Muslim world, under Western influence, started to promote notions of freedom and tolerance (see Black, 2008, 40). This brought the latter under the attack of hard-core Islamic intellectuals who accused them of being imitators of the colonizer (see Shalabī, 1998, 169). Here, al-Banna's account on democracy acknowledged the Western origins of democracy, propagating it in his writings, thus embodying this trend. Meanwhile, his focus on democracy concurred with CIPT's evident focus on it in debates on the state in Islam.

Nonetheless, his writings numerated several reservations on democratic rule. One, democracy was the political face of bourgeoisie, while capitalism[14] was the economic face of bourgeoisie (al-Bannā, 2004, 138, 146; see also al-Bannā 1994a, 29). Two, it allowed *cunning rulers* to deceive the masses to achieve absolute power. These rulers audaciously claimed that they enjoyed sweeping popular support, whereby the election and referenda results would come up with 99.9 per cent in favour of a particular candidate. To him, these figures are clear evidence of how people can be misled; they are evidence of how the electoral system, the backbone of democracy, can be manipulated (al-Bannā, 1984, 14–15; see al-Bannā, 1986a, 18). Three, democracy, according to him, focused on the individual (*al-Fard*), so it moved towards unleashing the individual rather than reforming him/her (al-Bannā, 1979a, 78). In addition, he argued that Qur'an views democracy as excessive with its freedoms,[15] to the extent that it reached chaos; it allowed the rich to exploit the poor, the old to be unfair to the young and the strong to enslave the weak (al-Bannā 1952/1999b, 130–1). There was no shift on his position regarding these reservations, as he maintained the imperfect character of democracy in the interviews: rule of the majority does not necessarily abide by the rule of law, as those who are rich and have access to decision-making structures could manipulate democratic rule (Interview, 27 October 2010).

At first glance, this particular critique of democracy might contradict his aforementioned support for freedom as stipulated by Islam. But he sought a balance between appreciating freedom and setting limits on it. To him, freedom, though vital, should not be left unleashed; when unrestrained, it leads humanity to war and atomic bombs destroying the world (al-Bannā, 1952/1999b). Likewise, economic freedom cannot function without a degree of organization between businessmen and the state on one hand, and businessmen and workers on the other (al-Bannā, 2005c, 263). To him, freedom should be intertwined with justice (al-Bannā, 1979a, 77). Similarly, it should be restrained by laws to protect against slander. Therefore, limitations on freedom are actually in place to protect others from violations that could be committed under its banner (al-Bannā, 1991a, 35).

In addition, al-Banna argued that democracy did not always protect freedom and even led sometimes to oppression. He invoked example of Germany's Hitler who reached power via democratic elections (al-Bannā, 2004, 139; 2000, 96). Likewise, one of democracy's pitfalls, to him, is that the democratic procedure based on 'majority rule' could end up oppressing freedom (al-Bannā, 2004, 139, and al-Bannā, 2000, 96). This way, not fully fascinated with democracy, he avoided the critique generally directed to intellectuals promoting Western patterns of rule and notions.

In fact, al-Banna didn't exhibit, in his writings, pure and exclusive fascination with the West. To him, early Islamic history, until the end of 'Umar b. al-Khattab's time, was better than democratic rule in today's world. He considered the Prophet's society of Madīna to be human (*Insan*), 'where it was secure under a government that knew no tyranny or authoritarianism, ruled by law and restrained by the people who held it accountable and guided it' (al-Bannā, 2005c, 198–9). This positive account on early Islam is one of the least-contested elements of the heritage and represents one common element with mainstream CIPT authorship. Al-Banna's profile sought, in part, the legitimacy embedded in, and driven from, the heritage. This demonstrates that even if an intellectual *breaks away* from part of the heritage, he/she cannot completely *free* their writings from it.

He considered Abi Bakr to be the first elected caliph[16] (al-Bannā, 2005c, 221). He even claimed Islam presented freedom of thought before democracy did (al-Bannā, 2000, 7). In the same direction, he claimed that Islam, not just as a religion but even more as a civilization, is better than democracy (al-Bannā, 2003b, 124). On the particular point of Abi Bakr and 'Umar, his account embodied the general trend in mainstream/tajdīd writings on early history of Islam as the golden age of the faith (see Khalaf 'Allāh, 2010, 5; Salvatore, 2007, 105).

As shown in Chapter 1, democracy and Shura are frequently juxtaposed in authorship on Islam, especially regarding the question of Islamic rule. Al-Banna endorsed this juxtaposition, asserting that Shura (al-Bannā, 1993, 76) and democracy are quite similar/compatible; Shura is, to him, one form of democracy (al-Bannā, 2010b, 34–5). He maintained that it leads to a democratic climate at all levels, starting from the family and continuing up to the state. Democratic climate is critical for Shura (al-Bannā, 1986b, 90, 72, respectively).

Nonetheless, he tended to regard Shura and democracy as synonyms. He encouraged others to present Shura in a new form adapting to current contexts, a form that is closer to democracy, even that democracy does not possess the deep impact of the word Shura over Muslim masses (al-Bannā, 2005c, 7). This is quite clear in his argument that states ruling Muslims need to practice democracy *or* Shura, implying the similarity between them (see al-Bannā, 1996b, 168).

In this regard, al-Banna heavily relied on Islamic early history to construct his arguments towards praising Shura; the Prophet, according to him, *restrained* (in a positive sense) his rule through the practice of Shura and frequently asked for consultation from others (al-Bannā, 2004, 120). The caliph was also selected through Shura until Mu'awiyya b. Abi Sufiyan turned it into despotic rule (*Mulk 'Aḍūd*) (al-Bannā, 2005c, 44). He also highlighted that Qur'an stipulated Shura (al-Bannā, 1984a, 110):

> 'Qur'an stipulates Shura and warns against tyranny and monopoly of power (*Infirad bi-l-Hukm*).' He also wrote: ' Shura is the means to practice rule in Islam.'(al-Bannā, 2004, 140, 144, respectively)

Interestingly, there are almost no negative accounts on Shura among intellectuals throughout the history of Islamic Thought. But there is a growing trend to highlight the non-binding nature of Shura (see al-Hibri, 1999a, 75), a position fortified by Qur'anic verses on Shura and one that is emphasized in comparison to democratic rule as applied today (al-Jābrī, 1992, 126). Opposing autocratic rule, supporting democracy and praising Shura, al-Banna, based on his understanding of the heritage, presented *practical* guarantees that power will not be abused. In his view, Qur'an decisively prohibits injustice and exploitation, all forms of coercion and authoritarianism (*Tasallut*) (al-Bannā, 2005c, 206). He maintained that Qur'an urged the masses to revolt against injustice (*al-Zulm*) and if they cannot face it, then they must do nothing less than emigrate to guard their dignity[17] (al-Bannā, 2004, 119). Islam, to him, rejects tyranny (see al-Bannā, 1995a, 11) and this position is congruent with his overall support for freedom and rejection of specific forms of rule.

The Islamic state

Towards the end of al-Banna's intellectual path, he expressed no preference for a defined place of religion in the state. This was especially true after he abandoned his prior conviction that a state is stipulated by Islam, based on his belief that authority taints values and ideologies, upon which religions are based (see al-Bannā, 2007a, 80; see also al-Bannā, 2003a, 53). In his appraisal, the state/the ruler always sought exploiting religion towards augmenting its/his power (Interview, 1 November 2010). For him, this is a truth that is not confined to Islam (al-Bannā, 2005c, 261; see also al-Bannā, 2010b, 340; and al-Bannā, 2001a, 53). This position was a strong shift in his intellectual path where he moved away, as stated earlier, from his prior overt support for an Islamic state/system (see al-Bannā, 1984a, 92), and setting guidelines for how it should function (al-Bannā, 1991a). Before this shift, he wrote:

> Those who believe that Islam does not include a state, separating between Islam and the idea of the state are in fact mistaken. (al-Bannā, 1994a, 12)

After the shift, he asserted Islam can never be associated with authority, as the right term is a Muslim Nation ('*Umma Muslima*) (al-Bannā, 2004, 142). Religions are, to him, about the preaching, not political rule. They are about guiding the rational society against economic exploitation and political tyranny (Interview, 29 January 2010). He wrote:

> The state of the Islamic nation is a civil state, does not claim Islam and does not practice Islamic tasks. (al-Bannā, 2003b, 43)

Yes, political rule was, to him, practised in Islamic early history,[18] but he argued early history of Islam is unique and can't be repeated (al-Bannā, 2004,

142). Plus, what the Prophet established in Madīna was more of a society than of a state (al-Bannā, 2005c, 197). Praising the traits of the Prophet as a leader of the nation, a military commander and a statesman (al-Bannā, 2004, 120, 99, respectively), he fortified his Islamic character. This way, his reference to early Islamic history, the least-contested phase of this history, was employed within the tajdīd appraisal as both unique and non-replicable (al-Bannā, 2003a, 7–8).

This shift on the state in Islam itself is one major element of the tajdīd profile of al-Banna, as deviating from the mainstream common conviction that there is politics/state in Islam. Thus, although his appraisal of the early history, as unique and embodying the spirit of Islam, is frequently depicted in the literature (see Ayubi, 1991a; Khalaf 'Allāh, 2010, 5; Krämer, 2000a, 32–3; Said, 1978), he eventually concluded that there is no Islamic state, in contradiction to the broad line of argument presented by his mainstream counterparts. This fortifies the assumption made in that both mainstream and tajdīd intellectuals usually build upon turāth/heritage, and on the way they diverge reaching different positions according to their hermeneutical convictions.

His rationale for opposing the Islamic state, in spite of political rule being part of early Islamic history, is based on the coercive traits of any state:

> The state, in the technical sense, should have a permanent army … police … and prisons, and it should impose taxes and Madīna had nothing of these, it was the case until 'Uthman assigned, while he was not in Madīna, an army to expel some deviants who took control of the city.[19] (al-Bannā, 2010b, 42)

Politics, in general, is not praised in his writings; he insisted it had a negative impact on religion, which is one reason for his rejection of the Islamic state. In this respect, he claimed politics *damaged* the body of heritage, mainly jurisprudence, and led it towards promoting submission and apathy on the part of the masses. Likewise, the construction of Sunna/Hadith through the juridical act of Proof (*Thubūt*)[20] is, in his account, guided and influenced by positions for/against political and/or juridical factions. According to him, these fell under the power of the strong desire to *invent* good Hadith as part of such factional struggles and contests (al-Bannā, 2004, 80).

But here are a few remarks: One, this is a similar line of argument to the one he made on the impact of the context of jurisprudence under autocratic rule, concluding that freedom and justice were not held central. Two, this is an argument that is quite central to the mainstream/tajdīd tension on the body of heritage depicted in Chapter 1; thus it is pivotal towards the positioning of al-Banna within the tajdīd stream. Three, in this account he presented an instance of him trying to affect the ultimate conception of the religious truth in Islam.

To sum up his position on this theme, he started out advocating for the Islamic state, but by the end of his intellectual life moved towards denying this state on the basis of authority ruining religion. This is the argument he used to validate the need for new Ijtihad after despotic history impacted the juridical element of the heritage. He reacted to the existing Shura-democracy juxtaposition and while he praised democracy, he also pinpointed several pitfalls in its theory and practice.

Shari'a but Ḥudūd scrutinized

Ḥudūd were applied in early history of the faith and the juridical effort on Shari'a, falling under jurisprudence, emerged afterwards. At the advent of modernization and the subsequent colonization of Muslim countries, the debate on Shari'a application emerged, as new institutional and legal orders were endorsed changing the landscape of Muslim societies. This constitutes one major and integral theme in CIPT authorship. Accordingly, al-Banna's conception of Shari'a and its application and his position on Western legal codes, applied nowadays in Muslim-dominated countries are approached against this background.

***Shari'a* qualified**

> It should be a given from the very beginning, that rules of Islamic *Shari'a* must be applied. (al-Bannā, 1995a, 153)

In the quote above, he capsulated his overall position on Shari'a application. In his earliest accounts on Shari'a, published under Sadat, he claimed it outweighed positive law, especially when the ineffective and cruel character of prison sentences are considered, compared to some ḥudūd, like that of theft, stipulated in Islamic Shari'a (al-Bannā, 1972, 172–6). Similarly, he believed positive law is embedded in social and economic structures, which bring the content of the law to bias towards the rich and powerful, a pitfall that law based on Qur'an does not suffer (al-Bannā, 1984, 71–9).

Zooming in on the theft penalty in Islam (*Ḥad al-Sariqa*), his clear admiration of the Islamic penalty could be easily established. He compared it to current penalties, mainly driven from Western penal codes, to show how efficient and sound the former is when compared to the latter (al-Bannā, 2010a, 134–9; see also al-Bannā, 2007a, 81; 1994a, 40). To him, Shari'a covers political, economic and social spheres (al-Bannā, 1994a, 24) and includes detrimental sins (*min Kabā'ir al'Ithm wa-l-Fawāḥish*), like adultery or drinking wine, which are punished with defined penalties (ḥudūd) (al-Bannā 2008a).

Similarly, he argued the legal penalty enacted in Egypt's penal code for a husband or wife murdering their spouse, after being caught in an act of adultery, did not abide by Qur'anic verses in defining the penalty. This, for him, represented a deviation from Qur'an (al-Bannā, 2008a, 14–19). Plus, he advocated the establishment of an Islamic peace court to settle armed struggle – among Muslims – between state and non-state actors which, for him, was part of the Qur'anic stipulation. To him, such a court should be established in compliance with the Qur'anic dictation (al-Bannā, 1986a, 98–120). In his own words:

> It is time for Muslims to know the rules of their religion; that the texts of verse number 9 of *Sūrat al-Ḥujurāt* and similar verses must be applied, it is neither for chanting by readers of Qur'an (*Qurrā'*) nor for academic knowledge. (al-Bannā, 1986b, 119)

So far, his appraisal of Shari'a does not only abide by the mainstream position advocating its application, but also argues for endorsing overlooked aspects of it, like Islamic courts. He defended it against laws based on positive law; that is, he stood in full conformity on the side of the Islamic in the secular/Islamic duality. However, in the paragraphs below, his strong deviation from mainstream, and outspoken adherence to tajdīd authorship, will become clear.

Three main qualifications move al-Banna closer to tajdīd than mainstream on the issue of Shari'a. First, Shari'a, to him, is justice,[21] and not simply penalties (ḥudūd). He wrote:

> Gentlemen, Sharī'a is not penalties 'ḥudūd', or keeping women at home or fighting arts and literature and not tolerating all means of entertainment ... Shari'a, in one word, gentlemen is 'justice' (*'Adl*), if you seek Shari'a, then apply justice; where the bad polarization between the poor, who have nothing and live in graveyards on one hand, and the rich, who have everything including tourists' compounds and palaces all over the world on the other does not exist any more. And the political polarization between rulers, who monopolize power, rule with fire and iron and spend state money on prisons and what they call domestic security on one hand, and the ruled, who can neither practice opposition nor contribute to rule on the other do not exist anymore. (al-Bannā, 2000, 91)

Second, ḥudūd, to him, represents a relatively minor part of Shari'a (al-Bannā, 1986a, 80). In his writings, the theme that should receive precedence and priority is the creed (*'Aqīda*), or the soul where Shari'a is the body. The faith needs to be deepened before any application of Shari'a can be of any significance (al-Bannā, 1998, 36–8). Third, he argued that some crimes, like adultery, cannot be proven except through an act that would contradict Islam, like spying. If an act is to be proven only through a violation of Islamic rules, then it's better not be proven. Furthermore, he made it clear that penalty is not the only way for redemption, there is also repentance, or doing good (*Ḥasanāt*) to omit bad deeds (*Saiyy'āt*) (al-Bannā, 2008a, 10–11).

This, along with his overall liberal profile regarding women's emancipation, such as his advocacy that women should not be obligated to wear the veil (al-Bannā, 2002a; see also al-Bannā, 2002c), women's eligibility to lead men in prayers if they excel in knowledge (al-Bannā, 2005a), and his opposition to the practice of female genital mutilation (al-Bannā, 2005b) constitute his deviation from mainstream intellectuals. Particularly, this liberal profile is where he collided with the religious institution al-Azhar, which largely adheres to mainstream understandings of Islam. In fact, al-Banna highlighted the various conditions or impediments set on the applicability of ḥudūd in today's world. This is congruent with the common argument among tajdīd intellectuals (see al-Ashmawy, 1994, 101) that the actual purpose of the penalties was not the punishment, rather deterrence (see Hakeem et al., 2012, 7–23).

Shari'a and positive law

Once again, the uprooting of Shari'a under modernization and colonization was associated with implanting Western-oriented patterns, institutions and laws. In result, the secular was portrayed as encroaching on the Islamic in CIPT. The larger theme on Shari'a revolved around its application after positive law co-regulated Muslim daily life. On the relation of Shari'a to positive law, al-Banna stressed two key dimensions: First, he insisted that its application at the time of the prophet was unique, but he largely presented it as non-replicable, which is a common claim by many tajdīd intellectuals, who usually highlight the vast differences between current practices of Shari'a application and its application in history. The past application, in his analysis, entailed nobility and a strong tendency to avoid ḥudūd application by the judge, as well as an equally-strong desire for salvation through the application of ḥudūd by the culprit/sinner (see al-Bannā, 2007a, 131–2; see also al-Bannā, 1986a, 177–8; 1994a, 39). Second, he emphasized adaptability; that is, laws governing society should cope with developments, when it is applied:

> The problem of religions is actually with time (*Zaman*), religions appeared thousands of years ago: Judaism more than three thousand years ago, Christianity more than two thousand years ago and the youngest is Islam, more than one thousand four hundred years ago.
>
> Time is neither an empty phenomenon, nor a rigid standard, nor just a vessel where incidents co-exist; rather, it represents an interaction of life and it is in society called progress, in the individual called growth. So, time is the embracer of growth, developments and events. (al-Bannā, 2010b, 45)

Once again, this emphasis on context is commonly propagated by tajdīd intellectuals in promoting tolerance towards new interpretations (Ḥanafī, 1983, 69; 78; 'Arkūn, 1995, 117). Through both arguments, al-Banna critically approached CIPT because his ultimate position defied the established mainstream conviction that ḥudūd should be applied. In this regard, his tajdīd profile towards introducing new interpretation is focused on the inevitability of change. This manifested in his assertion that the problem with the time factor is not with the general principles of belief in God, or the accompanying norms and values of good, justice, beauty and so on, rather with addressing worldly matters (*Duniāwiyāt*). To him, these matters should be dealt with in the same manner all social phenomena are dealt with; they should be subjected to progress and change. Sticking rigidly to rules turn them into obstacles in the way of reform (al-Bannā 2010b, 45–6).

Likewise, contemporaneity and its repercussions were highlighted in his account on Coptic demands vis-à-vis the Muslim majority in Egypt. Al-Banna agreed to their demand of Islamic jurisprudential revisions regarding 'Ahl al-Dhimma and 'Ahl al-Kitāb. To him, it is a duty to carry out such revisions; temporal rules (*'Aḥkām Zamāniyya*) versus absolute and constant values and creeds must be distinguished. To him, Jiziya was an old practice. Islam imposed it in exchange for protection and exemption from military service for non-Muslims, as this was the best arrangement available at the time (see al-Bannā, 2007a, 79; see also al-Bannā, 1996b, 156). On this, al-Banna embodied the tendency, depicted in Chapter 1, of the juridical terminology on 'Ahl al-Dhimma and Jiziya used as part of the history of Islam, after the Muslim landscape was altered and the logic for its application came to an end.

Largely concerned with the impact of time on Shari'a, he gave precedence to context towards advocating the non-exclusive nature of its application regarding particularities (*Juz'iyāt*), like marriage and divorce, usury prohibition and the penalties assigned to these. To him, Muslims are required by God to think about everything and to seek wisdom (*Ḥikma*). When this is done, it appears that God did not stipulate anything but for a reason (*'Illa*), this being justice or interest. In his writings, when Qur'an was revealed, it achieved these two higher norms. However, to him, sometimes progress overruns Qur'anic text. In this case, the latter may no longer provide wisdom and its initial reveal is no longer relevant. Thus, it retreats with it the provision concerned, because the latter goes hand in hand with the reason for its existence and/or absence (al-Bannā, 2010b, 46). In this regard, he reiterated norms usually consented as part of Islam such as rationale and reason that were not disputed as part of the heritage, to end up with his position on ḥudūd above.

Likewise, he provided evidence to his claim and position through examples of Islamic history on alterations applied to Shari'a application, such as when 'Umar b. al-Khattab stopped the practice of giving part of alms to those whose hearts are inclined towards Islam (*Mu'allafati Qulūbuhum*) (al-Bannā, 2010b, 46–7; see al-Bannā, 1996b, 131). In parallel, he also brought evidence from the contemporary world; al-Banna argued that all attempts for establishing a state to apply Shari'a failed and led to chaos, imposed restrictions (*Quiyud*), suspended freedom and hindered development, led to civil war and backwardness of the country. He used Sudan, Nigeria and Afghanistan as examples. They failed as Shari'a was imposed from ruling governments and not demanded by ruled nations. Thus, its application can only be based on popular initiative, restraining government monopoly of Shari'a (al-Bannā, 2010b, 42–3).

Nonetheless, his views on women's right to lead prayers, not wear the veil and the like imply he did not rigidly commit himself to the body of jurisprudence of Sunni Islam. His deviation from that body of mainstream authorship in CIPT is based on massive filtrations he applied to the Hadith tradition in his book Stripping Bukhari and Muslim (*Tajrid al-Bukhari wa Muslim*), filtrations that he based on the fact that Sunni collections were created long after the Prophet's death and there was an element of social prestige associated with telling Hadith back then (al-Bannā, 2008c, 7–11).

When it comes to ultimate positions, he deviated from the body of Sunni jurisprudence on women rights, repentance and the Islamic state. These are the most contested elements of his intellectual path (al-Bannā, 2006a; 2002c). Throughout his writings on these topics, he heavily used Qur'anic text, the least contested and most binding of all elements of the heritage (al-Bannā, 2006a,

9–13; 2003a, 12–37). This use of Qur'an is part of his attempt to establish his character as an Islamic intellectual engaged in renewing knowledge on Islam.

To sum up, al-Banna did not reject positive law, even if he numerated several reservations on Shari'a application in today's world. He didn't exclude positive law because, to him, suitability must be taken into account; worldly matters are to be dealt with accordingly. As pointed out above, if the reason why a penalty in Islam (*Ḥad*) is imposed does not exist anymore, then there is no logic in applying it. Therefore, positive law could regulate the matter and impose a penalty to the crime emanating from such developments. An initiative to apply Shari'a *should* come from the masses. If people would not push for it, laws would have its basis in positive law. In a capsule, he endorsed a three-folded stance on Shari'a. One, the call for Shari'a should come through the nation, not the state. Two, Shari'a is justice (*'Adl*). Three, there is a need for rational assessment of ḥudūd according to cause (*'Illa*) and positive law is not excluded, it has roles to play.

Violence: Jihad as activism

The vast military conquests, widely known as futūḥāt, expanded the Muslim empire drastically. Although usually depicted as a sign of glory and strength, the nature of these conquests as purely religious or a dictation of real politics is still debated today in CIPT, with no clear lines of demarcation between tajdīd and mainstream intellectuals. Yet, there's a general tendency to negate an offensive character of futūḥāṭ and converge on the fact that Islam knows no religious war, and reiterate the decent treatment of populations in the conquered lands. Similar records could be traced in Western scholarship on the conquests. Nonetheless, the conquests came to be linked to a critical debate on the general profile of Islam as a *violent religion* after the 11 September attacks and violence committed by several Islamist militant groups. Portraying Islam as a violent religion is believed to be instigated by a deliberate overemphasis on Islamist militancy in the West.

Still, CIPT writings maintain the dual nature of the term, entailing violent along with non-violent forms of activism. This does not represent a line of demarcation between mainstream and tajdīd, who mostly converge on condemning sporadic violence against civilians but insist on the right to use Jihad against occupation. Al-Banna's writings on Jihad is read against this background.

Futūḥāt in positive shadows

Within the duality of futūḥāt as part of the faith and a dictation of real politics, al-Banna did not present it as part of the Islamic faith/call, rather as a dictation instigated by *lack of alternatives*. The idea that the Islamic army would travel to other lands, call on people to convert to Islam and go back if they agree to convert, and voluntarily pay Jiziya if they disagree, to him, was too naive to even consider as an alternative to the conquests. So, the only viable alternative was that of war if non-Muslims resist the Islamic call. Converging with the cross-cutting argument on the non-aggressive nature of futūḥāt in Islamic history, in his views, the Islamic call was not to use violence in order to spread its message. Violence is only permissible in situations of self-defence; when attacked, the right to use force is established. He believed this is what happened in the Arab Peninsula during the time of the Prophet (al-Bannā, 2003a, 59–68).

Going back to the heritage and to the golden age of Islam, he maintained that futūḥāt were not intended to impose Islam on conquered lands; both Abi Bakr and 'Umar did not destroy churches and monasteries and actually prohibited Muslims from destroying them. To him, futūḥāt complied with the nature of things and dictations of human society; it was more of a survival war among different human communities (al-Bannā, 2004, 170). His positive account on the history of futūḥāt is summarized in this quote:

> It is without a doubt that the Islamic conquests (*Futūḥāt*) instigated progress, because it ended class rule based on privileges and inherited nobility, which deprived the masses from participation in public policy or freedom of labor, enjoying rights to a society based on equality and that no Arab is better than (*'A'jami*) 'non-Arab' but through piety and good deed (*al-'Amal al-Ṣāliḥ*). These conquests achieved the biggest melting among human communities, where Islam played the role of the reactor and the Arab language - as that of Qur'an - attained unity between different people.[22] (al-Bannā, 2003a, 61)

Although not a dictation of the faith, al-Banna affirmed that Islam contributed positively to the history of futūḥāt, as it provided some sense of mercy. As soon as the act of conquest was over, *Islamic peace* prevailed. Muslims were not allowed to steal the money, burn crops or destroy homes of the conquered and guaranteed freedom of creed for everyone. Comparing practices of Muslims as conquerors to those of Romans, he claimed the former were merciful, and the latter were brutal[23] (al-Bannā 2003a, 59–68). On this, he reiterated the common stance on futūḥāt among Muslim and non-Muslim accounts highlighting the decent treatment of conquered populations, especially compared to other non-Muslim conquests ('Arkūn, 1992, 115; Cleveland, 2000, 14–15, respectively).

Violence in relativism

As shown in Chapter 1, Abi Bakr launched wars against those who refrained from paying alms (*Zakāt*), after the death of the Prophet, known in history as apostasy wars (*Ḥurūb al-Ridda*). Because these wars were first launched by Abi Bakr, not the Prophet, their Islamic character was widely disputed as part of the faith. Highlighted earlier, al-Banna's liberal profile comprised overt advocacy of freedom, especially that of faith. He wrote and published a whole book to refute the argument that apostates should be penalized (al-Bannā, 2006a). He positioned what happened during the time of Abi Bakr within the context of real politics and not of Islam as a faith. To him, it was a war against those who refused to pay Zakāt and challenged Abi Bakr's authority, who started the aggression when they tried to take over Madīna (al-Bannā, 2006a, 28–9).

Therefore, to him, as much as futūḥāt were dictated by politics, so were the apostasy wars under Abi Bakr. Subsequently, these elements of Islamic history, which are today commonly used as part of linking Islam to violence are, in his account, not part of the faith of Islam and, accordingly, there is no reason to link the faith to violence. Still, the claims and arguments he presented do not constitute a position on the duality of tajdīd and mainstream. Even if the political nature of futūḥāt and apostasy wars is disputed (Tibawi, 1976, 53; Bielfeldt, 2004, 158), both camps converge on the non-aggressive nature of the faith of Islam.

Although he overtly opposed Islamist militancy against civilians, al-Banna contextualized violence endorsed by groups like al-Takfir wa-l-Hijra and al-Jihad in light of the violence by the Nasser regime. To him, Nasser's despicable torturing of prisoners was the key reason why these groups, whose leaders suffered in prisons, opted for violence (al-Bannā, 1996a, 91–2). He further highlighted this point during the interviews, when he maintained the Nasser regime resisted religion (Interview, 1 November 2010). This was also evident when he discussed the 11 September attacks on the United States. He wrote:

> The reality is that the 11 of September and its events are not, as some people think, a cause, rather a result. The Islamic society in contemporary times was controlled by wanton military rule that dominated the region, and the bitter hostility that grew between 'Abd al-Nasser and the Muslim Brotherhood; the discrimination he put them through and the torture and degradation he

> committed in his prisons, which developed a definite hostility between the regime and the Islamic stream. [24] (al-Bannā, 2004, 7)

In addition, he believed that the success attained by some political groups which opted for violence in the West, such as Syndicalism in France, Nihilism in Russia or Nazism in Germany, created an appropriate atmosphere for violent groups with Islamist calls (al-Bannā, 1996b, 91–2, 102–4). Here, he didn't differ from general authorship on the topic, which condemns this violence and signals prior injustice and oppression done to these groups towards explaining their use of violence.

Once again, much of Islamist militant activities carried out in the twentieth century were carried out under the banner of Jihad. As shown in Chapter 1, there is wide consensus on rejecting acts of sporadic violence against civilians, unless there is a clear state of occupation of lands. His account on these acts of violence falls within these broad lines. He differentiated between Jihad as struggle against occupation, which does not contradict Islam (Interview, 1 November 2010), and Jihad as irregular violent acts targeting civilians. In his view, Hasan al-Banna, the founder of the MB and his elder brother, called for the first, while violent Islamist groups opted for the second (al-Jihād, 2002b, 3–4; see 9).

In a similar vein, his writings on the role of MB's secret apparatus in fighting Israeli forces in Palestine signify his acceptance of the use of violence against occupation. In addition, to him, the large number of British troops in Egypt made it necessary to have such an apparatus, which admittedly at one point lacked discipline and became uncontrollable. Thus, his criticism was not directed to the use of violence, rather to its particular application (al-Bannā, 1996b, 64). Interpreting Jihad in ways conducive to assassinations and thuggery, to him, had nothing to do with Islam, he highlighted *wrongful* interpretations. His account on Islamist militancy falls at the intersection of his Islamic and political profiles; acts of violence he pointed out were not just part of the violence debate in CIPT but were also part of his discussing Egyptian politics.

Accepting violence under conditions of occupation in both early and modern Islamic history, al-Banna argued:

> Islam accepts combat, it even dictates it in self-defense .... Its strategic importance was evident in historical critical moments, as since Islam began, polytheists (*Mushrikūn*) wanted to abort it, and Muslims replied with combat that got them victory. The importance of Jihad was also evident during the colonial resistance time in the modern history ... it was not attacking others, nor an attempt to take their lands. ... coercion is alien to Jihad. (al-Bannā, 2002b, 8)

In other words, his appraisal of violence is not solely dependent on whether Islam permits it or not; he also approached it as a theme of politics. According to him, there must be an assessment of the potential for violent activities through a *utilitarian* conception of politics, violent groups committing violence in expression of their rejection and resistance to discrimination, for instance, without being able to launch a successful revolution, will end up committing individual acts of assassination or destroying buildings. Such acts do not affect ruling regimes, they result in more suppression instead. He, thus, concluded that these practices are useless (al-Bannā, 2004, 165).

His reference to backwardness of Muslims, combined with his account on colonial history above, manifests the recurrent nature of Said's Orientalist appraisal of authorship on Islam, where the West imposed *certain* understandings of the East through colonialism and its scholarship (Said, 1978, 43). It may have even signified Western fears and concerns through its scholarship on the East (Sardar, 1999, 13–14). Thus, al-Banna, although an intellectual who read Western literature (al-Bannā, 2009, 45–51), who firmly stood for freedoms and often contested mainstream CIPT contributions, didn't detach himself from the Orientalist discourse, symbolized in Said's writings and reiterated among many Muslim intellectuals on West/East relations.

To sum up, his appraisal of violence is partly formulated from within the heritage; he accepted forms of violence as acts of self-defence, including acts of liberation, but rejected those targeting civilians. Futūḥāt and apostasy wars are contextualized in his writings as acts of politics and power relations and not driven by faith. This touches upon the differentiation between Islam as faith and Muslim practices. Nonetheless, in accepting and rejecting forms of violence, he generally tended to seek relevance to the heritage, thus keeping his character as an Islamic intellectual.

Egyptian MB and Jihad

The MB in Egypt was a key source of contestation to successive ruling regime(s). The movement was banned in 1954 (Zahid, 2010, 79). Its members were jailed under Nasser, Sadat and Mubarak (Brown and Dunne, 2014), but it survived this long-term persecution. But MB political engagement cannot be understood apart from its social weight; the movement has an extended social base and regional network. This base is composed of both philanthropic engagement and businesses; they are involved in education and medical services, which offer services for reduced prices, and free education (see Clark, 2004; Zahid, 2010).

Many of those working abroad, particularly in oil-rich Arab countries, deposit their savings in Islamic investment businesses, which demand small interest rates and offer high revenues (see Hartmann, 2011, 111–12). The regional network added to the MB weight as an Islamist movement that is both entrenched and organized in more than one country (Pargeter, 2010, 15).

The core of MB political engagement could be traced back to Hasan al-Banna, to whom Islam was religion and state (Krämer, 2010; Ternisien, 2010, 51). In 1928, he started sending preachers (*Du'āh*) to countries geographically and culturally close to Egypt. These were countries of the Arab-East, Sudan and the Arab Gulf countries ('Abd al-Majīd, 2010, 71). Before the 1952 coup, the aforementioned secret apparatus, representing the MB military arm, was held accountable for the assassination of a judge and a prime minister, the bombing of several government buildings and a plot to overthrow the government. Hasan Al-Banna, founder of the movement and the elder brother of Jamal al-Banna, was in result assassinated by members of the secret police in 1949, in revenge for the assassination of the prime minister (Rutherford, 2008, 79).

Willing to engage in politics and supporting the Free Officers at the advent of the 1952 coup, the MB asked Nasser for a share in power, in exchange for its support and backing of the coup. This occurred only a few months before what is known as *The Crisis of 1954* – a crisis between Nasser and several military generals regarding the military return to its barracks. President Muhammad Najib, head of the RCC at the time, was in favour of a military withdrawal from politics (Brown, 2011).

After being warned to stop recruiting members from the country's police and armed forces, the movement was banned in January 1954 (Zahid, 2010, 79), and many MBs were jailed in the same year ('Abd al-Ghanii, 1993, 270). Families of MB detainees were persecuted; women who financially supported wives of imprisoned MB male members were arrested and detained ('Abd al-Hādī, 2011, 78). Imprisoned and tortured, many of them found haven in religiously conservative countries, such as Saudi Arabia (see Beattie, 2000, 114–15).

Yet, the regime gave two unintended boosts to the MB: first, the 1967 defeat played a critical role in the re-emergence of religious sentiments among Egyptians who felt they were punished for their lack of faith (see Makari, 2007, 55). Second, after the detention and then execution of Sayyid Qutb in 1966, the movement constantly expanded and established itself in most Arab countries (see Ben Jelloun, 2011, 54), due to the central and leading intellectual status of Qutb in the movement inside and outside Egypt (see Soffar, 2004, 1–14).

As stated in Chapter 2, Sadat regarded the MB as a counter-weight to leftists. But some qualification is due. In the period of 1972–5, Sadat used a group called *Shabab al-Islam* or Youth of Islam to counterbalance leftists and this group was not part of the MB ('Abd al-Majīd, 2010, 127). He started a gradual release of MB prisoners, including top figures like 'Umar al-Tilmisani, who took leadership of the movement after al-Hudaibi passed away. These releases encouraged MB exiles to return to Egypt, many of whom fled under Nasser. After years of working in other countries, they were able to establish businesses in Egypt upon their return (Beattie, 2000, 114–15).

Under Sadat, MB members were allowed to reclaim their Cairo headquarters and hold meetings inside mosques, continue their activities on university campuses and resume recruitment of new members (see Zahid, 2010, 82). Sadat's infitah contributed a boost to religious sentiments among Egyptians, as it caused social disturbances and materialism in society, people sought reference in Islamic ideals (McDermott, 1988, 188).

Under Mubarak, the movement sought electoral gains, starting the 1980s. In the first elections, 1984, they won eight seats; in 1987, they won thirty-six seats, a serious rise in their share and weight (Zahid, 2010, 100). Opting for violence under Mubarak was evidently employed by other political groups, working under the banner of Islam. Towards the end of the 1980s, Islamists disrupted musical concerts in universities and intimidated students of both sexes mingling in public (Bayat, 2010, 139). The violence started late in the 1970s, after several groups which evolved from Nasser's prisons opted for violence; these included al-Takfir wa-l-Hijra, but the MB was not involved in this violence (see Halverson, 2010, 88–91).

Regime persecution of the MB, under Mubarak, was quite blatant. A group of MB leaders were transferred to military courts and laws were issued to impair the movement's access to top syndicate positions. This was followed by arrest campaigns that varied in intensity and turned into a regularity after the 2005 MB electoral performance (Qandīl, 2010, 14). Verdicts issued by military courts were applied more quickly and were more severe than those of ordinary courts. The prosecutor was not obliged to present the source of his evidence and no judicial appeal was allowed (Rutherford, 2008, 87). From 2005 to 2010, the regime harassed and repressed several political groups including the MB (Dunne and Radwan, 2014, 252). Additionally, the government adopted a package of constitutional amendments in 2007 that prohibited the establishment of any party with a religious foundation (Rutherford, 2008, 187), in a deliberate attempt to block the movement from establishing a political party (Brown, 2011).

Countering oppression and contesting its blockage on the political sphere, the movement *preyed* on regime's brutality that the MB brought to public attention through media (see Bradely, 2008, 121–3). Meanwhile, the movement backed the judges club's proposed amendments to the law on the judiciary and expressed support for two judges, who were subjected to disciplinary proceedings for reporting fraud during the 2005 parliamentary elections (see Rutherford, 2008, 184). In the same direction, it gradually opted to deploy its social network to augment its oversight activities. Through charity networks, the Brotherhood's MPs could spot cases of corruption, consequences of governmental, social and economic policies, and to ultimately augment political support for their parliamentary activities (Brown and Hamzawy, 2010, 27).

Yet, even with the remarkable organizational skills on one hand and wide social network on the other (see Clark, 2004; Brown and Hamzawy, 2010), from the inside, the movement has a hierarchal authoritarian structure. Siblings of top figures in the MB were granted an almost automatic appeal regardless of their merit (see ʿAbd al-Munʿim, 2011, 13–18). Its organization does not allow much room for individual decision-making (al-ʿAjūz, 2011, 63). This tradition of hierarchal and top-centred politics goes back to the early days of the MB, when Hasan al-Banna repeatedly made unilateral decisions, completely bypassing the Guidance Office (Maktab al-ʾIrshad) (Pargeter, 2010, 16).

The 2011 uprising and the subsequent ouster of Mubarak opened up a window of political opportunities to the MB in Egypt. For the first time in their history, they could establish a political party and legally compete in elections as members of that party. Yet, after severing relations with the country's military and a popular call to oust Mursi in April 2013, the movement was back 'on the run', been subjected to large-scale legal and political persecution and was decidedly barred from the country's political sphere. The whole post-2011 MB record instigated intense debates on the pros and cons of the movement's political engagement and implications of its exclusion for Egypt's democratic transition (see al-Anani, 2015).

Al-Banna's appraisal of the MB is largely preoccupied with its political and social activism, focusing on the social network on one hand, and political engagement of the movement on the other. On both themes, he maintained, throughout his intellectual path, his admiration for its social activities. Towards the end of his life, he began to fluctuate on their political agenda and strongly criticized their engagement in politics. In fact, his position on the latter goes in line with his assertion that Islam has no state (2003a), although he asserted, during interviews, the strong political presence of the MB in the Egyptian street outweighed established political parties (Interview, 3 November 2010). By virtue of his personal profile, as brother of Hasan al-Banna, he had strong access to information. Also, al-Banna was jailed, as mentioned earlier, late in the 1940s because of his ties to the MB (al-Bannā, 1997, 7). The access al-Banna had to the MB during the 1930s and 1940s could be easily established through interviews, when he elaborated on their internal decision-making processes, socialization techniques, sports and concrete incidents of internal crisis and financial challenges (Interview, 10 November 2011; Interview, 15 November 2010).

Initially, the fact that the MB was never part of the regime under Nasser, Sadat and/or Mubarak meant intellectuals had more freedom to shed negative light on the movement. As the MB became a serious political rival to the three regimes, negatively presenting the MB was in fact an indirect, though unintended, *favour* to these regimes. The accounts of the movement in al-Banna's writings were mainly presented under Mubarak, with a very positive depiction of the movement's history, where al-Banna claimed the MB played a critical role in supporting the 1952 Free Officers move against the king. He also praised the populist non-bourgeoisie composition of the movement's leading figures (1996b, 77, 47, respectively; 1994a, 44).

But towards the end of Mubarak's rule, this positive depiction was hardly traceable, with negative appraisals of the prospect of movements working under the banner of Islam reaching power. He blamed the MB both for letting down Muhammad Najib and all other forces that stood for a return of civilian politics during the 1954 crisis, and for their drive to reach power, which according to him was not part of their original mission (2010b, 38–41, 53–4). Although it might be al-Banna's genuine conviction that led him to considerably shift on the MB in his writings, the severing of controls endorsed by the Mubarak regime against the movement cannot be overlooked. Put differently, his account on the movement might also be driven by the growing tension in its relation to the regime.

Note also, positive accounts of the MB that are traceable in al-Banna's writings pertain to the history of the movement. He mainly praised the time when his brother Hasan al-Banna served as the supreme guide of the movement, especially in 1936 when the movement raised funds for Palestinian leaders and in the 1948 Arab-Israeli crisis, where the MB played a *heroic* role in supporting the Arab cause (1996b, 46–9). Therefore, numerating the strengths of the MB in their early years established no contestation to the Mubarak regime, and this certainly did not fortify the MB position in this rivalry.

Identities: The religious 'in' the political

Under the broad theme of identity, there are both intra-identity aspects: dualities of Muslim versus Islamic, the Muslim versus the religiously devout Muslim, ordinary Muslims versus clerics (*'Ulamā'*) and certainly Sunnis versus Shiites. There are also inter-identity aspects: pertaining to how Muslims relate/should relate to non-Muslims. Terms like Dār al-'Islām/Dār al-Ḥarb; 'Ahl al-Dhimma and Jiziya constitute the juristic background of the larger CIPT debate on identity. These terms were coined at a time when Muslims were conquerors. Today, as Muslims are not spearheading human civilization, these terms are normally invoked for the purposes of discussing the juridical history of Islam.

Among mainstream and tajdīd intellectuals, lines of demarcation are still blurred on the issue of conversions from Islam as well as non-Muslims' right to hold state top positions, which were historically confined to Muslims. With the growing phenomenon of Muslims living as minorities in non-Muslim societies through labour immigration, other themes and juridical contributions became more central to CIPT and represented the need for revisiting juridical terms and establishing Minority Jurisprudence (*Fiqh al-'Aqalliyyāt*). Islamist militancy instigated and revived juridical discussions on Muslim/non-Muslim relations in the jurisprudence; sporadic violence against the state or society invoked a debate on how Muslims relate to their larger societies. Across mainstream/tajdīd writings on the matter, relation of Islam and the state/larger society is one of coexistence and cooperation.

Identity 'as' Orientalism

> Among all revealed religions, Islam shines as the most perfect of all, the last form and most refined of them. (al-Bannā, 1979a, 15)

As shown in Chapter 1, Muslim/East versus West is one of the identity classifications frequently depicted in CIPT, which is part of the larger juxtaposition instigated by colonial history between the Western colonizer and the Eastern colonized. Both acts of modernization and colonization brought the West closer to the Eastern/Muslim conscience and many of the revival and renewal intellectual efforts of the late nineteenth century were inspired by contact with the West (Black, 2008, 40). Al-Banna's account on identity resonated this West/East duality (see al-Bannā, 1979a, 86–90). In his writings, the West is mainly

Europe and/or European history, specific examples of European countries or the United States (see al-Bannā, 2002b, 58–61). The East is mostly country-based/national, focusing on one country (al-Bannā, 1986a, 21–36, 40–7). Likewise, the juxtaposition embedded in the duality of East-Islam/West was quite apparent in his appraisal of justice theory in Islamic and European Thought (al-Bannā, 1995c). In addition, his character as an Islamic intellectual is signified in his overt admiration to Islamic identity:

> We are still proud of almost fifty scientists, philosophers or Islamic thinkers who appeared during the flourishing of Islamic culture, we refer to what they presented to human civilization, that Europeans profited from them in medieval centuries. (al-Bannā, 1996b, 182)

Through this assessment, he indirectly addressed Said's Orientalism, which depicted the Orientalist scholarship as partly driven by the threat posed by the flourishing and expanding Islamic civilization to Europe/Christendom (Said, 1978, 59; Esposito, 1992, 37). Still, religion – Islam – is not the sole bond towards forming identity. To him, religion can be one attribute towards a larger identity, such as a national one:

> The collective spirit of the people, its national character, the various ties of history, traditions, customs, religions and political creeds, are the foundations that give millions of individuals one moral personality and holds it as a people. (al-Bannā, 1952/1999b, 123)

Although he acknowledged that all religions are traceable back to the same origin of Abraham, father of all Prophets (al-Bannā, 2003a, 206), he, like many Islamic intellectuals, highlighted some uniquenesses in Islam. Islam's extraordinary exhibition of God, its comprehensiveness and its basis of justice meant Islam excelled vis-à-vis other revealed religions (al-Bannā, 1979a, 12–17).

He did not only compare Islam to other religions but also to ideologies, again presenting Islam as better (al-Bannā, 1984a). Similarly, he argued Qur'anic verses stipulating freedom of belief are much better than Egypt's most liberal Constitution of 1923. Provisions of the latter were interpreted by the constituting committee, so that only religions based on revelation would be recognized (al-Bannā, 2003b, 26–8). This account on the 1923 Constitution is the exception to his very positive appraisal already noted earlier on this phase of Egyptian history. In Muslim societies, he depicted Islam as having an overwhelming identity, one that stretched to cover many aspects of community's self-consciousness. He wrote:

> Islam is the element of revolution and authenticity, it is the root for history and morality (*Nafsiyya*), it is the 'identity' of these societies and the most prominent of its constituents, it is the spiritual power that provokes and moves social, political and economic work. (al-Bannā, 1982, 111)

His account on Islam is very similar to that of Hodgson's Islamicate, where Islam comprises not just a spiritual creed, but also a comprehensive social system, with legislation, literature and Muslim lands (al-Bannā, 1982, 86). His Islamic and political profiles converged in his depiction of Islam as an identity that played a critical role in resistance and struggle against the colonizer both in Islamic history, where fighting was carried out under the auspices of Islam (specifically of Jihad) (al-Bannā, 2002b, 8), and in Egyptian history, during the wars of 1967 and 1973. He wrote:

> The Islamic identity played a critical role in defeating the Israelis, as the people [Egyptian people] viewed it as an Islamic battle, most of the soldiers fought while fasting ... as much as the 1967 defeat was a negative evidence of the defeat of a regime which antagonized Islam, the Ramadan victory was a positive evidence on the power of the religious passion and its capacity to win, penetrate all what Israel established. (al-Bannā, 1996b, 94–5)

As a rule of thumb, when Islam is invoked along with other religions in his writings, there is some visible preference to Islam. In more general terms, he outlined three features that associate with any religion, not just Islam; these are: one, sacred guidance through revelation to prophets and messengers does not differ from one religion to another. Two, addressing the individual is not something special about Islam, it is in the nature of any religion to address the individual (al-Bannā, 1979a, 40, 81, respectively). Three, in a society believing in some religion, this religion is the biggest factor in that society[25] (al-Bannā, 2001a, 56).

Egypt and Europe as identities

As an Islamic intellectual who spent most of his life in his home country, Egypt, he showed keen interest in debates circulating in the Egyptian public sphere. Many of his books were entirely devoted to addressing the country's political, social and economic problems (see al-Bannā, 1995d; 1987; 2006b). Even in books which revolved around concepts like democracy and seem to have nothing to do with his homeland, he came across Egyptian politics. His book New Democracy (*Dimuqratiyya Jadida*) was originally about democratic rule that transcends the procedural aspects of democracy into discussions on social security, pensions, healthcare and so on as part of state duties. However, a focus on Egypt is not to be mistaken throughout the different chapters of the book, where a whole chapter was devoted to the Egyptian national identity, women's status and workers in Egypt (al-Bannā, 1946, see 16–17, 169, 210, 231).

His book The Contemporary State (*al-Dawla al-'Asriyya*) mainly dealt with the modern state, how it evolved and the need to cope with it. A whole chapter was dedicated to a case study from the Egyptian working class, where he discussed the relation between the rulers and the ruled, starting the time of Muhammad 'Ali. He narrated on the failed efforts of the working class to coordinate and work together in order to form a real force and the missing role of the Egyptian intelligentsia in mobilizing this class (al-Bannā, 1982, 95–112).

Along with offering accounts of Egypt's Copts, MB and the military, he also discussed national – Egyptian – identity per se. He wrote:

> The national character expresses itself in everything, arts, literature, social custom, traditions, accent, conception of life, perception of objects. (al-Bannā, 1952/1999b, 122)
>
> The attempt [to establish a modern state] should follow a revolutionary manner, … because only the revolutionary logic … can save us from the trouble where we find ourselves, because only this logic can achieve that. (al-Bannā, 1982, 107)

Here, al-Banna spoke of Egypt and not of Islam. As shown before, history of Egypt, specifically the 1923 Constitution and the wars of 1967 and 1973, is discussed in his writings. He wrote of the Egyptian people, to whom he dedicated his book:

> And the people are the masters of all, and we all derive our pride from belonging to them and sticking to them, we measure our virtues to the extent we guard their honor and watching for their right … our obedience to their will. (al-Bannā, 1952/1999b, 172)[26]

Similarly, in books which, from the title, discuss Islam or CIPT or both, he often invoked the case of Egypt. For instance, in his book Rule by Qur'an and the Issue of Shari'a Application (*al-Hukm bi-l-Qur'an wa Qadiyyat Tatbiq al-Shari'a*), which addressed problems evident in democratic societies, he discussed Egypt although it was by no means a democracy when he wrote his book (al-Bannā, 1986a, 23). This was also the case in his book The Issue of Shari'a Application (*Qadiyyat Tatbiq al-Shari'a*) published in 1998, which assessed problems facing its application; he discussed Egypt's Copts as a religious minority (1998, 48, 75–6). To conclude on this point, he emphasized the *Egyptian* in no less intensity than he highlighted the *Islamic*. It was not only about discussing Egyptian politics, it was also showing that he belonged to Egypt, as his homeland. An intellectual, who presented him/herself as Islamic, can actually seek legitimacy in *other* identities without fearing that the former might diminish or jeopardize the latter.

Meanwhile, Europe, or the European, is the only identity al-Banna frequently addressed that he did not claim personal belonging, or even relation, to. In his writings, Europe is characterized by a frequent sense of comparison and juxtaposition to Islam and/or Muslim societies, which posited Europe as a parallel, if not contrasting, identity (al-Bannā, 1984a; 1995c). To him, Islamic rules enjoyed a moral and spiritual basis, which contributed to their effectiveness. He compared this to the European society, which cultivated a *legal sense* in the citizen that is incomparable to the moral one cultivated by Islam.[27]

Likewise, he juxtaposed the Islamic route to democracy through Shura vis-à-vis the European way of achieving Shura through democracy. For him, democracy does not lead to Shura because democracy is unleashed. But the opposite is true because unlike democracy, Shura entails a sense of *commitment* (al-Bannā, 1986b, 79–80). This point on democracy is consistent with his aforementioned reservations on it and his general positing of Islam as excelling vis-à-vis other religions and ideologies.

Al-Banna attributed this discrepancy to the logic dominating justice between Islamic and European Thought. To him, in Europe, religion has no real role, because it is pagan (*Wathaniyya*), it is driven by its passion and manipulated Christianity to shape it according to its own concepts. Conversely, he argued, Islam revolves around God. It takes all its departure points from the Creator, and through justice, Islam deals with crime and penalty (al-Bannā, 1995c, 116–21).

Nonetheless, his account on Europe was, in many instances, very positive. He did a great deal of Western readings, and admitted many of these were contemporary and European (see al-Bannā, 2008b, 13). Plus, he occasionally invoked European experience to model syndical historical examples (al-Bannā, 1993, see 39–54). To sum up, Europe, in his writings, is both an identity and a human community he compared, or at least juxtaposed, to Islam. When he did, he mostly gave preference to Islam; thus highlighted his Islamic character and legitimacy as an Islamic intellectual.

Identities, exclusion versus inclusion

Invoking early Islamic history, he highlighted The Madīna Document (*Wathīqat al-Madīna*),[28] which was a legal document regulating rights and duties of its *citizens* after the Prophet emigrated to Madīna, as an example of how national and religious identities can coexist. To him, this document established the notion of *one nation*; it exhibited citizenship, where the nation may consist of many different religions and origins, but all constitute one nation, within which each preserved its own character (al-Bannā, 2003a, 28). While in many instances he invoked the virtuous but non-replicable nature of early history as an argument against the call for strict application of ḥudūd, in this identity context, early history is presented as a model to be aspired. This is one rare instance of how the same elements of the heritage were simultaneously used in contrasting manners.

> In Egypt, Islam is the strongest faith for the Egyptian people … and the Egyptian society cannot be imagined without Islam. For where does Arabic, which was protected and treasured by Qur'an and Qur'an turned it into the standard language for what the Islamic world do; and where does history be; and where traditions, customs and feasts … etc come from; and above all, this is the conscience. For, all Muslims established their conscience in the shadow of the licit and the illicit (*Ḥalāl wa Ḥarām*). (al-Bannā, 2010b, 33)

A great deal of the literature on CIPT is preoccupied with two main sub-themes: Muslim versus non-Muslim and the Islamic identity in relation to national identity, where the common ground between Islam and Arab identities is usually emphasized (al-Ḥafiyān, 2006, 69; al-Jābrī, 1992; 15–31, 124). Al-Banna's conception, in this regard, is based on his appraisal that there is no contradiction and no mutual exclusivity traceable, as suggested in the quote above. The only contour he delineated was of extreme nationalism, that might turn into chauvinism. Nonetheless, he started out from his understanding of Islam's concept of the national and not the other way around, as he wrote:

> Islam recognizes this noble emotion and acknowledges it … an Islamic call cannot discard nationalism or see it as encroaching on it, to the contrary, it is part of it, because what intelligibly correct is also legally accepted, and because Islam does not oppose human emotions and sentiments, does not object to these, unless the latter exceeds moderation, whereby nationalism turns into 'chauvinism', turning people of one land to see themselves as above all others … but for a human to love his homeland, feels the special intimate relation binding him/her to it, is something that Islam recognizes and allows. (al-Bannā, 1996b, 154–5)

Likewise, he claimed religion in Arab societies is the base of its life and the origin of its conscience (, 17). He wrote of Islam not only as the most prominent of constituents of the Arab society, but also as one whose impact might outweigh that of the economic factor, which is usually, to him, the strongest factor in terms of impacting society (al-Bannā, 2000, 35; see al-Bannā, 2007a, 86, see also 51). On this point, he conformed to the array of CIPT contributions on the congruence of the Islamic and Arab identities.

This assumed coexistence between the Islamic and the national is congruent with his position on the role Islamic identity played in motivating soldiers in two Egyptian wars: the 1967 defeat and the 1973 victory (al-Bannā, 1996b, 94–5). His conviction that Islam rejects nationalism only when it leads to racist sentiments was clear once again when he addressed the war between Iraq and Iran. For him, Iraq incited the racist drive (*Naz'a 'Unsurriyya*), calling on other Arab countries to fight *Persians*. Al-Banna rejected such tendencies and wrote:

> As if Islam did not defeat this loophole; got rid of it; erased all differences between Arab and non-Arab and made all believers brothers. (al-Bannā, 1986a, 115)

Thus, Islam's acceptance of nationalism should be, in his view, limited by racist tendencies that nationalism might reach at one point. When it reaches exclusivity and racial hatred, then Islam not only rejects it, but also struggles against it. His understanding of Islam as a pluralistic religion (*Din Ta'addudi*)[29] is integral to his conception of the latter's relation to national identity as mutually not exclusive. To him, Islam, as religion, has allowed diversity and the Islamic society is supposed to be a pluralistic one (al-Bannā, 2003b, 34–5). He linked the plurality of Islam to the Sunni juridical rule of not judging people's destiny after death, be it heaven or hell (al-Bannā 2001a, 38–9). In fact, his conception of nationalism as a uniting force partly explains why he, as an Islamic intellectual, found no ground for rejecting it:

> It might happen, that the homeland might include -for historical reasons- non-Muslims. In this case, nationalism brings them together, whereby all are citizens that enjoy the same rights and have the same duties Muslims have. (al-Bannā, 1996b, 154–5)

Furthermore, he described the critical role religion played in Eastern societies as follows: 'Religions were in the origin of society formation, and they constituted conscience … Shari'a … and rule' (al-Bannā, 2010b, 33). To him, they guide the conscience of the masses in Egypt (al-Bannā, 2005c, 7; see also al-Bannā, 1996b, 33). 'Any civilizational project ignoring Islam will not touch the pulse of the masses, and will be born dead' (al-Bannā, 1995a,

35). Nonetheless, religion as part of public morale in Egypt is not restricted to Islam; Christianity is part of this social conscience he depicted (see al-Bannā, 2010b, 33). Particularly, in the case of Egypt, he highlighted the fact that Muslims were originally Copts who converted to Islam (al-Bannā, interview, 5 November 2010).

His non-conflictual perspective on identity is further promoted through his appraisal of the larger Islamic history, where Islamic societies did not repel non-Muslim communities. These were allowed existence and the freedom regarding their own rules. Similarly, they were offered protection for Jiziya, whereby women, children and the elderly were exempted from paying it[30] (al-Bannā, 2003b, 35). Here, the juridical terms of Jiziya are presented as part of history and not as applicable patterns, which is the general position endorsed across the mainstream/tajdīd duality.

Again conforming to the frequently used argument of drawing lines of demarcation between theory and practice of Islam in CIPT authorship (see Krämer, 2000a, 24; Salvatore, 2007, 105), he maintained that Islamic societies are frequently less pluralistic in nature than the religion of Islam. He argued that societies have gone through waves of narrow racism which imposed some sort of *loneliness*, not just between Muslims and non-Muslims, but also amongst Muslims themselves. Shiite separated from Sunni communities and each sect isolated itself. This is, to him, the by-product of corruption which sabotages everything: monotheism, jurisprudence, rule, women and so on (al-Bannā, 2003b, 35). This way, he assumed the influence of autocratic rule on jurisprudence negatively affected the larger society with the Sunni-Shiite towards the cleavage.

Coptic identity and inlcusion

As stated in Chapter 1, historically, Copts, non-Muslim religious communities, were treated as 'Ahl al-Dhimma in conquered territories by Muslim troops. According to this juridical notion, they did not enjoy equal rights as their Muslim counterparts, especially in terms of their access to rule (*Wilāiya*) (see 'Arkūn, 1992, 115). Today, and for the last eleven centuries, the majority of the country's population is Muslim; Egypt is no longer ruled under an Islamic caliphate. Legal codes and institutional settings, from the time of Muhammad ʿAli onwards, were largely inspired by, and often directly adopted from, Western *secular* models (see Dodwell, 2011, 237–9).

Often, Copts claim they enjoyed better conditions under Muhammad ʿAli and, his family afterwards, than under – Christian – England which invaded

Egypt in 1882 (see Milner, 1970; Mikhail, 1911, 12–13; Gruber, 2003, 81). Plus, ethnic differences in Egypt did not necessarily represent a major factor leading to political conflict, and trouble often also arose within an ethnic group (Tamura, 1985, 114.) However, under Republican Egypt (1952), the alleged discrimination against the country's Coptic minority usually escalated into, and was associated with, political violence. For instance, under Sadat in the 1970s, Copts were targeted by attacks and robberies at the hands of Islamist militants, likely at the belief that they constituted obstacles to the establishment of the Islamic state (see Halverson, 2010, 111). Likewise, during al-Khanka crisis, Coptic-Muslim relations were marred with communal violence – the crisis[31] started as clashes between Muslims and Copts, which erupted in the summer of 1971 (see McDermott, 1988; Muzikar, 1989, 109).

During this crisis, an authorized church was burned down; Shenouda III, the young patriarch of the time, called on fifty priests to march to Khanka on 12 November 1971, in protest (see McDermott, 1988, 89). It was a call against the instructions of authorities. As the crisis, and particularly the march led by Shenouda III, contested the regime on the status of the Coptic community, Sadat threatened to resort to Parliament and have Shenouda III stripped of his papal title (Beattie, 2000, 110).

Whereas regime-Coptic relations under Sadat began deteriorating with al-Khanka, the Coptic issue under Mubarak didn't confine to one particular incident or crisis. There was, for instance, al-Kusheh (1998–2000), which started out in Upper Egypt with a clash between a Muslim customer and a Coptic store owner. It escalated into communal violence and killed around twenty Coptic citizens (Eltahawy, 2000). Same with The News (*al-Nabaa*) crisis in 2001, when a newspaper published content of alleged sexual misconduct in one of the country's monasteries (U.S. Senate, 2001, 428; see also Khalil, 2001) and the conversion of Wafaa Costantine, a Coptic female in 2004, where the Church demanded, through mass protests, the state hand in Wafaa to the church (Amer, 2010).

Unlike Sadat, Mubarak did not seek confrontational measures. In fact, he attempted mitigating communal tension through concrete measures, including making, for the first time in Egypt's modern history, the seventh of January a national holiday in December 2002. He additionally appointed several Christian deputies from the back-then ruling NDP to the National assembly from 1984 to 2005 (see Makari, 2007, 70–88). Furthermore, al-Kusheh area was allotted two million dollars for developmental projects after the above-mentioned incident (Abou El-Magd, 2000). Wafaa Costantine, who fled after converting to Islam, was returned to the church (Amer, 2010). This evident inclination to *appease* the

Coptic community might be partly attributed to the fact that early in the 1990s, the regime/Islamists struggle resulted in Islamist militants targeting the country's Copts (see Bayat, 2007, 32–4). Yet, the cross-cutting stance of the three regimes was that there was no Coptic issue to address, and the Coptic diaspora pressure was regarded as a violation of Egypt's national sovereignty (see Hanna, 2013).

Remarkably, Coptic-Muslim relations were relatively good under Nasser and regime-church relations were seen as strong (Labīb, 2012, 15). But Copts were hit by the nationalization scheme after 1952, and access to occupations previously full of Copts was declining, which resulted in the emigration of thousands of middle-class Copts in the late 1950s and the 1960s. Yet, the communal tension never reached either the societal violence or the contestation posed to the regime under Sadat and Mubarak (see McDermott, 1988, 186).

The emigration of Copts, which started under Nasser, continued under Sadat and Mubarak. According to the Coptic Church, more than one million Copts left Egypt during the past three decades – 2004 (Marshall, 2004, 24). Copts leaving the country over the years developed into Copts of the diaspora (*'Aqbat al-Mahjar*) and constituted pressure on ruling regimes. This pressure was especially visible during the time of Mubarak, as the Coptic community sought greater protection and equal rights (see El Amrani, 2006).

But Coptic demands have *concrete* dimensions: discrimination against Copts' access to top state positions, the legal conditions set for building churches (the process of building a church ends up facing more impediments compared to that of mosques), and subjecting Copts to provisions of the family/personal status laws based on Islamic Shari'a (see Rowberry and Khalil, 2013, 120–1). Unsurprisingly, access to top state positions is the most critical, as it implies an assumed limitation imposed by the state regarding access to decision-making organs and state institutions in general. According to the late Muhammad Hasanain Haikal, one of the country's most prominent journalists, there has not been a single Copt among SCAF members in forty years – 2012 (see Rizq, 2012, 61).

After the 2011 uprising, the election of Muhammad Mursi as president in 2012 raised some concerns among the country's Copts regarding the potential for an eventual Islamization of the Egyptian society along with individual incidents of violence 'targeting Copts' (Tadros, 2013). Even that there were no clear measures by Mursi, or his associates, to Islamize the country, his ouster in July 2013 and the election of Sisi in 2014 might have relieved much of these concerns. The latter is largely seen as respectful of Copts and his ascent to power is believed to have their support, even that they are still underrepresented inside the security establishment, and sectarian violence was still traceable after his election (Yerkes, 2016). The Coptic diaspora continues to voice Coptic concerns and Sisi would have to pay attention to their activism in the West but having a non-Islamist president, in and on itself, was overtly welcomed by Egypt's Coptic community (Soliman, 2022).Their demands continue till this very day and they mainly revolve around their call for legislative reform and non-discriminatory practices to promote equality with their Muslim counterparts based on citizenship (Makar, 2016; Hoyle, 2020).

Naturally, writing on Coptic demands under Mubarak fell under the pressure of the Coptic diaspora which eventually increased sensitivity towards the debate in the public sphere,[32] but al-Banna's profile sought a balance between strong critique to church policy in crisis situations and a negative appraisal of regime policy regarding the Coptic community. For instance, he asserted that the parliament commission in charge of the investigation during al-Khanka crisis, under Sadat, argued both Muslim and Coptic clergy showed extreme sensitivity towards the slightest reference to the incident (2006b, 101). But in the same book, he emphasized violence committed by The Coptic Nation Association (Jamʿiyyat al-Umma al-Qibtiyya), the movement responsible for kidnapping the Orthodox Coptic Patriarch in 1954 and forcing him to sign a relinquishment of his position. He compared it to the MB as another political movement taking disguise in religion. He also held Sadat responsible, in part, for the extremist Islamist violence against Copts, as he allegedly gave a free hand to Islamist students in Asiyut University to combat his opponents (2006b, 84–9). Published under Mubarak, this account is an instance of the aforementioned trend to point out the vices of former, not current, regimes.

Likewise, after praising history of the Coptic patriarchy in Egypt, as guarding both the faith and citizenship, al-Banna depicted church policy under Shenouda III as contradictory, as it promoted secularist tendencies and still dug deep for Coptic sentiments in the Egyptian heritage (1994c, 167–70). Though not directly relating to Egypt's Copts, he published an entire book criticizing the speech of the Roman Pope Benedict the sixth on 12 September 2006 when he, in al-Banna's words, insulted the Prophet of Islam Muhammad (2006c). In the interviews, he summed up his position on Coptic claims of discrimination in a way that significantly adds to what he wrote in his books and articles on the matter. He acknowledged the discrimination claims as based on real incidents but also containing a great deal of exaggeration (Interview, 3 November 2010).

His accounts on the Coptic Church and Coptic communal violence were not chastized by the Mubarak regime, and I could highlight, in this regard, several factors. One, al-Banna's criticism was preoccupied with former regimes, and not that of Mubarak (2006b, 86–8). Two, even when he criticized Coptic policies or the Pope's statements, he always maintained that he was seeking unity and coexistence and extensively used references and documents to fortify his arguments in order to demonstrate an objective account (2006b, 190, 259–89; 2006c, 59, 128–56). Three, in his liberal profile, he deviated largely from mainstream Islamic jurisprudence especially in terms of freedom of faith (2008d), asserted pluralism as a feature of Islam and Islamic society (2001a), and labelled the Islamic state a *myth* (2003a). This multi-faceted profile coincided with Coptic concerns, as a religious minority, that fears denial of its basic rights under the prospect of Islamic rule (see Sharp, 2014; Armanios, 2013; Hanna, 2013). Thus, taken together, al-Banna addressed the Coptic issue without directly colliding with the Mubarak regime.

To wrap up, after an ideological shift in the 1990s, al-Banna conformed to the tajdīd line of argument that there is no state in Islam, out of the conviction that authority taints the faith, where the latter is employed for hegemonic purposes. Meanwhile, he responded to the existing juxtaposition of Shura and democracy, maintaining his Islamic profile, through positive accounts of Shura. A great deal of what he wrote on Shariʿa did not deviate from mainstream CIPT, especially asserting the need for Shariʿa application. Praising the Islamic theft penalty and rejecting some legal provisions in Egypt's penal code, based on their deviation from Islamic rules on the matter, implied he supported the application of ḥudūd. Yet, his larger more comprehensive account on Shariʿa emphasized the multiple impediments towards an application of ḥudūd today. In addition, he assigned ʿIlla the ultimate role of deciding on the applicability of any ḥad.

He is, by large, part of the CIPT discourse on futūḥāt, highlighting the *fair treatment* of non-Muslims propagated by Islamic intellectuals, although the conquests themselves were, to him, part of the history of Islam and not the faith. As Islamic intellectuals are not divided on resenting sporadic violence on one hand and accepting violence against occupation on the other, al-Banna, through conforming to these positions, didn't add to his Islamic renewal scheme. His account is also based on *pragmatic* assessments regarding the possibility of using violence as a means for change. Accordingly, his claims on the use of violence are not solely based on the dictations of the faith.

His writings on identity addressed three major constellations: the Islamic, the European/Western and the national. The latter was primarily concerned with Egypt and he asserted there was some overlap between the Islamic and the national. Through his overt admiration of Islam, positing it as better than ideologies of capitalism, socialism and even the European civilization, he promoted his character as an Islamic intellectual. Thus, he conformed to the general position of CIPT intellectuals on Islam as *generally better*. Still, he equally viewed Islam and other religions as a basis of belonging, and constituent of identity. His invoking of Europe within the colonial history of Muslim lands coincides with Said's account on Orientalism. Still, his Western readings could be seen in his positive accounts on democracy, which he recognized as a Western practice and his use of European syndical history as model for labour struggle to attain better conditions.

Through his overt focus on Egyptian identity, the political profile of the Islamic intellectual is embodied. He believed the religious and the national coexist, be this Arab or Egyptian, although he set conditions on national identity as to not reach chauvinism and end up with exclusions. Yet, he maintained his Islamic profile in his account on coexistence between the religious and the national, through depicting the Islamic perspective on nationalism and seeking the position of Islam on other identities.

Finally, the Islamic meta-language could be traced in his frequent invoking of the heritage towards establishing his claims, especially the least contested aspect of Islamic history, which is the golden age of the Prophet and his rightly guided caliphs. More generally, his accounts of the four major themes, delimited in Chapter 1, embody this meta-language. His renewal scheme was mainly embodied in his claim that the Islamic state is not part of the faith, highlighting the role of politics in shaping the content of jurisprudence, which is the common focus of tajdīd intellectuals towards introducing new interpretations.

4

Tariq al-Bishri on CIPT

Al-Bishri's multiple writings offered sufficient accounts for detecting his stances on CIPT themes and how he constructed his character as an Islamic intellectual. Yet, he, like Al-Banna, expressed overt interest and focus on matters of politics. As will be evident in this chapter, his Islamic and political profiles often overlapped throughout his intellectual path. Unlike al-Banna, he is a mainstream intellectual and there is neither intellectual nor societal contestation to his character as such. This chapter seeks answering three major questions: Where does al-Bishri stand on the four key CIPT themes? What are the elements of the heritage he utilized in establishing his Islamic profile and larger intellectual production? Where do his political and Islamic profiles intersect?

The state: Flexibly Islamic

As shown in Chapter 1, with the caliphate regarded as part of the historical practice, CIPT authorship addresses it as part of the turāth, not as a binding/re-applicable pattern of political rule. This signifies the dynamic nature of Islamic Political Thought. Today, Shura and democracy are largely juxtaposed. Other debates, such as the one regarding functions of the state in Islam or whether Western practices of party-politics and parliamentary elections could be compatible with Islam, are taking over instead.

Endorsing democratic and Western practices like elections, parliaments and political parties are not decisive lines of demarcation between mainstream and tajdīd intellectuals. Rather, it is the rejection of the Islamic state and, in many cases, the negation of the religious nature of the state and its practices in early Islamic history that constitutes demarcation lines.

The Egyptian state

Al-Bishri underwent a major shift in his intellectual path: he turned from a secularist/socialist to an Islamic intellectual. This shift became clear through both his critique of the communist movement (al-Haraka al-Shiyuʿiyya) in Egypt, and his position on the political engagement of the MB. In his critique of the communist movement, he called those who led it in Egypt *Jewish foreigners*. In his view, they were not much different from the Zionist movement and he did not regard MB's engagement in politics as exploiting religion anymore (al-Bishrī, 2002a, 22–9).

Just like al-Banna, he was immensely preoccupied with Egyptian history. In his books, there are long narrations on the country's governments, party politics and popular uprisings. In this respect, two key themes are frequently addressed. The first is the colonial influences on Egypt's political landscape, be it the state, or society. His appraisal of colonialism largely falls within the broad lines of Said's Orientalism, strongly emphasizing the impositions taking place through colonization of Muslim lands. It suffices to note that his general perspective on Western colonial history is that it was harmful, if not destructive, to the colonies (al-Bishrī, 1998, 63–4; 1991a, 20; 2002a, 45–6; 2005a, 123; 2007a, 37, 113). The second is his focus on al-Wafd Party[1] and his overt admiration of its history. In his book The Political Movement in Egypt 1945/1953 (*al-Haraka al-Siyasiyya fi Misr 1945/1953*), he devoted a complete chapter to discuss the party's political path and networks. He presented it as a party around which the masses gathered, which represented their demands of independence and freedom, labelling it Party of the Masses (Hizb al-Jamahir). He argued:

> Anyone interested in Egypt's political history, in the second quarter of the twentieth century, should stop for long at al-Wafd. (al-Bishrī, 2002a, 99–100)

In his writings, al-Wafd is presented as a party with a wide popular base, that not only stood for democracy, but also advocated it and broadened its political and social base (al-Bishrī, 1991a, 41, 72; see also 142). He called al-Wafd government democratic, referencing its broad popular support, which translated into votes in elections (al-Bishrī, 2012a, 14), but he argued that it was its indecisiveness and hesitation that confused all national and revolutionary forces (al-Bishrī, 2002a, 491) and claimed it was keen to curb freedoms in 1924 (al-Bishrī, 1987a, 94). Although he criticized al-Wafd government policy after it repealed the 1936 treaty,[2] his overall appraisal of the party was mostly a positive one. In fact, his accounts on the party indirectly reflected his appreciation for democratic politics and representative government. On both colonialism and al-Wafd, there was no drastic change throughout his intellectual path.

The democratic state

> I mean with democracy that system for managing society and running the state, which depends on objective institutional formations, and not on personal relations between officials. One that depends on the collectivism (*Jami'iyya*) in making decisions, and not on individuality (*al-Fardiyya*) in this regard. One that depends on multiplicity of entities and agencies practicing public affairs, and not on the oneness of these agencies. (al-Bishrī, 2003a, 177)

Out of his large focus on Egypt's history, many hints of his appreciation to democracy can be pinpointed. First, his admiration of al-Wafd as a democratically-elected party is one clue to it. Second, he claimed there was a connection between calls for independence and calls for democracy in Egyptian history because the slogan Egypt for the Egyptians (*Misr li-l-Misriyyun*) was used against foreign rulers. At the same time, the struggle was against a system of individual rule, which allowed the Khedive absolute authority (al-Bishrī, 1977, 17–18). Note that these accounts are, by and large, part of his political profile, where he discussed politics with no reference to Islamic heritage. Yet, he referred to this heritage in his appraisal of democracy differently, within a juxtaposition with Shura, that will be addressed below.

Just like with his account on al-Wafd, referring to its democratic election in a very positive context, he denounced state oppression and confiscation of basic political rights and urged for adopting collective decision-making (al-Bishrī, 1991a, 376; 2006a, 55). He also depicted the democratic regime as more competent in its ability to allow broader political participation, accept the establishment of various formations and adjust its policies, compared to other forms of government (al-Bishrī, interview, 25 October 2010).

Nonetheless, he did not necessarily associate collective decision-making with democracy. For instance, his strong appreciation of collective decision-making was evident in his book The Methodology for Studying Political Systems of Islamic World Countries (*Manhaj al-Nazar fi-l-Nuzum al-Siyasiyya li-Buldan al-ʿAlam al-'Islami*), where he didn't associate it with democracy (al-Bishrī, 2007a, 79–80). Likewise, in his book Studies in Egyptian Democracy (*Dirasat fi-l-Dimuqratiyya al-Misriyya*), he stressed the need for a division of powers as being a necessary prerequisite for political rule but with no mention of democracy (al-Bishrī, 1987a, 154–5). He attributed these exact same aspects to democracy elsewhere in his writings though (see al-Bishrī, 2008, 77).

This last remark may falsely imply that he is not comfortable with using the term 'Democracy' because of its Western origin and this would actually corroborate Said's Orientalist claim that the colonizer was seen only as colonizer by the colonized (Said, 1994, 189, 162, respectively). In such a scenario, Democracy, as a term, would be rejected due to the tendency to reject everything from the West and regard it as pure imposition. However, this is not the case for al-Bishri. He addressed democracy directly and praised it openly in some of his books. He argued liberal democracies possessed the qualities of including the totality of key political forces and the flexibility to adapt to marginal change (al-Bishrī, 2007a, 29). Similarly, in his appraisal of Egyptian politics in the early twentieth century, he described democracy as being wasted on the hands of al-Umma Party, which did not associate the call for democracy to that of national independence (al-Bishrī, 2007b, 20). In one of his lectures, in 1998, he contended multi-partism is just one form of pluralism and that other forms of the latter are needed as well. Pluralism has three key forms in his appraisal: (1) political pluralism and alternation of power, (2) pluralism in institutions of government so that decision-making is not monopolized by one entity and (3) pluralism in society so that social organizations engage in managing affairs of the respective society (al-Bishrī, 2015, 222–3).

Accordingly, his separate focus on particular elements of democratic rule, like separation of powers, pluralism or collective decision-making, meant that his appreciation for democracy related to the constituent elements of democratic rule, rather than simply promoting the wide-appealing term 'Democracy'. In other words, it is a focus on aspects of democratic rule, which are appreciated for their function (al-Bishrī, 2008, 71–87).

Just like al-Banna's account on democracy, al-Bishri expressed several reservations on it. To him, democracy depends on attaining an equilibrium among major actors, when new actors emerge or when events disrupt that equilibrium, efficacy of the democratic system ceases to function (al-Bishrī, 2007a, 29–30). Furthermore, although he, in the above quote, objected to individual rule (*Hukm Fardi*), he maintained it is not automatically associated with despotism or injustice. History has known individual rulers who made great strides of progress in their societies, he noted; they were rulers who provided an undeniable degree of social justice (al-Bishrī, 1991a, 223).

Nonetheless, he asserted that the chances of making *wrong* decisions and becoming despotic are higher in individual rule, as compared to when powers are divided among several organs and separation of powers is granted. On this, he drew an analogy between favouring individual rule, associated with great achievements, and the claim that horses and sailing ships won major wars (al-Bishrī, 1991a, 376). It is strongly believed this analogy was meant to refer to Nasser's rule of Egypt.

What he utterly rejected is personified rule (*al-Hukm al-Mushakhsan*). In his appraisal, in the last quarter of a century – in a smart and *safe* indirect gesture to Mubarak's rule – only two ministers presided the ministry of justice. Most top positions were personified and the job became the same thing as the person occupying it. This is why, he argued, more alternation obstructs job personification and inhibits despotic tendencies (al-Bishrī, 2006b, 39). He, thus, presented a very positive account on institutionalization:

> With the word 'institution', I mean a collective formation that organizes or surrounds a human community, bound together due to a sort of common gathering, through which a collective self replaces the individual selves of its members. It is based on interest-oriented bonds or harmonized intellectual formation capable of achieving this collective self; and replacing the individual selves inside the individuals. It seeks achieving the goals of common existence, whether to this institutional collectivity or to a larger community outside of this institutional collectivity. (al-Bishrī, 2007a, 45)

He praised, within the context of objecting to personified rule, modern ways of administration as being impersonal. In his account, these are based on stripping the position or job from the personality of the person holding it. So, incumbents are selected according to specialization and merit and work is organized in a way that does not depend on the personal experience of the job-taker (al-Bishrī, 2007a, 77–9). In a similar vein, he praised legitimacy and transparency of rules. For him, legislation is issued through a legislative body, which is supposedly constituted through the free election of its members. He argued its work should stay public, in a way that allows every one to follow even on the smallest detail. He claimed:

> The publicity of an institution's activity is also another basic guarantee for activity pertaining to public affairs, a real public activity. (al-Bishrī, 1987a, 154)

Through juxtaposing the East-Islam/West seen frequently in CIPT authorship, al-Bishri sought a delicate balance between praising modern Western practices and not defaming practices prevalent in Islamic history. This was expressed in two parallel accounts. The first, through comparing the modern administrative practices with administration in Islamic history, which according to him lacked institutionalization but was part of the way administrative work was organized throughout history. The second, in his position on adopting foreign patterns of rule. By taking what works from the West and assuming it is going to work in Muslim-dominated countries, the role of context is erroneously reduced. This is because, to him, Western systems were developed in a context not jeopardized by external aggression. Thus, when these systems were applied in Muslim societies under colonialism, the reception and functions of these systems were utterly different (al-Bishrī, 2007a, 77–9, 8–13, respectively). Here, he completely adhered to the notion, propagated by Said, that the colonizer was perceived only as a colonizer, although the latter presented his mission as that of enlightenment.

Moreover, his description of individual rule, which prevailed in Islamic history for centuries, as not necessarily oppressive as well as his appraisal of non-institutionalized administrative practices in Islamic history, manifests his keen attachment to the heritage of Islam. Consistent with this account, al-Bishri criticized the claim that application of democracy must inevitably be intertwined with the endorsement of the secular positive legal codes/reference (Marji'iyya) (al-Bishrī, 2007b, 101).

Democracy with freedom

Treating democracy as a system of rule with pros and cons is common in CIPT writings; this is common among Islamic intellectuals. Wahba al-Zuhili, a reputable jurist and head of the Association of al-Sham Scholars, presented democracy as the fruit of a long struggle against despotic rule in the West, as well as one that is, at the level of theory and rhetoric, different from its real practice (al-Zuḥīlī, 2006, 448–9). As pointed out in Chapter 1, addressing the relation between democracy and Islam is a common concern of intellectual and jurisprudential scholarship. On this, al-Bishri didn't claim Shura is the same thing as democracy (see al-Jabri, 2009, 122–6), he overtly made this point when he negated democracy and *Mashura* are the same. He wrote:

> Democracy is not consultation, it is an organizational order (Nasaq) for decision-making, and acting in a collective manner, on the basis of distribution of authorities, specializations, and making decisions within collective, not individual, entities. (al-Bishrī, 1991a, 123)

Nonetheless, in his writings, Shura is a general principle relating to plurality ('Akthariyya) in studying matters, researching them and subsequent making of decisions. This general principle could be applied in many ways and in different manners, with models organized, modified and altered according to needs/stipulations of the surrounding environment and historical conditions (al-Bishrī, 2008, 85). Here, he highlighted the role of context, which is actually the aspect usually emphasized by tajdīd intellectuals towards introducing new interpretations. His ultimate position, though, does not represent a deviation from mainstream CIPT claims.

Democracy does not necessarily entail guarding freedoms; this guarding comes through liberal, as opposed to illiberal, democracy (Zakaria, 1997). Al-Bishri endorsed a very similar conception. To him, democracy does not guarantee individual freedoms, although these freedoms and their safeguards provide the right atmosphere for democratic organization to function. Freedom is, consequently, one of the conditions of a democratic construct (al-Bishrī, 1987a, 143). Furthermore, he outspokenly admired the 1923 Constitution as an unprecedented document of rule because it was one based on rights and freedoms. He highly valued rights and freedoms allowing collectivities of individuals to organize and act. This is why he resented the attempt to curb freedoms stipulated in the constitution drafted by former king of Egypt Faruq, who, through adding a reservation to articles on freedoms 'for the guarding of the social system', allowed the administrative apparatus to curb them (al-Bishrī, 1987a, 56, 63–4). Likewise, his critique of al-Wafd's tendency to restrict freedoms in 1924 is another gesture manifesting his strong appreciation of the latter. In commenting on the party's position on the king's initiative, he wrote:

> Al-Wafd curbed people's freedoms -its only political prop- and the leadership [of al-Wafd], by virtue of its nationalism, stayed hanging in the air, with his back naked. (al-Bishrī, 1987a, 94)

Nonetheless, his emphasis on freedom of collectivities is associated with his rejection of what he calls *logical simplifications* that the individual is the basic unit of the society (*labanat al-Mujtama'*). To him, the individual is always found inside a unit of society, and the system acquires its vividness from the establishment of these units, the latter's activity and interaction. In his own words,

> Nationalism does not contain individuals, Islamic unity does not include individuals, "Egyptianism" (*al-Misriyya*), Iraqism (*al-'Iraqiyya*), or Moroccanism (*al-Maghribiyya*) does not contain individuals. They, rather, contain communities (*Jama'at*), representing belonging units, each one of these being capable of self-initiative (*al-Inbi'ath al-Dhati*), with motion flowing from its inside, using its special generators. (al-Bishrī, 2007a, 42–3)

A similar concern for the community was evident in his account on his own experience that one's capabilities can do him/her good, but it is better to benefit one's community by pushing the institution where one works, or the community to which one belongs, a bit farther (al-Bishrī, 2002b, 92). Thus, he asserted that freedom should not be taken to mean individual freedom vis-à-vis the community or the collective unit (*al-Wihda al-Jama'iyya*) to which one belongs. Because, in this sense, freedom would have a destructive connotation to the collective construct (*al-Biniya al-Jami'iyya*), leading to dispersion of individuals; an individual never existed but within a community (al-Bishrī, 2007b, 31–2). To conclude on this point, he appreciated freedom and criticized political forces which suppressed it. Still, he opposed the individualistic conception associated with freedom which ignores the collective character of human societies. He objected to treating freedom as the 'one and only norm' to guide human societies; he sought a balance between both positions.

Yet, his appraisal of democracy can't be fully grasped without coming across his account on the Egyptian military. As stated in Chapter 3, before the 2011 uprising, the only period where the military had a clear political involvement and on which abundant information is available is the time of the 1952 coup; though al-Bishri referred to it as the revolution. He presented a detailed account on this period (1991a; 2002a, 539–58), which was largely concerned with historical analysis. But his writings spotted several pitfalls: he noted the strong control of the RCC over drafting the 1953 Constitution, where new political parties and streams were weakly represented. Additionally, the merging of the executive and legislative powers under the upper hand of the executive and the growing intelligence apparatus and repression against the MB and other forces are also discussed. He associated these features with a general sense of withdrawal from politics in the Egyptian society (1991a, 203, 211, 319–35).

Still, to him, the strengths of the *revolution* outweighed its weaknesses (2002b, 61), and its military component directly related to the Palestinian liberation cause (2006c, 15) – the cause which was frequently addressed in his writings (see 2002c, 77–100; 2003b). Furthermore, he related the Egyptian military to a segment of popular political forces that appeared and grew in the 1930s – a segment that played a role in shaping public opinion in Egypt (al-Bishrī, 1991a, 13, 138, respectively).

Interestingly, his overall assessment of the political role of the military does not clearly fall along the lines of either acceptance or rejection. It is more or less about its implications by virtue of the strategic position and centrality of the military to the ruling regime (1991a, 90–1). Nonetheless, several aspects combine towards an implicit position that does not favour military involvement in politics. Some factors add up to a faint likelihood al-Bishri would applaud any space for the military in civilian politics: One, the aforementioned lack of information about a political role of the military, as an institution before the 2011 uprising. Two, pitfalls he associated with the 1952 coup, and his overall positive stance towards democracy (2007a). Three, his claim on the indispensability of pluralism in society (2008, 51–7). Before the 2011 uprising, his writings on the military, which were mainly historical in nature, reflect the relative availability of information on the 1952 period (see Abdel-Malek, 1971; Beattie, 1994) and the growing secrecy on its political role, if any, afterwards. Presenting his largest account on the 1952 period under Mubarak, there was no ground for him to collide with the regime.

In fact, the strongest critique he ever directed to the military came after the 2011 uprising – where he numerated several shortcomings in the June 2012 addendum – that stripped the president from many of his prerogatives and granted SCAF the legislative function of the dissolved National Assembly. Among other things, al-Bishri maintained this addendum was illegal and flawed, both in form and content, not to mention that it contradicted and annulled the March 2011 constitutional declaration and contributed a relapse in the democratic transition that was evolving since Mubarak's ouster (2012b, 229–46).

Few years later, it became even more salient and overt that he detested a role for the military in civilian politics. A relatively thorough account on the military's interventions in 2011 and 2013 was presented in his book The 25th of January Revolution and The Struggle for Authority (*Thawrat 25 Yanayir wa-l-Sira' hawl al-Sulta*), months before Sisi's election for his first presidential term, where al-Bishri maintained that the intervention in 2013 was a coup against a democratically elected president – Muhammad Mursi (2014, 176). Although in this book, he asserted the pivotal roles the military played throughout the country's modern history, he insisted that the 2013 ouster was not only erroneous but also destructive to Egypt's democratic transition, a stance that goes in harmony with his overall admiration for democratic practices and his disdain for autocratic/despotic settings.

In fact, his account on the military in this book (2014) signified the importance of reading an intellectual's writings as a whole because only through reading them together can one fully capture his/her stances. It is worth noting that al-Bishri wasn't reportedly subjected to any form of prosecution/persecution because of his post-2011 appraisals of SCAF and/or the military. One can think of a few factors in this regard. On one hand, there was his use of legal terminology in some of his negative appraisals, like that presented in the June 2012 addendum. On the other, as pointed out earlier, there was his old age (he was around eighty years old) and juridical status as a renowned former judge in the Egyptian State Council and head of the Committee which drafted the constitutional amendments of March 2011. In sum, his account on the Egyptian military reveals not only his overt commitment to democratic rule but also a distinction between the military's role in guarding the national and territorial integrity of countries and its interference in civilian politics.

Religion in the state

Throughout his writings, al-Bishri maintained that religion played and still plays a role in society. Commenting on 'Ali 'Abd al-Raziq, the renowned Egyptian jurist whose juristic appraisal of the caliphate was discussed in Chapter 1, he argued:

> 'Ali 'Abd al-Rāziq, in his denial of Islam's government, strictly separated between the spiritual seigniory (*Wilāiya*) of the prophet, and that of the government and authority; between Islamic guidance (*al-Hidāiya al-'Islāmiyya*) and the system of life. He separated religious and political leadership, which has its roots in the duality of the church and the state in the West. This is from an intellectual philosophical dimension. For the political dimension, his separation of state from religion contains stripping religion of the possibilities of organizing life. (al-Bishrī, 2007b, 30)

In this quote, he invoked CIPT heritage to make his claim that religion has a role in the state, and this stance will be fortified in his position on Shari'a application below. His position on Islam in the state could be established as supportive in three different instances:

First is his own intellectual shift, which resulted in a change in his position towards the MB political engagement, which is discussed in some detail later in this section. It was problematic to him when he first addressed it in 1972 (al-Bishrī, 2002a, 27–9), but he turned to accept political engagement of groups and/or parties which claim religious identity after this shift. Thus, he accepted religion's role in society, as the involvement of religious groups in politics entails a chance for the latter to enter government through elections and influence policies that might eventually even affect state structure and organs.

Second is his discussion of laws and institutions coming from the West, which were new to the environment, compared to traditional social settings and laws prevalent in Egypt or in Arab and Islamic countries at large before colonialism. These traditional settings, where religion is central, enjoyed popular acceptance according to al-Bishri. For him, a law must reflect the norms and values prevailing in society in order for the law to be effective, followed or have legitimacy. On this, he compared people dealing with taxes and paying *Zakāt*, where people try to reduce the amount of taxes to be paid but tend to pay *Zakāt* in excess (al-Bishrī, 2008, 63).

Third, his assertion that Islam, unlike Christianity, regulates worldly matters (al-Bishrī, 2011a, 22; 2007b, 59) implied that religion can exist at the level of the state. He asserted Islam's comprehensiveness (*Shumūl al-'Islām*) as an original feature and indispensable characteristic of the faith. He went further to argue that Islam would not be complete without this comprehensiveness (al-Bishrī, 2005b, 27).

It is worth noting that this comprehensiveness is a frequently used argument by mainstream intellectuals to maintain that the application of Shari'a or regulating politics according to Islamic historical practices is different from the separation of powers in the West (al-Shāmī, 2012, 19; 'Abd al-Fattāḥ, 2008, 35). Nonetheless, in Western history, the separation of the religious and the worldly, the sacred and the profane, the spiritual and temporal was not as simple as it is depicted today (Krämer, 2000a, 81: see also Warde, 2000, 237). On state-church separation, he adhered strongly to mainstream authorship on the matter which differentiated between history of Islam and that of Christianity (see al-Zuḥīlī, 2006, 383), through his aforementioned account on the differing receptions of positive law in the West and in Muslim countries during colonization.

Intersecting his Islamic and political profiles, he asserted that religion was part of the political and public spheres in Egypt. In his account, the Muslim Youth (*al-Shubban al-Muslimun*) and the MB appeared because there was a general Islamic orientation in society (*Tawajjuh Islami 'Am*). He argued that this orientation was also clear in the works of intellectuals of the time. In his appraisal, due to domestic and international developments, Islam did not find reasonable political expression, and the MB appeared to help compensate for this absence (al-Bishrī, 2002a, 44–5; see also al-Bishrī, 2008, 38). Likewise, he frequently emphasized the wide popular appeal the movement enjoyed among the Egyptian masses (al-Bishrī, 2002a, 28; see also al-Bishrī, 2006a, 105).

In a similar vein, his appraisal of Islamic banking in Egypt, which was associated with wide juridical debates, represents another convergence of his Islamic and political profiles. In his book The Islamic Secular Dialogue (*al-Hiwar al-Islami al-'Almani*), al-Bishri discussed this issue at some length. He claimed the rise of this sector was the byproduct of a religious inclination prevalent among the masses in Egypt towards licit gaining (*al-Kasb al-Ḥalāl*). Both paying *Zakāt* and avoiding usury (*Ribā*) are examples of such an inclination (al-Bishrī, 1996a, 75–82). In this regard, he didn't question the Islamic nature of these transactions; the larger issue, to him, was that of accepting/rejecting economic businesses carried out under the banner of Islam. He criticized some aspects of their performance, but his criticism did not reach the level of complete condemnation or overt rejection.

A core theme in his writings, when it comes to religion in the state, is the aforementioned political engagement of the Egyptian MB. Notably, there was a significant shift in al-Bishri's account on the movement, which actually related to his larger shift from secularism to Islam (2002b, 263–4). His accounts before this shift, namely under Nasser, were quite harsh and depicted the movement as confiscating Islam in its program and using religion for its own interest. As highlighted in Chapter 2, he labelled the secret apparatus as *the terrorist organization of the MB* (2002a, 117–19, 127). After this shift, his writings on the MB highlighted the Nasser regime's harassment of the movement (1991c, 285), the larger exclusion of Islamist calls from the mid-1950s till the early 1970s (2002b, 107) as well as their strengths and weight in the Egyptian society (al-Bishrī, 2002a, 28, 44–5; see also al-Bishrī, 2006a, 105).

Nonetheless, before and after the shift, al-Bishri's overall account on the MB is relatively small. When he addressed them in his book (*al-Haraka al-Siyasiyya*) (2002a), it was part of a larger focus on the political and historical context directly preceding the 1952 coup. Likewise, after his ideological shift to Islam, he wrote few phrases on the MB stance on Arab identity and their role in Palestine, within larger foci that fall within his accounts on Islamic and Arab identity (al-Bishrī, 2008, 38). Other issues were more central to his intellectual path, like identity, Shari'a application, Islamic thought and political history of Egypt. Throughout decades of intellectual production, he did not present a huge account on the MB like the one he presented on the Coptic issue or on the pre-1952 history of political movements. Accordingly, the regime persecution suffered by the MB under Nasser, Sadat and Mubarak could not constitute a restraint on his writings in this regard, due to his relatively strong interest in other themes.

Both the exceptional political engagement of the MB after the 2011 uprising, that ousted the long-time Egyptian president Mubarak, and Mursi's ouster in July 2013 reflected in some focus on the movement in al-Bishri's writings from 2011 onwards. The key, and recurrent, appraisal he made in this regard was bi-folded: on one hand, he asserted the strong popular base and sheer political experience of the movement (al-Bishrī, 2013, 91), but on the other, he criticized some of its post-2011 political decisions, especially after Mursi's November 2012 constitutional declaration (al-Bishrī, 2014, 37, 99).

As stated above, he expressed clear support for democratic rule, admiration for principles of collective decision-making and separation of powers, and maintained that Shura should be moulded by circumstances. The idea of context, surroundings and circumstances, which should be taken into account in his writings on Shura, helps the reader understand why he didn't decidedly and articulately define particular criteria for rule or the structure of the state in Islam. In Islamic history, there was no one fixed form of political rule. The succession of the rightly guided caliphs was put to an end with the rule of Umayyads, which was hereditary. After which came different Islamic dynasties, which officially ended when the Turkish modern state was founded in 1923 (see al-Ashmawy, 1994, 16). Today, several Muslim-dominated countries, like Saudi Arabia, Morocco and Jordan, are ruled by monarchies, while others, such as Egypt, Tunisia and Algeria are republican. These changing patterns of rule make it difficult for an Islamic intellectual, even if mainstream, to advocate one specific mould to embody Islamic rule and claim that it should subsequently be replicated across countries.

To sum up, the critique al-Bishri directed towards ʿAbd al-Raziq asserts that he perceived Islam, in its early history, as both government and spiritual authority. His understanding of Islam as comprehensive meant he accepted religion at the level of the state. In addition, his profile, as a mainstream Islamic intellectual, fortified the assumption that he accepted the notion that Islam exists/should exist in the state. As shown in Chapter 1, mainstream intellectuals do not normally exclude the prospect of an Islamic state, although they may diverge on details thereof. But there is nothing in his intellectual production suggesting he stood for a certain pattern of political rule – inspired or derived from Islamic history – that *must* inevitably be endorsed. There is also no good reason, based on his writings, to assume he assigned religion a particular function at the level of the state.

Shariʿa: Historically rivalled traditions

Ḥudūd were applied in early Islamic history and the juridical effort, known as jurisprudence, emerged afterwards. The advent of both modernization and colonization in Muslim countries instigated the debate on Shariʿa application, as new institutional and legal orders were adopted, changing the landscape of

Muslim societies and representing one key theme in CIPT debates. Accordingly, al-Bishri's conception of Shariʿa and its application as well as his position on Western legal codes applied in Muslim-dominated countries are approached against this background.

As stated in the introduction, he is a retired judge, who studied not only law but also jurisprudence (*Fiqh*). This study, along with his prestigious judicial position, numerous publications and intellectual engagement in the public sphere of Egypt constitute his *credentials* as an intellectual. Particularly, his study of jurisprudence gave him extra merit on the Shariʿa debate, as he provided a relatively elaborate account on the history of Shariʿa application and used juridical terminology. In addition, studying jurisprudence established his Islamic character and exempted him from the contestation associated with a lack of juridical training that intellectuals such as Jamal al-Banna are faced with.

Historical Perspective on Shariʿa

Much of what he wrote on Shariʿa can be summarized in his appraisal of the historical and current status of Shariʿa in Muslim countries. He started with a depiction of the heritage, particularly from Islamic history, which he used to construct his overall account on Shariʿa. He wrote:

> For the legal system, there is no doubt that Islam was the one prevailing in our-Islamic- countries, as thought, culture, politics, religion, creed and system, until the ends of the eighteenth century. (al-Bishrī, 1987b, 618)

In his appraisal, Islamic Shariʿa connected the system of rights, values and manners (al-Bishrī, 2005b, 35); its jurisprudence acknowledged pluralism and diversity in solutions within a framework allowed by the text (al-Bishrī, 2011a, 75). As evident in the quote, he argued that until the beginning of the nineteenth century, Shariʿa was a sovereign system of rights; it acted as a regulator of individual and group behaviour and as a source of values and legitimacy in society (al-Bishrī, 1988a, 9).

In fact, his account, in this respect, converged with historical accounts in CIPT, which claimed that the nineteenth century witnessed a major alteration in legal codes. Back then, Shariʿa courts were stripped from their privileged status, and autonomy vis-à-vis state authority and Islamic law came to be supervised by various statute laws (see Arabi, 2001, 13). This alteration was, again as shown in Chapter 1, a reason to pose the question on Shariʿa application in CIPT today, after modernization and colonization brought positive institutional and legal orders to Muslim lands. He invoked this historical element as part of his account on the prospect for applying Shariʿa in Muslim societies today. But he used this societal dimension to make his call for its application, especially since he, as shown above, emphasized the un-rootedness of Western practices and laws imposed by the colonizer on Muslim lands. During the interviews, he argued that establishing binding regulations on positive law, away from societal norms and codes of conduct, which are closer in nature to the content of Islamic Shariʿa, ends up with citizens falling into a state of confusion (Interview, 16 July 2011). He argued:

> And although we studied and study Islamic Shariʿa in a reasonable manner in law school, what is emphasized in terms of majority of her [law school] legal methods, are the predominant codes coming from the West, and especially those coming from France. Missions from us travelled and still travel to France to learn law sciences. A scientist from us is refined through resorting to French references in terms of rules, laws and jurisprudence. A student is taught that the history of his law goes back to the Romans, then the European ecclesiastical law, then codes of Napoleon. This way, a complete and stable legal and historical structure based on that link is constructed inside us. But for Shariʿa, it is marginalized (*Mazwiyya*) in the field of personal status and family law. And we called the movement of alienating Shariʿa and inserting French legislations, we called it (judicial and legislative reform). (al-Bishrī, 2002a, 50)

In a similar vein, he argued that Shariʿa constituted a source of legitimacy for any ruler of any Islamic country until the nineteenth century. However, he differentiated between Shariʿa as a source of legitimate political rule on one hand, and such rule being successful, representative or democratic on the other. Thus, he detached himself and his intellectual production from individual instances of Shariʿa application in history. He neither defended nor denounced specific Shariʿa applications; he only argued that it was the source of legitimacy for the ruler and that it was applied. He also admitted that Islamic history experienced authoritarian rule, which he described as *defective* application of Shariʿa (al-Bishrī, 2005a, 75–7). Yet, this appraisal concurs with the aforementioned accounts of ruling elites in Islamic history allying with mainstream Sunni jurists who promoted popular obedience, thus, cementing their political rule with the legitimacy of Islam (Ayubi, 1995, 84; Black, 2008, 30).

Al-Bishri actually exhibited consistency in his intellectual profile; he praised the representative character of democracy and acknowledged the history of Islam was largely despotic. Thus, he seemed to be aware of the kind of counterargument that might result from his appraisal of Shariʿa application in the history of Islam, as insinuating he might accept or promote despotic rule.

Again deriving from the heritage, he maintained that rules of Islamic jurisprudence accumulated through the direct relation between the people and jurists; through this direct relation, branches of jurisprudence thrived (al-Bishrī, 2005a, 104). What he claimed, in this regard, is actually congruent with similar accounts, which confirmed that historically, for long centuries, there was no attempt to set rules towards institutionalizing Ijtihad and to identify its status and authority within the state (Kamali, 2008, 163; see also Griffel, 2007).

His positive appraisal of Shariʿa could be traced in his assertion that it allows for progressive interpretations of women rights. In an introduction to a book titled Woman and Political Activity: An Islamic Vision (*al-Mar'a wa-l-ʿAmal al-Siyasi: Ru'ya 'Islamiyya*), by Heba Raouf Ezzat (1995), he maintained that women can hold positions of mandate (*Wilāya*) and that no Islamic text deprives women of this right. The same applies to mixing with the other sex (*'Ikhtilāṭ*) for purposes of work; he argued it isn't a sin that requires prohibition or penalty (al-Bishrī, 2015, 128–45).

In a similar vein, in his writings, juxtaposition between Shariʿa and positive law is preoccupied with overt preference to Shariʿa. This is especially true in his criticism of the secular *perspective* which, he argued, has a tendency to emphasize an evaluation of legal systems based on criteria such as freedom and justice. He phrased the matter in terms of faith and civilizational struggle between the imported and the inherited (*al-Wāfid wa-l-Mawrūth*) (al-Bishrī, 2002a, 50–1). Plus, his preference for Shariʿa became clearer when he asserted that evaluating legal codes in such a manner strays away from the roots and creed and even attempts to weaken Islam through altering social conditions and relations among people in a way that contradicts Shariʿa and its rules (al-Bishrī, 2005a, 105). Last but not least, he stressed that there is no way to claim the merit of legislation taken from Latins, Germans and Saxons, compared to Islamic Shariʿa (al-Bishrī, 1998, 39), and criticized the way Western legal codes prevailed at the cost of alienating the latter. Accordingly, his account on Shariʿa, as rivalled by positive legal codes coming from the colonizer and imposed on Muslim populations (colonized), is basically a parallel account to the key tenets of Orientalism, presented by Said. At the same time, it is an embodiment of the secular/Islamic duality which tends to be a tense intellectual and societal debate in Muslim-dominated countries (see al-Ghazālī, 1987, 133–6; al-Qaraḍāwī, 1997b).

Shariʿa and positive law

In addition to the historical rivalry between Shariʿa and positive law and the assumed top-down imposition of positive law on Muslim populations, he claimed that some Islamic rules totally contradict positive law. In 2010, the Coptic Pope refused to carry out a court sentence because he viewed the sentence as contradicting the Bible. Al-Bishri criticized him for this and, in his criticism, he gave examples of al-Azhar abiding by court sentences to pay certain amounts of money and the interest thereof, stipulated by positive law, even though al-Azhar regarded this interest as contradicting Shariʿa and Qur'anic text (al-Bishrī, 2011a, 12–14).

Here, it might be relevant to link his stance on money interest as violating Shariʿa and his aforementioned account on Islamic businesses. It was already established that he did not question the righteousness of Islamic transactions or the idea of having Islamic economic businesses per se, although he criticized other aspects relating to their actual performance. With this appraisal, it could be inferred that he recognized that these businesses conducted licit Islamic economic activities. But because of the economic rivalry between them and the Mubarak regime, it would have been risky to openly assert the legitimacy of these businesses, as he may have faced public persecution.

In spite of these accounts on the historical rivalry and positive law contradicting Shariʿa on interest rates, expressed by several mainstream CIPT intellectuals/jurists such as Yusuf al-Qaradawi (see Soliman, 2004, 273), al-Bishri spotted compatibility between Shariʿa and positive law regarding medical transplants. According to him, Shariʿa does not differ from positive law in defining death and its symptoms. They are also alike in their prohibiting and criminalizing of human murder; organ transplants are regarded similarly in terms of the conditions of necessity (*Ḍarūra*)[3] (al-Bishrī, 2001, 12–14). But he is not alone in his assessment of such convergences; others have also depicted them regarding, for instance, the definition and prohibition of crimes against internal and external security of the state (al-Zuḥīlī, 2006, 373–4).

Yet, this is not to insinuate he gave up on his preference for Islam in the juxtaposition between the Islamic and the secular. He even argued that the secular both augments state authority and destroys existing collectivities; he wrote:

> Today's rulers in the existing secular regimes, we see their powers broader, larger and more massive in the lives of people than yesterday's rulers. Today's man cannot practice his daily life, but through a huge set of rules and relations where

> the state is part in these, and that are established by rule institutions. (*Mu'assasat al-Hukm*). And this is among the impacts of positive systems in our societies, because positive law became subject to the law of the ruler. (al-Bishrī, 2005a, 96)

These traditional institutions and belonging units, according to him, preserved social balance for the community. The state came to substitute these formations and monopolized public action away from what he termed self-management entities (*Haiy'aat al-Idara al-dhatiyya*). Self-management entities include syndicates, communities and the like. To him, the positivist secular orientation granted the state permission to undertake all these functions. For, if the state is to carry out all these tasks, it should have the power to do so and also possess the source of authority according to which these tasks would be regulated. It would not just have the power to legislate but also, in turn, be the source of legislation (al-Bishrī, 2005a, 119).

On this point, and aside from his view on positive law as augmenting state authority compared to Shari'a, his preference for a strong autonomous society rather than a big state could be easily singled out. This is partly consistent with both his emphasis on the rootedness of Shari'a in Islamic societies till the end of the eighteenth century on one hand, and his emphasis on the autonomous nature of juristic tutorship in Islamic history on the other. Similarly, he denounced a centralized state as one that negatively influenced society; through its control, social institutions diminish (al-Bishrī, 1996c, 80–2). It is a state that is relatively weak in its ability to combat military occupation, compared to less centralized ones. He also claimed that a less centralized state is one that is associated with a strong civil society (al-Bishrī, 2002c, 20–2, 75).

This feature represents another instance of convergence of the Islamic and political profiles of the intellectual. His arguments are not solely based on the heritage, be this the text of Qur'an or Hadith, history of Islam or jurisprudence. It is his frequent emphasis on the societal entrenchment of Shari'a in society and its role in the evolution of identity clusters, as arguments for Shari'a application. That is, he capitalized on the representative nature of Shari'a in addition to referencing CIPT heritage.

In many instances, the duality of the Islamic and the secular is strongly traced in his use of the term 'secular' together with the term 'positive'. He used this *secular positive* term in more than one book (see al-Bishrī, 2005a, 119; 1996a, 34). He also used them simultaneously in his assessment of the secular feature/influence on Egypt's national movement (al-Bishrī, 2002b, 156–8). He addressed the relation between Islam and the secular as two different, and often opposing, intellectual streams, where the secular is depicted as originating from outside Islam and religion in establishing systems, defining relations and behavioural patterns (al-Bishrī, 1996a, 8).

Therefore, to him, Muslim countries turned away from Shari'a towards positive law as the source of legitimacy, but the secular ignores religion. The positive and the Islamic are, thus, largely portrayed historically and intellectually as opposites. Nonetheless, as shown above, he did not claim that Islamic and positive laws are two complete opposites when it comes to their content; some congruence could be traced. This is why a careful reading of al-Bishri's writings shows two parallel dualities of Shari'a and positive law. They are legal systems on one hand, but they are also historical experiences and key propositions on the other (see al-Bishrī, 2005a, 119–24; 1996a, 7–9). This differentiation is clearest in his assessment of the Islamic and the secular positive systems. He wrote:

> We might find similarity in details between a system based on secular positive foundations and another one based on Islamic foundations. But this similarity concerns vocabulary and miscellaneous (*Mufradat wa Nathriyyat*). There remains the disagreement in the dominating perspective, regarding the general goals sought by society, the latter conception of the public interest, and the meaning of progress and renaissance, as they are known. (al-Bishrī, 1996a, 34)

Once again, his main objection was directed to the way positive law was implanted in Muslim societies rather than its actual content. He addressed how positive law, along with social institutions, came to rule without being socially rooted in society. Specifically, ruling elites opted for simple addition, rather than intellectual and civilizational selection, when dealing with the duality of the inherited and the imported, in order to form harmonized intellectual and social institutions, based on modernizing the inherited and authenticating the new (*Ta'ṣīl al-Muḥdath*) (al-Bishrī, 1988, 278; see also al-Bishrī, 2007a, 24).

Shari'a in multiple lights

More than once, he maintained Shari'a was/is still a constant demand of Islamist movements (see al-Bishrī, 1998, 25; 2002a, 50–1). Thus, Shari'a application is presented not just in terms of a legal or intellectual debate but also as part of a societal demand of groups of citizens. He even argued that Shari'a was part of the national cultural heritage of Egypt's Copts. He wrote:

> I did put in it [the last chapter of the book] the idea, that in the framework of complete equality and participation between citizens, even if their religions are

> different, Islamic Shari'a can be applied. And that if it is part of Islamic religious affairs for Muslim citizens, it is part of the national cultural heritage of Christian citizens, as long as citizenship rights, in terms not just of equality, but also of participation are guarded. I presented forms of intellectual attempts in this regard. (al-Bishrī, 2002b, 174)

His overall account on Copts was always framed within his assertion of unity and solidarity. His account on Shari'a emphasized equality and participation as conditions for its application, as well as a ceiling for citizens' demands (al-Bishrī, 1998, 65–6; see also al-Bishrī, 2002b, 234). This point will become clearer in the section below on identity. His appraisal of Shari'a, as part of the national heritage of Copts, goes in line with his claim that it played a unifying role. It was, to him, unifying for non-Arab national minorities like Kurds and Berbers (al-Bishrī, 1998, 39). Although the Arab and Islamic are commonly presented as congruent in CIPT writings, regarding Shari'a as a unifying element among Arabs and non-Arabs is quite particular to his account on identities.

In line with his admiration to Shari'a is his parallel appreciation of jurisprudence. He argued that Islamic jurisprudence possessed the necessary tools and means towards responsiveness to realities (al-Bishrī, 1998, 39). Though 'responsiveness to realities' does not necessarily guarantee equality among Muslim and non-Muslim citizens, which is, to him, integral to applying Shari'a, he asserted that Fiqh can realize equality and participation:

> But I say, there is now in jurisprudential 'Ijtihādāt what guarantees the principle of citizenship in political thought, and achieves equality and participation in applied jurisprudence, from within existing theories, be these Islamic jurisprudence or political thought. (al-Bishrī, 2002b, 181)

Nonetheless, as discussed in Chapter 1, although the exclusion of non-Muslims from top state positions is not a line of demarcation between mainstream and tajdīd intellectuals, mainstream CIPT authorship still comprises voices which argue for maintaining this exclusion. Accordingly, because of this division amongst mainstream intellectuals on the matter, al-Bishri, partly concerned with conformity to jurisprudence as a mainstream intellectual, presented the notion of citizenship and equality between citizens as Ijtihad. This goes, hand in hand, with his assertion that ijtihad on legal frameworks, based on Shari'a, suffered stagnation for long centuries (al-Bishrī, 1987b, 617).

There is no contradiction between his positive appraisal of Shari'a and the state of stagnation he claimed. To him, Shari'a itself was not stagnant, rather the juridical and intellectual Ijtihad on it was. Although insisting on the societal character of the call for Shariʿa application, he did not ignore the counter-force resisting this application. To him, there must be some coexistence between both camps; he wrote:

> The call for applying Islamic Shariʿa, represents one of the most important pillars of the Islamic stream call. It might even be the most important of this stream's demands, which this stream considers to be a principle and essence, and a reason for its call. Insisting on its application on one side, and its rejection on another side constitute an area of inevitable collision, and a source of conflict and provoking conscious and unconscious responses. It might incite kinship (*ʿAṣabiyya*) and hatred. As much as it prevails for each party that, the other is the obstacle in the way of its existence, emancipation and self-actualization, as much as hatred, fanaticism are incited. (al-Bishrī, 1998, 65)

Yet, he boosted his character as an Islamic intellectual when he maintained the call for Shariʿa is a religious obligation. He argued:

> And when we, lay a system based on Islamic legitimacy, taking the latter to be its origin; one that considers Shariʿa to be the source of legitimacy and origin of arbitration, we are then choosing something we are religiously-ordered (*Ma'mūrūn*) to do. For, there is a faith side, that cannot be denied, dictating the application of Shariʿa. (al-Bishrī, 2005a, 75)

Taken together, his focus on the societal character of the Shariʿa call along with its status as a religious obligation spared him the criticism of *over-legalizing Islam*, which could happen if it is presented as a law-based faith (see Kamali, 2008, 1–6). His understanding of Shariʿa application is multifaceted, it is part of an existing intellectual debate and a demand on the part of Islamist movements that is faced with counter-demands against its application. It is also, to him, a religious obligation and a source of legitimacy for political rule in history.

Along with his earlier emphasis on how Shariʿa was marginalized in Egypt's legal system, his association of positive law with augmenting authority of the state in Islamic and Arab countries, it becomes clear he did not stand against Shariʿa application. To the contrary, he supported it, but the particularities of how Shariʿa should be applied and if and how positive law can integrate such an application cannot be securely delimited.

Once again, his reservation on positive law is not about its content as such; rather about the way in which it was imposed. He believed it led to a duplication (*Izdiwaj*) in society at the time of colonization, between the inherited and the imported, a duplication that he denounced. For, in his analysis, rulers, at that time, did not adopt a comprehensive renewal scheme and they did not care that the new would emerge from the old. Rather, they kept old terms of thought, institutions and people and established new institutions with new thought and men (al-Bishrī, 2007a, 24). Because he recognized areas of convergence between both Shari'a and positive law, and asserted the need for reform and the state of stagnation in Islamic jurisprudence, it could be safely argued he did not reject Western legal codes in their entirety (see al-Bishrī, 1987b, 617; 1988, 278, 282).

Violence: Jihad as liberation

As shown in Chapter 1, three key elements to the violent theme in CIPT persist: futūḥāt, Islamist militancy and the juristic notion of Jihad. Among Islamic intellectuals, there is a strong appreciation of futūḥāt, as a sign of civilizational superiority in Islamic history. The violence theme, instigated by Islamist militancy, invoked futūḥāt within the relation of Islam to promoting violence. Jihad itself is presented as both violent and non-violent action across the mainstream/tajdīd duality. But the debate on violence does not represent a clear division between both camps; there is a rejection of sporadic violence against civilians but an acceptance of violence towards liberation of lands. This is the background on Jihad in Islam, as one key CIPT theme to al-Bishri's writings.

Non-violent activism

In his writings, he addressed political action (*al-'Amal al-Siyasi*), political activity (*al-Nashat al-Siyasi*) and the like. When he used these terms, he mainly referred to political parties and journalism. This was the case when he discussed political activism of 'Ahmed Lutfi al-Sayyid, a known Egyptian politician and a co-founder of al-Umma Party. Al-Sayyid was the editor of *Al-Jarida* newspaper, then became a member of al-Wafd Party and finally a member of the Constitutional Liberals (al-Ahrar al-Dusturiun). Interestingly, al-Bishri did not view al-Sayyid's involvement through political parties as his effective political action; rather, his ever-lasting political influence was, to him, the political ideas Lutfi publicly presented in the early twentieth century, when he ran *Al-Jarida* (al-Bishrī, 2002b, 38–40).

A similar focus on journalism was seen in his account on the New National Party (al-Watani al-Jadid). He wrote about party founder Fathi Radwan's involvement in political action (*al-'Amal al-Siyasi*), referring to the party newspaper The New Banner (*al-Liwaa' al-Jadid*) (al-Bishrī, 2002a, 24). Journalism was again depicted as one of the most effective means of mass gathering for political action (al-Bishrī, 1987a, 63). He referred to the role of strong critique in newspapers as pushing the government to repeal the 1936 treaty with the Brits after the 1951 Egyptian-British negotiations yielded significant discontent (al-Bishrī, 2002a, 418).

In fact, this evident focus on the act of writing may partly explain his own interest in authorship. The large accounts he offered on political movements in pre-republican Egyptian history, his writings on the country's Copts (2004) and his smaller, more diversified accounts on Islamic Shari'a, identity and secularism should be read in light of his own appreciation of writing on politics (al-Bishrī, 2002b, 7–8).

Nonetheless, political engagement, to him, involved more than party politics or journalism. He drew attention to demonstrations and strikes as popular motion (*Taharruk Jamahiri*), when he addressed the societal reaction towards the Egyptian-British negotiations in 1946 and 1947. He also referred to secret political action, as in the case of The Democratic Movement for National Liberation (*al-Haiy'a al-Dimuqratiyya li-l-Taharrur al-Watani*), one of the most active Marxist organizations in terms of popular engagement back in 1950s in Egypt, which secretly established labour unions in rural areas (al-Bishrī, 2002a, 421, 536, respectively). He pointed out that this movement supported al-Wafd candidates for the 1950–1 elections and participated in organizing demonstrations and meetings with the party's youth (al-Bishrī, 2002a, 516). Likewise, he acknowledged *using weapons* as political action in his account on the Palestinian struggle. Violence as a means is, to him, more suitable to combat settlements, compared to peaceful ways of protesting endorsed by al-Wafd (al-Bishrī, 2004, 731–2).

Yet, his appreciation for party politics is evident in his account on the multiple restrictions on the Egyptian party system, which, in his words, fell under a ceiling imposed since multi-partism was launched in the late 1970s up until 1991. It was a ceiling that prevented political parties from moving upward and expanding out of the scope imposed on them (al-Bishrī, 1991b, 9). Similarly, he argued there were active groups that could not establish political parties in Egypt in the 1980s (al-Bishrī, 2007c, 19); he wrote:

> That a party system, leading to the existence of a group of parties, not representing the political, social and cultural conditions of the country, would be established: and that what exists 'legally' does not exist in reality: and the real does not exist 'legally'; and that this gap and this discrepancy remain between what is real and what the law recognizes its legitimacy and existence; that this situation is there could lead to a Schizophrenia in 'legitimacy', making it difficult to manage society. (al-Bishrī, 1992, 21)

Political activism was evident again in his appraisal of popular mobilization, that could be based on traditional institutions, like small families and extended ones. He affirmed that political action involves activity inside any *popular cluster* classified along the lines of profession, craftsmanship, neighbourhood or intellectual activity (al-Bishrī, 1991a, 372–3). Note here his appreciation of plurality at the level of society which concurs with his positive accounts on jurisprudential plurality in Islamic history, and his negative appraisal of positive law, above, as augmenting state authority towards diminishing the power and plurality of autonomous clusters.

Particularly, his appreciation of plurality was again evident in his account on al-Azhar. Although presided either by Maliki or Shafiʿi Imams, two of the four major schools in the Sunni jurisprudence, al-Azhar taught the content and methodology of all four schools. According to him, this fact implied that jurisprudential disagreements did not lead to one school excluding the others. He argued this was closer to pluralism and the diversity of the different parties concerned, parties that acknowledged coexistence in the framework of a general comprehensive cultural reference (al-Bishrī, 2011b, 12–13).

In fact, his account above doesn't necessarily contradict Western scholarship on Islam that claimed individual rule was caused by historical reality and *oneness* of the God (see Krämer, 2000b, 56–7). The question of oneness versus plurality invoked more profound questions of structure, freedoms and rights, as well as the legitimacy of diversity of interests and opinions in Islam. Whether or not Islam accepts any sort of organization, party and parliament is already under discussion (Krämer, 1994, 40). Interestingly, the multiplicity of jurisprudential schools and their coexistence is, as shown in Chapter 1, the argument usually employed by tajdīd intellectuals towards promoting new interpretations in CIPT. This is an instance exhibiting the convergence between mainstream and tajdīd, emanating from the fact that both camps react to the same CIPT self-imposing themes, and the almost unified body of heritage they both use in their intellectual production on Islam and the Islamicate.

Violence as a logic

Violence, to al-Bishri, is largely presented within the contours of *feasibility*. This was the case in his assessment of Egyptian politics under British colonization. He wrote:

> The strength of al-Wafd was based in its large popular support, the strength of the British emanated from the presence of the occupation army in conditions

> where the popular movement could not challenge it using violence. (al-Bishrī, 1991a, 41)

Likewise, in his appraisal of the integration of the Palestinian cause into goals of the Egyptian national movement, he presented violence versus peaceful legitimate means. To him, the criterion for deciding on the use of violence was feasibility or effectiveness. That is, there is a need to explore means of struggle compatible with colonialism, which was implanted using *the power of weapons*. He argued that this meant legitimate peaceful means of struggle were incapable of combating it (al-Bishrī, 1991a, 60). This same duality of violence vis-à-vis peaceful means was reiterated in his appraisal of the history of fighting colonialism in general; he wrote:

> Today, our crisis is not in Western colonization, which we experience more as a threat and siege, penetration and pressures on our political will, than as a direct military occupation and direct rule. We lived through all that in the nineteenth century and the first half of the twentieth century. But we fought it using peaceful means, when peaceful means worked, and we resisted it with violence and weaponry, when it was a must for resistance to opt for this way. Sometimes, we decided for one and not the other; and sometimes we used both, when using them together was possible and helpful. (al-Bishrī, 2005c, 7)

In fact, to him, the availability of non-violent means/channels of legitimate claims to violated rights is critical towards deciding on the use of violence. More precisely, when legitimate claims are blocked, violence can take place. His professional background as a judge is visible in his account on claims to violated rights. If two parties are not sure that courts will serve them justice, then they would probably resort to violence (al-Bishrī, 2006b, 33).

Although propagated as the highest value in Islam, there is much diversity in determining the exact connotation of the term 'Justice', especially when justice and equality are addressed together. Justice is a term usually employed to cover a wide field of political, social, ethical and legal dimensions (see Krämer, 2007, 23, 31; 2011, 78). Nonetheless, al-Bishri's focus on justice is not exclusively invoked as an Islamic term but also as a civil value, pertaining to the assumed damage associated with denying/violating rights.

Conversely, when there are channels for political expression, violence, according to him, is not employed. Egypt's Free Officers, he argued, did not resort to political assassinations partly because of the atmosphere of freedom of expression and popular political action prevalent after the government of Saʿdiyyin was toppled (al-Bishrī, 2002a, 550). Committed within a free environment or blocked channels, he claimed violence stays largely subjective and relative; it is shaped by the ideas and positions of those committing it; he wrote:

> An incident pertaining to a community going out with weapons on others, shows in the news as revolution, or rebellion, or terrorism, or disobedience. The way the incident was described contains political thought and it contains a political position. (al-Bishrī, 2002b, 56–7)

As suggested through earlier accounts, he expressed strong interest in, and support to, the Palestinian cause, which he addressed within the framework of the Islamic term 'Jihad' (al-Bishrī, 2006c, 22; see also al-Bishrī, 1998, 12). He used Jihad within his Islamic profile when he discussed the Islamic governor (*al-Wālī*) arming his soldiers with the religious spirit (al-Bishrī, 2002a, 34). But the term falls at the intersection of his political and Islamic profiles in his appraisal of the role of civil society in mobilization for Jihad, liberation of the land and the moral power deriving from Islam in this respect (al-Bishrī, 2002c, 22).

To him, Jihad is one of the constants (*Thawābit*) of Islamic rules. It is an Islamic duty that does not change (al-Bishrī, 2005a, 107). As shown in Chapter 1, the scope of *Thawābit* and *Mutaghaiyyrāt* is one major anchor to the mainstream-tajdīd contestation. Through their revisions to the body of Islamic heritage, tajdīd intellectuals challenge mainstream conceptions on both Islam and the larger Islamicate (see Ḥanafī, 1990; 'Arkūn, 1992, 114; Ayubi, 1995, 84). Mainstream intellectuals, however, insist there must be limits to Ijtihad and tajdīd, where Mu'āmalāt, for instance, but not rituals, would be open to renewal (Farrūkh, 1986, 9–10).

He is evidently part of the larger tradition that highlights the double nature of the term 'Jihad', as composed of both violent and non-violent forms of action. For instance, on the subject of the relation between national and religious identities, he argued that, for nationalists, there can be no obstacle to the religious pan (*al-Jami'a al-Diniyya*); there is a bond of Jihad against *invading conquerors* (al-Bishrī, 1998, 11). Here, he referred to colonialism and the pursuit of independence. If combating colonialism includes violence as a means of liberation, then Jihad actually has, in his writings, a connotation of using violence. However, if colonialism is viewed as larger than military occupation, then Jihad is broader than violence and might include other aspects, like working on reducing dependency on the West, boycotting markets or the like. This was traceable in his account on colonialism and/or independence. He stressed the need to acquire independence of its political, economic and social forms (al-Bishrī, 2008, 13, 86–7; al-Bishrī, 2007a, 113; al-Bishrī, 1978, 27).

As shown in Chapter 1, Jihad was invoked within the contemporary phenomenon of violent activism by several groups working under the banner of Islam (Lane and Redissi, 2004, 18, 32; see also Krämer, 1994). Although al-Bishri didn't negate these acts, he generally condemned them in his writings and even disassociated them from their alleged Islamic character. In his writings, they contradict Islamic tolerance, its protection for one's self and money, citizens and places of worship (al-Bishrī, 1998, 48). This denouncement of violent acts against civilians, carried out in the name of Islam, is shared by most CIPT intellectuals, who assert Islam neither calls nor tolerates such crimes (al-Ghazālī, 1987, 103; al-Saʿīd, 2004), even when this sort of violence is attributed to political oppression and economic hardships (see Al-Zuḥīlī, 2006, 368, 377–8).

Violence from above

CIPT debates are not separate accounts; in many instances, they intersect. Al-Bishri presented this intersection of violence by presenting it within state struggle for identity. Namely, he addressed both Ottomans' keenness to keep their racial dominance over different nations/races and the Men of Union and Progress (Rijāl al-ʾIttiḥād wa-l-Taraqqī) an Arab national movement in the caliphate state (*Dawlat al-Khilāfa*) that resisted the Ottoman Empire (al-Bishrī, 1998, 13).

Although the state has the legal right to use coercion (see Demirovic, 2007, 24), it can also commit violence in an illegal sense. As shown in various sections of Chapter 2, the state resorted to detaining political opponents, torture in prisons and was linked to physical attacks on journalists transgressing particular red lines. Thus, the issue of legality becomes central in conceiving state use of violence. Al-Bishri's account on such practices asserted its illegitimate character, which he both resented and frequently linked to authoritarian rule (see al-Bishrī, 1991a, 62–4, 150; 2006a, 33).

In his accounts on Egypt's political history, he reiterated the illegitimate use of violence by the state, when a demonstration was conspired by the regime to break into Egypt's State Council and physically attacked its back-then president, Dr. ʿAbd al-Razzaq al-Sanhuri (al-Bishrī, 2006b, 14–16). Likewise, in his book Historical Personalities (*Shakhsiyyat Tarikhiyya*), he praised a court sentence by Saʿd Zaghlul, a key political figure in Egypt's history, leader of the 1919 Revolution and former leader of al-Wafd. This ruling was against political torture and violent measures carried out by men of the administration, such as police officers, on citizens. Al-Bishri praised the verdict as embarking on a just system inspired by

Zaghlul's thought and principles and not on the system the government created (al-Bishrī, 1996b, 27). His admiration of al-Wafd highlighted earlier and the strong appeal of Zaghlul's profile in al-Bishri's intellectual path can be spotted in several of his books (al-Bishrī, 2002a; 2002b). It also partly explains why one of the three books he published after the 2011 uprising was completely dedicated to Zaghlul's biography and nationalist struggle (al-Bishrī, 2012a).

Furthermore, his account on the state's use of violence embodied a classification and differentiation between legitimate and illegitimate forms. Although he rejected the use of violence towards racial dominance or infringing on judicial independence above, he fully accepted its use in fighting crime. For instance, he argued that *violence should be faced with counter-violence.* His objection was to the use of violence, as a logic, through which the state deals with political opposition (see al-Bishrī, 1991a, 318; 2002b, 310). In his own words,

> Violence, in our estimate, is neither rejected in itself, nor accepted in itself. It is one way for resolving political conflicts. Judging whether it is right or wrong is a field of the science of politics. It necessarily concerns necessity, possibility and feasibility. Violence is the means most exposing people to damages ..... It is the most costly means. The winner in it is a loser, to the degree of what he lost and was costed. (al-Bishrī, 2002c, 46)

Meanwhile, in his account on Coptic demonstrations, he highlighted violence coming from social or communal groups against the state that was not faced with counter-violence from the latter. In al-Nabaa incident, Copts gathered for days in rejection of published material on alleged sexual misconduct in a monastery. He commented on government response to the demonstrators' long gathering and throwing stones on police forces as *tolerant* (al-Bishrī, 2002b, 215). Briefly put, his account on violence is not solely defined along the lines of the Jihad theme; the decision to resort to violence is equally guided by context. Nonetheless, he set parallel criteria for accepting or rejecting violence which, in his appraisal, is a very subjective matter. He endorsed violence against occupation but rejected sporadic violence against civilians. Likewise, he accepted use of violence by the state, as long as it is used to combat crime, not to suppress opposition.

Identities: Unifying pluralism

Under the broad theme of identity, there are both intra-identity debates – with dualities of Muslim versus Islamic, Muslim versus religiously devout Muslim, ordinary Muslims versus clerics (*'Ulamā'*) and Sunnis versus Shiites – and Inter-identity debates, which pre-occupy with how Muslims relate/should relate to non-Muslims. Terms like Dār al-'Islām/Dār al-Ḥarb, 'Ahl al-Dhimma and Jiziya constitute the juristic background of the CIPT theme on identity. These terms were coined at a time when Muslims were conquerors. Today, as Muslims are not leading human civilization, these terms, when invoked, are used mostly for the purposes of display of the juridical history.

Lines of demarcation between mainstream and tajdīd are still blurred on the issue of conversions from Islam and on non-Muslims' right to hold state top positions, historically confined to Muslims. Yet, tajdīd intellectuals are more unified in this regard. With Muslims living as minorities in non-Muslim societies, through labour emigration to the West, other themes and juridical contributions became more central to CIPT and represented the need for a redefinition of the juridical terms and establishing Minority Jurisprudence (*Fiqh al-'Aqalliyyāt*). Sporadic violence against the state or society invoked a debate on how Muslims relate to their larger societies. Across mainstream-tajdīd writings on the matter, the relation between Islam and the state is one of coexistence and cooperation. Nonetheless, violence against the latter, by Islamist militants, was/is largely instigated by a potential for conflict between Islam and these entities.

Contouring the 'We'

His account on identity is largely inclusive rather than exclusive, as will be evident in this section. The inclusive emphasis was already evident earlier in this chapter, seen in his appraisal of Shari'a as unifying Arab and non-Arab Muslim minorities on one hand and to Arab Muslims and non-Muslims on the other. Most significant is his emphasis on divisions as establishing inter-connectedness between communities, where a person participates in more than one community and communities overlap (al-Bishrī, 2007a, 44; see also al-Bishrī, 2008, 50–1). He wrote:

> For instance, Egyptians, this human community, which lives in the Eastern corner of Africa. They are Egyptians, in terms of territory, Arabs in terms of language, Muslims in terms of Religion. And in conceiving all that comes through multiplicity of criteria of classifications. This multiplicity helps in defining features and these features overlap and co-exist; for, not each criterion is separate from the others and not every description detached from the other. Circles of identities overlap with one another. (al-Bishrī, 2000, 7)

In parallel, he presented himself as an intellectual within the contours of more than one identity. Throughout his intellectual path, he spoke of himself as part of the Egyptian, Muslim and Arab masses (al-Bishrī, 2006a, 10; 2011b, 9; 2002c, 23; 2003b, 18). To him, belonging to one or more community/ies is not an act of free choice, it is binding. On this, there is more than one quote:

> If we put conditions for us to confess the origin of our belonging, we thereby subject our belonging to choice. we would be associating it to us, not associating ourselves to it. We would be judging it, rather than judging according to it. We do not choose our Egyptian or our Arab identities and we do not choose the basis of our community. (al-Bishrī, 2005a, 93)
>
> Our matter with its totalities and origins is a matter of identity and belonging. For instance: we are Egyptians. And our 'Egyptianity' is imposed on us by necessity. Out of this comes its power of subjection and compliance, as a measure of appraisal (*Mashra' li-l-Nazar*) and a criterion for arbitration. (al-Bishrī, 2007b, 10)
>
> We do not choose Arabism and we do not choose Islam, they are imposed on us. And territoriality (*al-Quṭriyya*) is destined on the Egyptian, the Iraqi and the Moroccan. Each in his land. And a human being does not choose his language; and he does not choose his father and his mother. (al-Bishrī, 1991c, 280)

In spite of the many instances revealing his identity circles being the Islamic, Arab and Egyptian, his particular pride of his *Egyptian-ness* is quite remarkable, he elaborately wrote:

> Colonizing Egypt was different from that of many other colonized countries. The Britons came to it in September 1882 to find in it a state composed of a cabinet and an elected parliament, of ministries and agencies and administrations, of a regular army and police, and local administrations and judicial bodies. A state that was constructed in three quarters of a century – until it became, according to the criteria of the nineteenth century, complete in existence and pillars. It is the same state that, with its army and administrations, was able forty years ago to resist European ambitions and to defeat the Ottoman state and jeopardize existence of the latter. The state that could establish a strong unified state, stretching from the middle of Africa in the South to the borders of Turkey in the North. The state that presented a more advanced pattern of rule than that of the Turkish Ottoman one, prevailing in the Middle East. A state that founded established schools, sent missions, that eagerly acquired from the sciences and arts of the West. They [the British] found in it a populace with a high degree of unity, enjoying a large extent of national maturity. (al-Bishrī, 2012a, 15)

Nonetheless, in line with the inclusive perspective on identities above, these three identities are not, in his accounts, presented as competing. He stated it clearly that these identities do not rank among each other. He wrote:

> Our Islamism, 'Egyptian-ness' and Arabism are an alloy. The differences among the elements are not separating; for the alloy is united in its elements and in harmony. (al-Bishrī, 2002b, 168)

On this, he fortified the argument that an Islamic intellectual can still present as belonging to other identity circles, at no risk of losing their Islamic character, due to such concurrent affiliation with another identity.

The West as identity

Like al-Banna, he addressed the West as a counter-identity. This is evident in his prolonged discussion of colonization and its impact on colonized societies. Laws and perspectives came from a different context, based on a different society, history and culture. The social and political institutions were imposed through colonization. In these discussions, he juxtaposed the West not just to Islam but also to the Arab and/or the Orient. That is, it is treated as a multifaceted entity or unit, not merely geographic but also civilizational (see al-Bishrī, 2007b, 31; 2008, 63). This juxtaposition is quite salient in his appraisal of contemporaneity (*al-Mu'āṣara*), which, to him, eventually led to dominance by the Western as features of the age (*Khaṣā'iṣ al-'Aṣr*). The future of the West, thus, became the future of Muslims and Arabs, and its life and societies became their aspired virtuous state (al-Bishrī, 2007b, 52). Similarly, his appraisal of colonization, and Western social and political institutions that came with it, versus traditional ones, maintained the juxtaposition. Al-Bishri argued:

> We can say that the main challenge faced by our Arab and Islamic communities in the last two centuries was generally that of how to face historical greediness and how to reach the model necessary for the community to rise and stand together, with which it can face the dangers. On the basis of this criterion, we realize that when we look at traditional and modern social and political institutions, we find that the right and the good (*al-Ṣawāb wa-l-Naf'*) were not correlative, because the ultimate value is in using these right and good in social reform, and in how efficient the adopted forms for that use are. (al-Bishrī, 2008, 61)

The West and East were again juxtaposed on political parties, between Western understanding and actual experience in Muslim/Oriental countries. A political party in the West represented interests of a social group, such as industry men, bankers or peasants, while in Muslim and Oriental societies it had a different function and acted as national parties or the entities that led national liberation movements. According to him, these were collective; in the eyes and conscience of their members, they represented the nation in its totality (al-Bishrī, 2007a, 28–34).

Taken together, these accounts of the West/East-Islam juxtaposition coincide with Said's Orientalist accounts, which were reiterated by many CIPT intellectuals. Nonetheless, he neither defamed the West nor presented the Islamic as intrinsically better in the juxtaposition. The competitive edge of Shari'a, as shown earlier, compared to positive law was, to him, the fact that it has its roots in Muslim countries. It is not the content of Shari'a per se that is superior. In his writings, the West is defamed in his appraisal of colonialism because of acts of colonization that were damaging and imposed. However, he did not criticize the West per se.

Plus, the West was interchangeably referred to as secular, within his account on colonization, depicting the secular as a counter-force vis-à-vis Islam. This is quite clear in his account on secularism implanted as political and social theories, which were criteria for arbitration and source of legitimacy towards the late nineteenth century and early twentieth century (al-Bishrī, 1996a, 8, 20). He wrote:

> When I write about the relationship [between Islam and secularism], I mean with Islam a method (*Manhajan*) regarding Islam as the source of legitimacy, the criterion for arbitration, the framework resorted to in social and political systems and behavioral patterns; whereas secularism -I think- is dropping that matter, and emerging from other than Islam, and other than Religion in establishing systems, and drawing relations and patterns of behavior. (al-Bishrī, 1996a, 8)

This might be the case because of his focus on the Western origins of secularism; he wrote: 'For the secularism we know in our countries is from the Christian West and Christianity didn't comprise legislations or legislative rules regarding earthly affairs' (al-Bishrī, 2019, 18). Nonetheless, his account on the West praised both the division of labour among different entities and collective decision-making. These two aspects, to him, represent a shift from government of individuals to government of institutions; a shift that he applauded and called for, in order to enrich Islamic constitutional and administrative systems (al-Bishrī, 2007a, 79–80). The same occurred with judicial principles of trial levels and multiplicity of judges on a single case. These, amongst others, are Western practices that he claimed '*enriched and improved Shari'a Judiciary* (*al-Qaḍā' al-Shar'ī*), *late in the nineteenth century*' (al-Bishrī, 2011b, 27). In the interviews, he was clear that he had no hatred against the West per se and that he found it critical for the Muslim and Arab world to learn and derive from particular Western achievements in fields like natural sciences, economic affairs and administrative structures (Interview, 15 August 2011). As shown earlier, his objection was to the manner in which Western ideals were imposed, as he believed it was done in a way that caused a split in society (al-Bishrī, 2002a, 50; see also al-Bishrī, 2007a, 24–5; 2008, 58). Likewise, his appreciation of democracy, a practice that evolved in Western countries, meant the West itself was not rejected (see al-Bishrī, 2008, 77; 2007a, 79–80).

Ranking the National and the Religious

In his appraisal, territoriality (*al-Quṭriyya*) had a damaging effect on identity and self-perception. He argued that history was sorted out along territorial classifications resulting in attempts at unity to be regarded as annexation (*Ḍam*) or opening (*fatḥ*) (al-Bishrī, 2005a); he wrote:

> And in a history limited to the Egyptian territory, *al-Mu'iz li-Din Illah al-Fatimi* [the fourth Fatimid caliph] would look like a conqueror (*Fātiḥan*) or invader (*Ghāziyan*). (al-Bishrī, 2005a, 77)

Here, he was preoccupied with the question of territoriality, which is a phenomenon commonly disdained in CIPT (al-Jābrī, 1990b, 94; see also Brunner, 2004, 82). Nonetheless, consistent with his inclusive approach to identity, he argued there is a need to seek commonalities without exclusion or mutual destruction (see al-Bishrī, 2008, 32–3). Shari'a, in his accounts, was one point of convergence between religious and national streams (al-Bishrī, 1998, 39). Egyptian identity, to him, did not collide with Islamic identity during the time of the caliphate (*al-Khilāfa*) (al-Bishrī, 2008, 52–3). He maintained that the political pan, across many centuries, was established on the basis of religion and creed; and Egypt was, in the eyes of Muslims, part of this more comprehensive political pan (al-Bishrī, 2002b, 175). This was also clear in his account on Egyptian identity versus Islamic identity of the Ottoman Empire. He wrote:

> The national pan, that evolved in Egypt, went throughout the last century -the nineteenth century- without struggle with the Islamic creed, or with the concept comprising it. It does not seem that 'Egyptianity' appeared back then as a call

> for secession from the larger pan (*al-Jāmi'a al-'Ashmal*), because Egypt was, at that time, already separated from that larger pan. It also does not look like the Islamic position did not tolerate this movement. (al-Bishrī, 2002a, 36)

Likewise, he argued that the national (*Qawmiyya*) and the religious reject fragmentation and seek unity; he wrote:

> And both the national and religious bonds embark upon rejecting fragmentation, and targeting collectiveness. And they include combat (*Jihad*) against aggression and control, and seek harmony and peace with other weak nations. (al-Bishrī, 1998, 12)

Accordingly, his accounts on the Islamic/Arab are largely congruent, as the Islamic and Arab streams had a close relation due to their cultural overlap, which created clear blending (al-Bishrī, 2008, 22). In the same direction, he argued that the Ottoman rule, which had a religious appearance, endorsed a semi-national rule, inclined to control other nationalities. He argued that this is the reason for the emergence of national movements (al-Bishrī, 1998, 12). On the relation between Arab and Islamic, he wrote:

> It is true that someone who advocates Arabism is called Arabist, and the Islamic is called Islamist, but the deep sources are the same in many of the joints of the national and the Islamic idea. (al-Bishrī, 2008, 22)

This is perhaps why he often invoked the Islamic and the Arab together; it further validates his perspective on both identities as historically overlapping (see al-Bishrī, 1998, 56; 2002c, 70, 74, 79; 2006c, 22; 2007a, 83, 105; 2007b, 61, 63; 2008, 30, 38, 61). This overlap between Islamic and Arab identities was eloquently summarized in this quote:

> And when we talk in any field of thought or activity in our foregoing history, we do not distinguish much between the Arab and the Islamic. (al-Bishrī, 2005b, 105)

Although he depicted them as closely related and overlapping, as identities and intellectual streams, he made a significant qualification on the matter. He argued that Islam existed first, as identity, and that the Arab came from within. For instance, in Egypt, Arabism appeared from within the circles of the aforementioned al-Shubban al-Muslimun in the 1930s (al-Bishrī, 2008, 22). He maintained that Islam and Arabism differ only when it comes to secularism, which Shami Arabism adopted and propagated, on one hand, and the Egyptian *sentiments* of 1919 on the other. Here, he presented a trilogy of Islam, Arabism and secularism, where Arabism is closer to Islam, as much as it is farther from secularism and vice versa (al-Bishrī, 1989, 37; 1998, 90–1).

On this, he claimed the secular, which originated from the West, stood between the Arab and the Islamic. With this appraisal, he somehow added to the damaging features of colonialism and its dividing impact on identities which originally converged and overlapped. The same coexistence he claimed between Islamic and Arab could be argued in his stance on how religious identities relate. His general position on the Coptic question is presented within the framework of a call for unity and solidarity; there is, and should be, no intellectual struggle between Islam and Christianity (al-Bishrī, 2002b, 158). This quote captures his call for unity:

> All we seek through our talks and debates is to reach the biggest possible amount of cohesion for our national community among all its elements and components, and to realize what we could call the main political stream that embraces the whole community and accepts its sub-variations, and that each sub-formation in this national community finds what assures it for its existence and continuity along other sub-formations. (al-Bishrī, 2011a, 7)

In addition to his claim that Ijtihad in jurisprudence can recognize equality between Muslims and non-Muslims, his stance regarding equal rights of Copts is based on his reading of Qur'an and Hadith. He maintained that there is no definitive text in Islam that denies complete citizenship in the homeland for non-Muslims who take part in the land's struggle and development (al-Bishrī, 2004, 844). Here, he presented his position on Copts' eligibility to hold top state positions without contradicting his Islamic profile. He asserted that excluding Copts from these positions, based on a theoretical concept of different treatment, can end up with two societies and damage unity (al-Bishrī, 1998, 37–8).

Interestingly, although an Islamic mainstream intellectual, he gave precedence, in case of conflict, to the national versus the religious. This feature will become more salient in the following section on Coptic identity. To him, the national and the religious must be allowed to freely function within two concurrent boundaries. One, the national should have precedence vis-à-vis the religious identity, but Coptic demands should not aspire anything beyond equality and participation (al-Bishrī, 1998, 65–6; see also al-Bishrī, 2002b, 234). Two, intellectual and political disagreement could be tolerated as long as they abide by strict respect for the national community (al-Bishrī, 2002b, 254).

The boundaries he set were clearest in his account on the church's decision not to carry out a court verdict in 2008, allowing the remarriage of divorced

Copts. Though granting the church the right to object and claim *wrongness* of the verdict, al-Bishri objected to its refusal to carry out the verdict; he wrote:

> But for the church not to carry out a final verdict, this is a disobedience against the state (*Khurūj ʿalā al-Dawla*), judicially and legally, with the state representing the national community, and this is a disobedience on the prevailing legitimacy in the society. (al-Bishrī, 2011a, 12)

Similarly, he referred to his demand to apply the law for financial supervision (audit) by the Central Agency for Financial Auditing (al-Jihaz al-Markazi li-l-Muhasabat) on financial matters of the church. His argument, in this regard, is that the church is a public enterprise – according to legal, jurisprudential and judicial terms in Egypt – and thus must be subjected to general provisions of the relevant Egyptian legal codes (al-Bishrī, 2011a, 51). In return, there must be equality in the eligibility to participate in public activity among all citizens (al-Bishrī, 2008, 72). Accordingly, on the basis of citizenship, Copts should be eligible to run for all positions:

> What is important is the stance from the national community. Political stances vary among citizens, even if their religions are different, but what should be warned against is that a political stance develops and polarizes the people of one religion, towards what the latter conceive as a benefit to them, regardless of the benefit of their community in general. Because -the private benefit here is a factional one jeopardizing the collective belonging of the citizens and loosen its fabric. (al-Bishrī, 1998, 54)

Therefore, he identified himself with more than one circle of identity. Identities, to him, are not matters of choice. There is nothing to imply he had preference for one of his identity circles compared to another. He was very proud of being Egyptian. The West is, in many instances, a counter-identity; still, there was some good input from the West. His general approach to the identity question is historical, with a focus on inter-identity aspects. He showed focus on Coptic demands, with two key ingredients. One, supporting their right to hold top state positions and the general right for full equality and participation. Two, demonstrating the necessity to keep within the boundaries of national identity and not to seek a sorting out of history.

Coptic identity within citizenship

Al-Bishri wrote his nine-hundred-page account on Coptic-Muslim relations under Sadat; it was published in 1980. Under Nasser, many Copts started immigrating due to an increasing negative sentiment regarding the loss of the professional and economic privileges they enjoyed before the 1952 coup, but without incidents where the regime directly collided with the Coptic Church or the larger Coptic community (see Doorn-Harder, 2005, 26–8). This was different from the situation under Sadat, when regime-church relations severed during al-Khanka incidents onwards. His account on the relations is, therefore, a reflection both of the Coptic affair as a prolonged debate in Egypt's public sphere and of developments under Sadat. Still, the greatest part of this book was preoccupied with the pre-1952 history (2004).

Under Mubarak, in 2002, he commented on various individual incidents of Coptic-Muslim friction. But he published a small book on the Coptic issue in 2005 (*al-Jamā'a al–Waṭaniyya Baiyn al-'Uzla wa-l-'Indimāj*) (2005d), where he maintained that the regime was lenient towards them, even when their protests involved violence. He even argued that the regime's reaction to protests by Muslims was relatively harsher than that towards similar ones by Copts (al-Bishrī, 2002b, 215–17). This appraisal was not to collide with the Mubarak regime as the pressure of the Coptic diaspora was, as illustrated more than once, based on allegations that Copts are discriminated against. His account on external actors using the Coptic community, as a means towards achieving their agendas/aims (2004, 138; see also 1996c, 34), actually served the Mubarak regime to mitigate this pressure. Moreover, he directly attributed the increasing tendency towards heating up the Coptic issue to its diaspora (2002b, 234). His blaming of this diaspora for severing the debate on the Coptic issue converged with the state narrative, under Mubarak, depicting it as infringing on the country's national sovereignty and parallel accounts in the press.

Nonetheless, the comparative lack of a genuine large production, on his part, about the Coptic issue under Mubarak might relate to two parallel factors: one, he already offered an extensive account on Copts, written under Sadat, which was first published in 1980, and was republished more than once under Mubarak (Mūrū, 1991, 4). Two, as shown earlier, the Coptic diaspora pressure on the regime regarding the status of Copts, along with reported cases of conversions, translated into great sensitivity in publicly addressing the topic (see El Amrani, 2006; Hanna 2013).

After the 2011 uprising, he openly criticized the Coptic Church under Pope Shenouda III for isolating the community from the larger Egyptian nation (al-Bishrī, 2011a, 24–5, 51). His book The State and the Church (*al-Dawla wa-l-Kanīsa*) appeared during the first interim period when it was strongly expected that the Islamist MB would have a *big* share of votes at the advent of competitive elections (see Lavi, 2012). There could, thus, be no risk of colliding with the regime through direct critique of the head of the Coptic Church. In 2015, he presented much of his stances on the Coptic issue in one chapter in a book, which is a collection of some of his earlier writings, titled Intellectual Readings and Egyptian Concerns (*Qirā'āt Fikriyya wa-Humūm Miṣriyya*). Although all three introductions, included in this chapter on Copts, were originally published before 2011, this chapter summarized much of his long-time account on them, regarding the capacity of Shariʿa to allow equality among citizens, his call for this equality and the role Coptic diaspora plays in inciting dissent within the community (2015, 253–80).

Before and after the 2011 uprising, he maintained two key claims regarding allegations of discrimination: *One*, citizenship as a binding concept on all communities, through which no community would enjoy a privileged status vis-à-vis the other (see 1991c, 282; 1998, 91). *Two*, the capacity of Islamic jurisprudence to guarantee equality among citizens (see 2011a, 27, 75). This way, he stroke a balance between standing against communal discrimination and maintaining his Islamic profile, as presenting this equality as congruent with Islamic Shariʿa.

Generally, he tended to quote and use multiple references; his writing style is often similar to those of academicians. During interviews, this style was evident in his assessment of the Coptic discrimination claims, when he differentiated between Coptic status inside the judiciary, which he claimed showed no discrimination, and other sectors that might really embody exclusion of Copts, like that of the head of state universities or governor positions (interview, 6 September 2011). But across his writings on the topic, he didn't portray ruling regimes as infringing on Coptic rights.

In conclusion, al-Bishri's account on the state is multifaceted, with long narrations on the history of Egypt and his admiration for representative politics and democratic rule that were evident, particularly in his accounts on al-Wafd. His ideological shift to Islam was manifested in his appraisals of the state, where he came to accept the involvement of groups working under the banner of Islam in politics, something he rejected before his shift. While he maintained Shura is a stipulation of Islam, he argued it was flexible enough to accommodate democratic rule. He supported the merge of the historical practice of Shura and the modern forms of representative government, like parliaments and party politics.

Still, his appreciation for democracy is based on collective decision-making, institutional character and division of powers, not a fascination with democracy per se. Especially important to him was the rootedness of rules regulating state/society; it was critical towards his assessment of any political or legal setting. Since democracy is a Western practice, it did not have its roots in Islam and that fact was, in his view, its main problem when applied to Muslim societies. Unlike al-Banna, who offered long accounts on defaming despotic rule prevalent in Islamic history, al-Bishri maintained individual rule, in itself, was not a synonym to despotism. In consistency with the general mainstream stance on the state in Islam, he asserted Islam has a role at the level of the state, without necessarily advocating a particular form of an Islamic state.

Through stressing the historical dimension of Shariʿa, as a source of legitimacy and code of conduct, he established its rootedness in Muslim societies. This is a point he used to show preference to Shariʿa when juxtaposed to positive law, in a way similar to the juxtaposition in Orientalism which depicted colonialism as largely damaging because its patterns were viewed as an imposition from outside. Still, he differentiated between Shariʿa as a source of political legitimacy and how representative/autocratic this rule was. As a whole, positive law is not rejected because of its secular/Western character but because of the way it encroached on societies.

Emphasizing the factors leading to violent activism, he argued that resorting to violence is more effective than other non-violent means towards combatting colonial occupation, and when channels for non-violent claims to rights are blocked. On this matter, his Islamic and political profiles intersect with examples from the colonial history of Muslim lands and Egyptʿs contemporary history. Jihad is one Islamic constant in his writings and one that was used to boost the spirit of soldiers. He did endorse the dual nature of Jihād as comprising both violent and non-violent activities, which is common in the writings of CIPT intellectuals, especially because, to him, colonialism is more than just military presence and can take other political, economic and social forms. Rejecting contemporary Islamist militancy, while recognizing violence against occupation, put his writings in line with larger CIPT discussions on the matter.

Identities are, in his view, inclusive in nature. Through multiple communities, interconnectedness grows, which is congruent with his appraisal of Shariʿa as unifying Arab and non-Arab Muslim minorities. His political profile manifested in his emphasis on Egypt as identity, embracing all political and social streams. Still, he presented himself as Muslim, Arab and Egyptian. Identity, to him, is not a matter of choice. Largely concerned with colonial history, he depicted the West as the identity of the colonizer, juxtaposed it to Islam and also to secularism. The secular was depicted as encroaching on the Islamic, mainly through positive law. Expectedly, he denounced the colonizer who imposed legal and institutional settings, but praised democracy's impersonalized administrative practices coming from the West.

Though negatively assessed in his writings, territoriality (Quṭriyya) did not exclude/negate religious identity. In his accounts on modern Islamic history, he maintained the coexistence of both the national and the religious. Thus, through depicting this history, he presented his overall stance on identities as guided by their inclusive nature. Still, he positioned the cleavage between the Arab and the Islamic as pertaining to the secular, which is an instance of the damaging colonial impact on Muslim countries. Unlike al-Banna, who departed from the Islamic in his view that the national and the Islamic coexist, al-Bishri maintained that the national should have precedence over the religious in cases of conflict. This can be seen in his appraisal of the Coptic Church's attitude towards a court verdict contradicting biblical rules.

Finally, the logic of counterargument was traced more than once in his writings. When he came across Shariʿa as a source of legitimacy for political rule, he anticipated a counterargument that this rule was largely despotic. Likewise, he argued that democracy must not necessarily be associated with secular/positive references and/or laws; the counterargument here is that democracy is a Western practice which developed in a secular environment and thus could not function without it.

Conclusion

When I embarked upon this research, more than a decade ago, I was overwhelmed by the abundance of writings on CIPT, an abundance that constituted a double-edged weapon. On one hand, one starts from a good deal of academic scholarship, but on the other, it's quite challenging to contribute an addition to it. Yet, after reading across time, themes and sometimes languages too, it became clear a balance between particular interest in the writings of an Islamic intellectual and the contexts in which he/she contributed their writings is much needed.

Through its different chapters, I tried answering several questions that pertained to the elements constituting the meta-language that an Islamic intellectual would have to react to, take a stance on or simply discuss. In the background of the analysis were Salvatore's meta-language and Foucault's desire to know and desire for truth. Hermeneutics, specifically the notion of a hermeneutic circle, guided much of the reading as well as research design. Reading the bulk of the intellectual production by al-Banna and al-Bishri, along with conducting semi-structured interviews, the material used in writing this book was collected during fieldwork visits to Cairo over the span of eight months (2010–11).

CIPT was defined as spoken and written language seeking reference from Islamic heritage towards establishing claims and/or arguments, with the ultimate aim of promoting Islam as a political program or code of conduct, on the various manifestations of power, both at the levels of state and society, starting the Second World War onwards. But several basic assumptions were central to my work. These could be summarized as follows: one, in the intellectual's public sphere, there is a meta-language that comprises key CIPT debates and the use of Islamic heritage towards making claims on Islam and the larger Islamicate. Two, self-imposing themes are strongly moulded through struggles and domination taking place inside and/or outside the public sphere. Three, intellectuals are restrained, at varying degrees, through these, but an intellectual often addresses CIPT themes through their respective claims to *true discourse.*

For any intellectual claiming to contribute to CIPT, there are two key elements which constitute power of the Islamic meta-language:

One is the four major themes: State in Islam, Shari'a application, Violence as Jihad and Identity. An intellectual claiming to be *Islamic* inevitably addresses most, if not all, of these themes in his/her writings. Within each of these themes there are debates, or sub-themes, defining what elements are most relevant, but centrality of particular sub-themes changed over time. For instance, today, the question of the caliphate is not invoked as a possible alternative for political rule, rather as part of Islamic history. The same is true for Islamic conquests, which were commonly employed as a manifestation of the flourishing civilization in the past. Nowadays, it is used as part of a larger conceptualization and counter-conceptualization on Islam's relation to violence. Likewise, Muslim/non-Muslim relations, which were grasped through the lens of juridical terms of 'Ahl al-Dhimma and Jiziya, are currently presented differently, with notions of citizenship and equality taking over much of the discussions.

The second is the use of Islamic heritage in constructing claims and/or arguments. The heritage is mainly composed of Qur'an, Sunna, Islamic history, and philosophical and juridical contributions to Islam. Navigating through tens of CIPT publications, the key line of demarcation between its mainstream and tajdīd intellectuals is the differing positions towards the heritage. But the latter, as we know it today, underwent modifications, largely shaped by real politics. This fact partly explains the duality where mainstream intellectuals claim what the religious truth entails and their tajdīd counterparts challenge them on the same truth.

Yet, as expected, using the heritage in making claims and arguments led to a considerable common ground between both camps on several CIPT sub-themes. As much as mainstream/tajdīd intellectuals diverge on particular aspects, like the notion of the Islamic state or the application of ḥudūd, they do converge on futūḥāt. It is considered glorious in its assumed fairness to the conquered, even if the Islamic basis of these conquests is disputed. They also converge on resenting sporadic violence but not the use of violence in struggle against occupation. This is also the case for identity; though presented within various dualities of inter-/intra-identities, mainstream/tajdīd intellectuals do not disagree regarding the centrality of Islamic identity and its coexistence with other forms of identity.

Moreover, Said's Orientalism reflected through several elements of CIPT themes across the mainstream/tajdīd duality. It was strongly evident through the Democracy/Shura juxtaposition under discussions on the State in Islam and the Shari'a application debates, after colonization brought Western institutional settings to Muslim lands. It was also traceable in another juxtaposition between Shari'a and positive law. Nonetheless, tajdīd intellectuals challenge large segments of Islamic heritage, especially the significant attention paid, and commitment, to the four Sunni schools of jurisprudence by their mainstream counterparts. They use particular aspects of the heritage, such as early Islamic history and Qur'an, in establishing their claims on one hand and stress the impact of, and give more weight to, the role of real politics on the body of the heritage as it developed throughout Islamic history on the other. Their highlight of real politics is usually aimed at excluding, or at least marginalizing, some elements of this heritage, which are normally acknowledged and endorsed by their mainstream counterparts.

Both al-Banna and al-Bishri spent most of their lives in Egypt and were, thus, also preoccupied with political debates in the Egyptian public sphere. In this respect, chances of escaping the authority of ruling regimes over their writings were not significant. This could be safely attributed to the punitive power possessed and exercised by autocratic ruling regimes. Under Egypt's successive regimes, discussions in the public sphere were kept within regime-defined contours. This control was motivated by the fear of deliberation, persuasion and potential mobilization that might jeopardize the dominant position of the ruling regime in the political sphere. Towards attaining control, particular red lines were made public through cases of direct harassment of prominent intellectuals/journalists/novelists, which the respective regimes wanted out of discussion.

All three regimes of Nasser, Sadat and Mubarak sought to delineate contours and jeopardize the moral/physical integrity of those involved in the country's public sphere in very similar ways. Although the structures and measures employed by the three regimes in setting red lines were quite similar, red lines were maintained within a duality of must/may penalize under Mubarak. Government corruption was not necessarily reason for harassment, while those criticizing Mubarak in person, his family finances and Jamal's succession were inevitably harassed. Under Mubarak, al-Banna and al-Bishri were faced with more avenues for expression, with private media and internet proliferating. However, content on these outlets was still controlled by the regime through the use of laws and arrests. Because the two intellectuals mainly presented their work in the form of books, they were less susceptible to the common harassment practiced against press and new media. Accordingly, the medium used to disseminate information/views, not just the content of the latter, was a decisive element towards regime harassment.

In spite of al-Banna being persecuted shortly after the 1952 coup, for using the word Coup to refer to the military intervention ousting King Faruq, and al-Bishri colliding with Mubarak on the judicial 1992 State Council incident, both intellectuals succeeded in maintaining their inclusion in the public sphere. Other public figures, such as Hilmi Sallam or Ihsan ʿAbd al-Qudus, were decidedly excluded by ruling regime/s. Red lines revolved, inter alia, around direct critique of the head of the state: the president. Through critique of ex-regimes, brief accounts and/or generalized statements, the two intellectuals could achieve a balance between addressing *tense topics* and avoiding direct harassment.

However, more than once, their writings indirectly promoted dominance of the ruling regime. For instance, when al-Banna criticized capitalism and advocated socialism, which was the guiding ideology of Nasser's socio-economic revisions, he indirectly served propaganda to the regime. Likewise, al-Bishri – before his ideological shift into an Islamic intellectual – in his depiction of the Muslim Brotherhood as a group confiscating religion and labelling their secret apparatus a *terrorist organization*, promoted the regime's dominant position vis-à-vis one of its strongest political rivals. The same occurred with al-Banna's account on pluripartidism in the late 1970s as not contradicting Islam, at a time when Sadat decided to open up the political sphere and enacted a law in 1977 which was the basis of the establishment of political parties. Additionally, in his writings on Nasser's oppressive measures against parliamentary opposition, he further fortified the legitimacy of the Sadat regime, which sought to break away from the legacy of his predecessor.

Nonetheless, several instances in their intellectual production exhibited an element of *silence*, where particular ideas were deliberately not presented at all or presented briefly or at a later point in time, probably at the anticipation of potential persecution. This was the case, under Mubarak, with al-Banna's Islamic renewal profile and al-Bishri's account on judicial autonomy in Egypt without mentioning his own personal experience in that regard and their strong tendency to present ex-regime critique.

A turning point in Egyptian modern history was at the 2011 uprising, with major reshuffling in the country's political sphere. Yet, political oppression and economic hardships persisted and, thus, the themes for contesting *the regime* stayed largely the same. Al-Banna's first book after the uprising embodied the alteration in the political sphere, mainly through addressing the revolutionaries and in overtly defaming the Mubarak regime. Likewise, al-Bishri's book on the Coptic Church, published after the uprising, comprised a stronger tone of critique to the church and its pope as compared to his two prior accounts on Copts published under Mubarak. His book about the 2011 uprising, published in 2012, also embodied the regime alteration, as it included overt and strong critique to the Mubarak regime.

Before and after the 2011 uprising, challenging mainstream conceptions of Islam in Egypt was commonly associated with moral exclusion. In this respect, exclusion depended on other variables, like regime secular orientation and/or the punitive power enjoyed by the religious formal institution, al-Azhar, which played an evident role in regulating the religious truth. But al-Azhar, which confiscated two of al-Banna's books under Mubarak, could neither entirely exclude him from contributing to CIPT debates nor strip him of his character as an intellectual in the Egyptian public sphere. Al-Azhar's monitoring of the religious truth had to do, at least partly, with the three regimes seeking to maintain its cooperation, as they needed, and relied on, religious clergy to promote their dominant position. This feature translated into the public sphere being controlled and monitored by both successive ruling regimes and al-Azhar, which co-defined its contours.

Aside from the different controls exercised over their public sphere, their Islamic and political profiles intersected more than once. For al-Banna, this was traceable in his account on Islam as central to the Egyptian masses, particularly when he addressed the role of Islamic sentiments in the wars of 1967 and 1973. His account on military rule addressed this issue as both part of Egyptian politics, which related directly to the theme of the military in civilian politics on one hand and as one dimension of the concern about forms of rule in Islam on the other.

Al-Bishri also exhibited similar intersections. In his account on Copts, which was largely preoccupied with the claims of Egypt's largest religious minority, he addressed the questions of Shariʿa application and identity in Islam. This was also the case with his account on the role of civil society regarding mobilization for Jihad and the moral power emanating from Islam in this regard. It was also clear when he made claims on the criteria for the legitimate use of violence, where he used examples from colonial history of Muslim lands and contemporary history of Egypt.

They both boosted their character as Islamic intellectuals in different ways. Al-Banna did through his outspoken admiration and preference to Islam, positing it as better than ideologies of capitalism and socialism. He generally conformed to the common position of CIPT intellectuals on Islam as *better*.

Plus, he reacted to the Islamic meta-language, both through his addressing of all the four key CIPT themes, as well as his frequent invoking of the heritage towards establishing his claims. This is especially true regarding the most binding of all elements, Qur'an, and the most highly-regarded aspect of Islamic history, the golden age of the Prophet and his companions. Al-Bishri boosted his Islamic character not just through invoking the heritage in establishing his claims and reacting to CIPT key themes but also through his overtly positive appraisal of Shari'a when he asserted its unifying role to Arab and non-Arab Muslim minorities, his emphasis of the rootedness of Shari'a in Muslim societies and employing this rootedness to give preference to Shari'a when juxtaposed with positive law.

The renewal scheme of al-Banna is easily traced in his stance on Shari'a, where he argued that ḥudūd application depended on 'Illa and a comparison of the historical practices to today's world. On this, he used the heritage towards offering his *new* interpretation. 'Illa is an established juridical term used in Qur'anic hermeneutics, and the practice of ḥudūd application in Islamic history is well documented. It is known, and acknowledged, as part of the consented body of Sunni heritage. The deviance comes from his use of 'Illa as determinant of definitive text and his position on the ḥudūd application practice in history as part of a non-replicable golden age, making the conclusion that ḥudūd might be suspended if 'Illa changed.

Moreover, he filtered the Hadith tradition according to consistency with Qur'an. He based this on the acknowledged historical fact of Hadith being collected long after death of the Prophet and that it was a source of social prestige back then to present Hadith collections. This way, he attempted a *sorting out* of the heritage, in its Hadith element. Similarly, on the Islamic state, he used history. The fact that authoritarian rule prevailed for long centuries in Islamic history, to him, translated into an overt emphasis on obedience in jurisprudence. Thus, he adopted the tajdīd stance to highlight the role of real politics in the construction of the body of Islamic heritage, consented today, towards establishing his renewal stances.

In fact, al-Banna's intellectual production signified tajdīd intellectuals' tendency to take note of the hierarchy among elements comprised in this heritage, as some elements evidently enjoy larger weight than others and this is why he heavily employed these towards presenting his new interpretations. But the main strategy he employed towards establishing his tajdīd profile can be summarized in sorting out the heritage through asserting contexts affected its content, especially the body of Hadith and the jurisprudence.

As a mainstream intellectual, al-Bishri didn't seek to sort out this heritage in the way tajdīd intellectuals do. Yet, the discrepancy between al-Banna and al-Bishri's use of the heritage is remarkable and reflects their different positions on CIPT. Whereas al-Banna extensively used Qur'anic verses and early history of Islam, especially when he contested mainstream stances, al-Bishri rarely used Qur'anic verses and his accounts were not overwhelmingly occupied with early Islamic history. This is especially true when his writings are compared to those of al-Banna. His books on political movements in pre-republican Egypt, first published in 1972; his large account on Egypt's Copts, first published in 1980; or his book on Egypt's judicial independence published in 2006 were not even presented from an Islamic perspective. While he referred to the text, especially Qur'an and Hadith, much less frequently than al-Banna, his character as an Islamic intellectual is not contested in Egypt or the larger Muslim world. This signifies the little relevance of writing style compared to ultimate positions on CIPT themes and the heritage in the practice of classifying Islamic intellectuals along the mainstream/tajdīd duality in Muslim societies.

Still, when juxtaposing their intellectual production, their respective thematic foci partly elucidate their emphasis on particular elements of the heritage. For instance, al-Banna's concern for ideals of freedom and justice were better suited to his reference to the golden age of Islam, as compared with subsequent periods of Islamic history. Likewise, al-Bishri's strong interest in the colonial history of Muslim lands made it suitable for him to frequently discuss modern Islamic history.

In a capsule, on the four key CIPT themes, al-Banna shifted from claiming there is a state in Islam to rejecting this state, argued Shari'a application should be defined through 'Illa, strongly defended the use of violence against occupation and denounced using sporadic violence against civilians. To him, identities coexist and nationalism shouldn't reach the level of chauvinism. Al-Bishri maintained Islam has a role at the level of the state but didn't argue for a particular form of rule, Shari'a is deeply rooted in Muslim societies and could be applied, violence against occupation is justifiable and repression offers the fertile soil for violence to thrive. To him, identities overlap and they are not a matter of choice, but national identity should take precedence in case of conflict.

Nonetheless, both share some significant common ground, such as the assertion that Shura is stipulated in Islam, in their appraisal of democratic rule, their tendency to find analogies or relevance between Shura and democracy, their rejection of authoritarian practices, and their praise of the plurality of the jurisprudential community once prevalent in Islamic history. Similarly, al-Banna praised the divine law as free from human subjectivity, and al-Bishri praised the rootedness of Shariʿa among Muslims as a code of conduct and manners. On Jihad and violence, their accounts are almost identical. To them, violence against civilians is not acceptable, while violence towards liberation may be allowed. Even regarding the effectiveness of the use of violence, which has nothing to do with their Islamic profile, both converged on that resorting to violent acts is determined through other factors. To al-Banna, it was through the prospect of change using violence, and to al-Bishri, it was through the availability of non-violent means of reclaiming violated rights. The same with identity, both regard themselves as belonging to multiple identity circles: Muslim, Arab and Egyptian. They emphasized their identity as Egyptians and highlighted the role of Islam in moral mobilization and the inclusive nature of identity circles.

Plus, their writings converged on Orientalism in more than one occasion. Al-Banna linked the West to colonization but still praised democracy and syndicalism in Europe. Al-Bishri depicted the West as the colonizer which imposed institutional settings and positioned the cleavage between the Arab and the Islamic as pertaining to the secular, but praised the impersonal administrative practices and the logic of different trial levels coming from the West.

Meanwhile, they clearly diverged on the Islamic state and ḥudūd application. Plus, in his critique of democracy, al-Banna argued that it could be easily manipulated by the powerful and the rich, while al-Bishri criticized its dependence on equilibrium among different actors, an equilibrium which is vital to the functioning of democracy. They also diverged in their assessment of individual rule. Al-Banna openly criticized individual rule and linked it to despotism, while al-Bishri maintained individual rule – while representing a risk to infringe on rights and freedoms – is not necessarily despotic.

To sum up, Islamic intellectuals don't exist in vacuum, they live in contexts that shape their writings in various manners. Often, they have to deal with authorities that set red lines on what could, and couldn't, be discussed. They also need to address particular themes that *self-impose* on those engaged in the public sphere. Yet, an intellectual who claims to be Islamic has to promote this character through accounts on Islam and its heritage. Those who claim tajdīd usually offer new interpretations and challenge the consented body of knowledge, advocated by their mainstream counterparts; it is basically a contestation of accounts on the religious truth. Al-Banna and al-Bishri, through their many writings, embodied all these intricacies, and an adequate reading of their intellectual production was only made possible through their various contexts.

Notes

Introduction

1 See al-Ashmawy, Muhammad Saiid (1987), *L'Islamisme Contre l'Islame* (Islamism Against Islam), Cairo: Edition al-Fikr, where he maintained there was no state in Islam.

2 An Egyptian professor of Philosophy, who faced societal criticism and legal charges in the 1990s because of his publications on Islam and tajdīd. One of his key ideas in this regard is that heritage was strongly shaped by its context; thus, cannot be taken as binding rules and should be dealt with accordingly. For his whole thesis on tajdīd, see his book, *al-Turāth wa-l-Tajdīd* (Heritage and Renewal), Arab Centre for Publications and Research, 1980.

3 Abu Zaid faced legal charges of apostasy based on a new reading of the Qur'anic text he suggested in one of his tenure papers. For a good account on Abu Zaid and his charges, see: Al-Azm, Sadik Jalal (1981), 'Orientalism and Orientalism in Reverse', reprinted in *Orientalism: A Reader*, A. L. Macfie (ed.), Edinburgh: Edinburgh University Press, 4; and al-ʻAwwā, Muḥammad Salīm (2003), *al-Ḥaq fī-l-Taʻbīr* (Freedom of Expression), 2nd edn, Cairo, Dar El Shorouk.

4 With 'not-mainstream', here I imply their assumed deviation from commonly circulated conceptions on Islam and its heritage. It is not, by any means, an attempt to either promote or belittle these contributions as irrelevant. Examples for such writings are al-Banna's stance on the veil, see al-Bannā, Jamāl (2002), *al-Ḥijāb* (The Veil), Cairo: Dar al-Fikr al-Islami; al-ʻAshmawy's stance on the Islamic state; see: al-Ashmawy, Muhammad Saiid (1987), *L'Islamisme Contre l'Islame.*

5 Tariq al-Bishri, one of the two intellectuals studied, published a book titled (2008), *Naḥw Ṭaiyyār 'Asāsī li-l-'Umma* (Towards a Main Stream of the Nation), 1st edn, al-Jazīra papers (no. 8), al-Jazīra Center for Studies (available online at https://studies.aljazeera.net/ar/ebooks/book-1152), in which he discussed a key or mainstream of the nation, but it was, among other things, about national consciousness catalyzed by a unified cause. It's different from what I propose here to distinguish mainstream and not-mainstream contributions to CIPT.

6 Mostly, the term legitimacy pertains to the justification of the political regime ruling in a community of human beings. Legitimacy enhances the stability of political rule. So, when it is missing, coercion is usually employed as an alternative. For more on the term, see Fuchs, Dieter (2007), 'Legitimität' (Legitimacy), in Dieter Fuchs

and Edeltraud Roller (eds), *Lexikon Politik: Hunderte Grundbegriffe* (Lexicon of Politics: Hundreds of Basic Terms), Stuttgart: Phillip Reclam jun., 158–61.

7 The term 'Realpolitik' originally comes from German and connotes 'politics of the real'. The term first appeared in 1853, as a critique of the liberal policies of German politicians not reflecting realism. Realism is based on the distinction between the actual and the 'should be' or the supposed, basing conception and action in the political sphere on the concept of power and the drive to self-preservation: Scruton, Roger (2007), *The Palgrave Macmillan Dictionary of Political Thought*, 3rd edn, New York: Palgrave Macmillan, 582. Its underlying rationale is utilitarian politics, maximizing benefits and minimizing costs in making decisions, Camus, Albert (2012), 'Realismus' (Realism), in Werner Pfennig (ed.), *Definitionen Moderne Politikwissenschaft: Die Sammlung Pfennig* (Definitions of Modern Political Science: the Pfennig Collections, Shwalbach: Wochen Schau Verlag, 162–3.

8 His writings on Islam also reflected his focus on Marxism, long after he stopped being a socialist thinker. See for instance, al-Bannā, Jamāl (1984), *Wūjūh al-'I'itilāf wa-l-'Ikhtilāf Baiyn al-Ra'smāliyya wa-l-Shiyū'iyya wa-l-'Islām* (Aspects of Similarity and Difference between Capitalism, Socialism and Islam), Cairo: Dār al-Fikr al-'Islāmī; al-Bannā, Jamāl (2003), *Mawqifunā Min al-'Almāniyya, al-Qawmiyya, al-'Ishtrākiyya* (Our Position towards Secularism, Nationalism, Socialism), Cairo: Dar al-Fikr al-Islami.

9 His concern and devotion to the labour force continued long after he held that position. See, for instance, al-Bannā, Jamāl (1989), *al-Ḥurriyya al-Niqābiyya* (Syndical Freedom), in three parts, Cairo: Dar al-Fikr al-Islami; al-Bannā, Jamāl (1995), *al-Niqābāt al-Mihaniyya al-Miṣriyya fī Ma'rakat al-Baqāa'* (Professional Syndicates in Egypt in the Survival Battle), Cairo: Dar al-Fikr al-Islami.

10 He published a book of his sister's diaries as a sign of gratitude to her support for his project. See al-Bannā, Jamāl (commentator) (2009a), *Dhikraiyāt Fawziyya al-Bannā bī-Qalamihā* (Memoirs of Fawziyya al-Banna with Her Pen), Cairo: Dar al-Fikr al-Islami.

11 He had a clear secularist orientation in the 1960s, but gradually shifted away from it in the seventies. He publicly became an Islamic intellectual in 1983. Still, he admired Islamic jurisprudence long before he underwent this shift. For more, see al-Bishrī, Ṭāriq (2014), *Thawrat 25 Yanāyir wa-l-Ṣirā' ḥawl al-Sulṭa* (The 25th of January Revolution and the Struggle for Authority), Cairo: Dar El Bashir, 68.

12 See Ghuraiyyba, 'Ibrāhīm (2008), 'al-'Amal al-'Islāmī wa Fiqh al-Marḥala' (Islamic Work and the Phase Jurisprudence), *al-Ghad Newspaper*, 22 November, http://www.alghad.jo/?news=7930.

13 Mainstream Islam will be addressed in Chapter 1 and al-Bishri's mainstream positions will be discussed in Chapter 4, tackling his intellectual production at length.

14 Kifaya will be addressed in Chapter 2, as part of the mobilization facing the Mubarak regime. For a good account on the movement, its composition and activism, see Ezzeldeen, Nahed (2010), 'Protest Movements in Egypt: The Case of Kefaya', in Dimitar Bechev and Isabel Schäfer (eds), *Agents of Change in the Mediterranean*, Ramses2, Working paper 14/10, May, 29–42, https://t.ly/YmbE.

15 See for instance, Justice al-Bishri, Tariq (2012), 'Charter Writing Constituent Assembly Balanced', *Ikhwan Web*, Muslim Brotherhood's official English Website, 28 March, http://www.ikhwanweb.com/article.php?id=29820.

16 The Law 46/1972 and executive controls over the office of public prosecution diminish judicial autonomy in Egypt. For this, see Said, Mohamed Sayed (2008), 'A Political Analysis of the Egyptian Judges' Revolt', in Nathalie Bernard-Maugiron (ed.), *Judges and Political Reform in Egypt*, Cairo: American University in Cairo Press, 21–3. More generally, autocratic regimes could strongly subordinate the judiciary through employing specific strategies, like using incentives to facilitate co-opting judges, planning fragmented judiciaries and so on. For this, see Moustafa, Tamir, and Tom Ginsburg (eds) (2008), 'The Functions of Courts in Authoritarian Politics', in *Rule by Law: The Politics of Courts in Authoritarian Regimes*, New York: Cambridge University Press, 14.

17 On the MB status in Egypt, see Brown, Nathan J., and Amr Hamzawy (2010), *Between Religion and Politics*, Washington, DC: Carnegie Endowment for International Peace; Ben Jelloun, Tahar (2011), *Arabischer Frühling: Vom Wiedererlangen der Arabischen Würde* (Arab Spring: From Restoring Arab Dignity), Bonn: Bundeszentrale für Politische Bildung.

18 For the history of Hermeneutics, see Dilthey, W. (1996), *Hermeneutics and the Study of History*, Princeton, NJ: Princeton University Press.

1 Contemporary Islamic political thought

1 Enayat attempted offering such a definition, but his contribution was quite general, see (Enayat) 'Ināyit, Ḥāmid (1984), *al-Fikr as-Siyāsī al-'Islāmī al-Mu'āṣir* (Contemporary Islamic Political Thought) trans. 'Ibrāhīm al-Disūkī Shitā, Cairo: Madbouly Library.

2 Although Hasan al-Banna was mainly an Islamic figure, not an intellectual, he attempted intellectual contributions through his messages (*Rasā'il*). See for instance, Krämer, Gudrun (2010), *Hassan al-Banna*, Oxford: One World.

3 This is the general trend of the aforementioned studies, except for 'Imara's study on 'Abd al-Raziq, which was mainly focused on the incident of stripping the latter from his jurisprudential Azhar position. See: 'Imāra, Muḥammad (1972), *al-'Islām wa*

'Uṣūl al-Ḥukm li-'Alī 'Abd al-Rāziq (Islam and Origins of Rule of 'Ali 'Abd al-Raziq), Beirut: Arabic Institute for Studies and Publication.

4 Mainstream intellectuals differentiate between turāth al-Waḥi (Revelation), the Qur'an, complimented by Sunna, which should be left intact, pure and authentic, and turāth, which involves human contribution regarding explanation/ interpretation of the revelation. See Farrūkh,'Umar (1986), *Tajdīd fī-l-Muslimīn, lā fī-l-'Islām*, Beirut: Dar al-Kitāb al-'Arabī, 15.

5 See on Islamic history, Hūwaidī, Fahmī (1987), *Taziyīf al-Wa'ī* (Forging the Conscience), Cairo: Dar El Shorouq, 49.

6 'Ilm al-Kalam developed as a science, in part, to defend Islamic beliefs. On Islamic Theology, see Masud, Muhammad Khalid (2009), 'Islamic Modernism', in Muhammad Khalid Masud, Armando Salvatore and Martin Van Bruinessen (eds), *Islam and Modernity: Key Debates and Issues*, Edinburgh: Edinburgh University Press, 238–9.

7 For a larger account on these groups, see al-'Abiīrī, al-Sayyid (2007), *al-Firaq al-'Islāmiyya Baiyn al-Qadīm wa-l-Ḥadīth* (Islamic Groups between the Old and the Modern), Cairo: Dār al-Ḥadīth, 97–101.

8 For the importance of 'Ijmā' as an Islamic term and its application in the history of Islam, see 'Iqbāl, Muḥammad (2010), *Tajdīd al-Fikr al-Dīnī fī-l-'Islām* (Renewing Religious Thought in Islam), trans. 'Abbās Maḥmūd, Cairo: al-Haiy'a al-Miṣriyya al-'Āmma lī-l-Kitāb, 38.

9 For 'Ijmā' to be binding, there are two conditions: One, there is no physical or moral pressure exercised on the scholar towards reaching it. Two, it should be based on definitive evidence (Dalīl Qaṭ'ī). For this view, see Faḍl 'Allāh, Mahdī (1995), *al-'Aql wa-l-Sharī'a: Mabāḥith fī-l-'Ipistomoljiyya al-'Arabiyya al-'Islāmiyya* (Intellect and Shari'a: Research in Arab and Islamic Epistemology), Beirut: Dār al-Ṭalī'a, 19.

10 For the debate on 'Ijmā' and its binding force, see: al-'Āṣī, al-Sayyid Aḥmad 'Abd al-Maqṣūd (2009), *'Aqīdat al-'Ikhwān al-Muslimīn fī Mizān al-Kitāb wa-l-Sunna min Khilāl Mu'assisihā* (Creed of the Muslim Brotherhood on the Scale on the Holy Qur'an and Sunna, through its Founder), al-Mansoura: Dar al-Wafaa, 97–8.

11 Under the Ottomans, religious jurists were part of the political elite. For this, see Krämer, Gudrun (2013), *Geschichte des Islam* (History of Islam), 3rd edn, München: Deutscher Taschenbuch Verlag, 209.

12 This is also the Gramscian concept of the religious institution as promoter of the state hegemony. See for this: Gramsci, Antonio (1986), *Zu Politik, Geschichte und Kultur: ausgewählte Schriften* (On Politics, History and Culture: Selected Writings), Leipzig: Philipp Recalm jun Press, 222–6.

13 The term turāth had been frequently addressed in Arab writings on Arab/Islamic discourse. See, for instance, Sīdā, 'Abd al-Bāsiṭ (1990), *al-Wad'iyya al-Manṭiqiyya wa-l-Turāth al-'Arabī* (Logical Positivism and The Arab Heritage), Beirut: Dār al-Farābī; and Ṣāliḥ, Farḥān (1983), *Jadaliyyat al-'Ilāqa Baiyn al-Fikr al-'Arabī*

wa-l-Turāth (The Dialectic of the Relation between Arabic Thought and the Heritage), Beirut: Dār al-Ḥadātha.

14 There is a whole parallel jurisprudence concerning transactions, like sales, purchase trades and the like in the Shiite community, under the school of Ja'farism. For this, see al-Ṣādiq, Ja'far (2012), *Islamic Law: According to Ja'fari School of Jurisprudence: Transactions*, vol. 2 (Oakland, CA: CreateSpace Independent Publishing Platform.

15 Contemporary linguistically refers to 'the present' or 'a person living at the same time or of the same age as another'. For this definition, see *Longman Active Study Dictionary of English* (2010), 5th revised edn, London: Pearson Longman, 132.

16 This was mainly achieved through the interviews.

17 Examples of writings of pure juridical nature include: Attia, Jamal El-Din (2008), *Towards a Realization of the Higher Intents of Islamic Law: Maqasid al-Shari'ah, a Functional Approach*, London: Cromwell Press; and al-Zuḥīlī, Wahbā (2006), *Qaḍāiyā al-Fiqh wa-l-Fikr al-Mu'āṣir* (Issues of Jurisprudence and Contemporary Thought), Damascus: Dār al-Fikr.

18 Compare for instance: al-Qaraḍāwī, Yūsuf (1985), *Sharī'at al-'Islām: Ṣāliḥa li-l-Taṭbīq fī Kul Zamān wa Makān* (Islam's Shari'a: Applicable in Every Time and Place), Cairo: Dār al-Ṣaḥwa for Publications and 'Abū Zaid, Naṣr Ḥāmid (1995), *Al-Tafkīr fī Zaman al-Takfīr: Ḍid al-Jahl wa-l-Zaiyf wa-l-Khurāfa* (Thinking in the Age of Excommunication: Against Ignorance, Falsification and Superstition), Cairo: Madbouly Library.

19 The term is used to connote countries with a majority population of Muslims. This is compared to other terms, like Dār al-'Islām, where the majority of the population are not necessarily Muslims but it is where Muslims rule. See for that view al-Jubailī, Zainab al-Ghazālī (2000), *Naḥw Ba'th Jadīd* (Towards a New Revival), Cairo: Dar at-Tawzi' wa-l-Nashr al-Islamiyya, 100–1. The opposite term is Dār al-Ḥarb, which is either the land where Muslims do not rule and do not have a treaty committing this land not to attack Muslims, or the land which is adjacent to Dār al-'Islām, but where Muslims do not rule; and both Muslims and non-Muslims do not enjoy the safety and security they enjoyed in early Islamic history. For this, see al-Shihābī, 'Ibrāhīm Yiḥiyā (1992), *Mafhūm al-Ḥarb wa-l-Salām fī-l-'Islām: Ṣirā'āt wa Ḥurūb..'am Tafā'ul wa Salām?* (The Concept of War and Peace in Islam: Struggles and Wars or Interaction and Peace?), Libya: Tripoli, Kulliyyat al-Da'wa al-'Islāmiyya, 128.

20 See: Weisman, Steven R. (1991), 'Japanese Translator of Rushdie Book Found Slain', *New York Times*, 13 July, http://www.nytimes.com/books/99/04/18/specials/rushdie-translator.html.

21 The themes of the Islamic meta-language identified in this chapter were also traced more in the writings of contemporary intellectuals, like Muhammad Salim

al-'Awwa, Muhammad Imara, Muhammad 'Abid al-Jabri and the like. Many sources used in writing this chapter are examples of the focus on these major themes.

22 'Abd al-Raziq was regarded as a figure like Taha Husein and al-'Aqqad, who called for adapting the heritage to the requirements of the modern civilization, and were ready to sacrifice, in different degrees, the content of clear religious text (Ẓāhir al-Naṣ). See 'Amīn, Jalāl (1989), *Naḥw Tafsīr Jadīd li-'Azmat al-'Iqtiṣād wa-l-Mujtama' fī Miṣr* (Towards a New Interpretation of the Crisis of the Economy and Society in Egypt), Cairo: Madbouly Library, 143.

23 For a detailed account on theocracies and the history of the term, see McLean, Iain (ed.) (1996), *Oxford Concise Dictionary of Politics*, Oxford: Oxford University Press, 495.

24 Generally, this rapidity is associated with globalization and not only to media. Globalization produces various effects in several fields. See, for instance, Plattner, Marc F. (2002), 'Globalization and Self-Government', *Journal of Democracy*, Vol. 13, No. 3, 54–67; Duschinsky, Michael Pinto (2002), 'Financial Politics: A Global View', *Journal of Democracy*, Vol. 13, No. 4, 69, 86.

25 A good example for this trend is al-Banna speaking to the media about the confiscation of one of his books on women in Islam; for the newspaper interview on the matter, see: 'Abd al-Ḥalīm, Hishām (2008), 'al-Mufakkir al-'Islāmī Jamal al-Bannā...' (The Islamic Thinker Jamal al-Banna...), *al-Maṣrī al-Yūm*, 14 June, http://today.almasryalyoum.com/article2.aspx?ArticleID=109171.

26 Nonetheless, there is also a belief that media contributed to generalizations and making general judgements. See, for that point, al-Juhainī, Aḥmad, and Muḥammad Muṣṭafā (2005), *al-'Islām wa-l-'Ākhar* (Islam and the Other), Cairo: al-Haiyaa al-Misriyya al-'Amma li-l-Kitab, 33.

27 Shura is generally seen as not binding to the ruler. Nonetheless, there are few authors who maintain that shura is binding. See, for instance, al-Fanjarī, 'Aḥmad Shawqī (2010), *Kaiyfa Naḥkum bī-l-'Islām fī Dawla 'Aṣriyya* (How Can we Rule by Islam in a Modern State), Cairo: al-Haiy'a al-Miṣrriyya al-'Āmma li-l-Kitāb, 192–205.

28 Sūrat 'Āl 'Imrān, verse 159; Sūrat al-Shūrā, verse 38.

29 For a fair account on the concept of Maṣlaḥa in classical and contemporary Islamic discourse, see Opwis, Felicitas (2007), 'Islamic Law and Legal Change in Classical and Contemporary Islamic Theory', in Abbas Ammanat and Frank Griffel (eds), *Shari'a: Islamic Law in the Contemporary Context*, 121–57, Stanford, CA: Stanford University Press.

30 Mu'āmalāt include dealings pertaining to money, property, contracts, selling, buying, usury, donations, insolvency and so on. for this, see al-Fiqī, Muḥammad 'Alī 'Uthmān (1986), *Fiqh al-Mu'āmalāt: Dirāsa Muqārana* (Mu'amalat Jurisprudence: A Comparative Study), Riyad: Dār al-Marrīkh.

31 For example: Sūrat al-Nisā', verses 60–5; Sūrat al-Nūr, verses 47–51.

32 The term is found in Qur'an, Sūrat al-Tawba, verse 60, as one of the categories receiving Zakāt in Islam.

33 The exact juridical term is *Maṣāliḥ Murrsala* or general interests, which, according to mainstream jurisprudence, can be used to establish shari'a rules, when no definitive text *Naṣ Qaṭ'ī* exists. See for this: Faḍl 'Allāh, Mahdī (1995), *al-'Aql wa-l-Sharī'a: Mabāḥith fī-l-'Ipistomoljiyya al-'Arabiyya al-'Islāmiyya*, Beirut: Dār al-Ṭalī'a, 82.

34 The golden age ended with Mu'awiya b. Abi Sufiyan, turning the state into a coercive body ruling 'over' society (al-Jābrī, 1990b, 107).

35 This logic of separating earthly dictations, power relations and human desires on one hand and religious rules on the other is not confined to the issue of violence. For instance, ending the caliphate by Mu'awiyya b. 'Abi Sufian was analysed along the lines of this separation. See, for instance, 'Idrīs, 'Aḥmad (2011), *al-Fikr al-Siyāsī fī-l-'Islām; Wījhat Naẓar 'Ukhrā* (Political Thought in Islam: Another Point of View), Cairo: al-Haiy'a al-Miṣriyya al-'Āmma li-l-Kitāb.

36 These are referred to as Dhimmis, and were generally treated better than other categories of non-Muslims. For more on the term, see Björkmann, W. (1933), 'Kāfir', in *Brill's First Encyclopedia of Islam 1913–1936*, Vol. 4, the Netherlands, Leiden: E. J. Brill, 618–20.

37 The inhabitants of Islamic colonies supposedly enjoyed better treatment than the citizens of Roman and Persian colonies. For details on that point, see al-Juhainī and Muṣṭafā (2005), *al-'Islām wa-l-'Ākhar* (Islam and the Other), 49–50.

38 Usually piety is set as the sole criterion for the believer in relation to his creator, for such a view, see 'Abd al-'Azīz, Jum'a 'Amīn (2003), *Qirā'a fī Rakā'iz al-Mashrū' al-Ḥaḍārī al-'Islāmī* (a Reading into the Pillars of the Islamic Civilizational Project), Cairo: Dar al-Da'wa, 133.

39 Many authors tend to relate these movements' opting for violence to state oppression, particularly to political torture. For this view, see Qaraḍāwī, Yūsuf (1997a), *Mustaqbal al-'Uṣūliyya al-'Islāmiyya* (Future of Islamic Fundamentalism), Cairo: Wahba library, 17–22. See also 'Abd al-'Azīz, Jum'a 'Amīn (2003), *Qirā'a fī Rakā'iz al-Mashrū' al-Ḥaḍārī al-'Islāmī* (A Reading into the Pillars of the Islamic Civilizational Project), Cairo: Dar al-Da'wa, 157.

40 For a brief history of how violence, as a means for change, started in the 1970s in Egypt, among Islamic movements, see Ḥusām Tammām (ed.) (2012), *'Abd al-Mun'im 'Abū al-Futūḥ*: *Shāhid 'Alā Tārīkh al-Ḥaraka al-'Islāmiyya fī Miṣr 1970-1984* ('Abd al-Mun'im 'Abū al-Futūḥ: a Witness on the History of the Islamic Movement in Egypt 1970-1984), 2nd edn, Cairo: Dar El Shorouk, 64–70.

41 For more on Islam turning into an integral component to the functioning of European societies, see Ḥamzāwī, 'Amr (2005), 'Tarābuṭāt 'al-Hawiyya wa-l-Dīn

fī 'Urūpā (Linkages of Identity and Religion in Europe)', in Nādia Musṭafā (ed.), *al-Hawiyya al-'Islāmiyya fī 'Ūrūbā..'Ishkāliyyāt al-'Indimāj* (Islamic Identity in Europe..the Problematics of Integration), Cairo: Program for Dialogue of Civilizations, 138.

42 Ḥisba was to be practiced by al-Muḥtasib, who had opinions regarding customs and traditions and would receive income from the state. For further details on Ḥisba, see al-Kīlānī, 'Abū Zaid (1987), *Ta'ṣīl wa Tanẓīm al-Sulṭa fī-l-Tashrī'āt al-Waḍ'iyya wa-l-Sharī'a al-'Islāmiyya* (Authenticating and Regulating of Authority in Positive Legislations and Islamic Shari'a), Jordan: Dār al-Bashīr, 185–7.

43 The historical struggle reflected in debates on the authenticity of Hadith-telling among Sunnis, Shiites and Kharijites, where each group tried to monopolize the Prophetic Hadith especially that Sunna regulated matters of politics and authority. For more details, see 'Arkūn, Muḥammad (1992), *al-Fikr al-'Islāmī: Naqd wa 'Ijtihād* (Islamic Thought: Critique and Ijtihad), trans. Hāshim Ṣāliḥ, Beirut: Dar al-Saqi, 101–2.

44 There is also Dār al-'Ahd (land of the treaty), where Dār al-'Islām, according to a treaty, is obliged to defend another community and Dār al-Ḥiyād (land of neutrality), where Muslims live and freely practice their religion, although the rule itself is not Islamic. For these terms, see al-Shihābī, 'Ibrāhīm Yiḥiyā (1992), *Mafhūm al-Ḥarb wa-l-Salām fī-l-'Islām: Ṣirā'āt wa Ḥurūb..'am Tafā'ul wa Salām?*, Libya: Tripoli, Kulliyyat al-Da'wa al-'Islāmiyya, 129.

45 One consideration is the fact that the definitive text prohibits non-Muslims from leading the Muslim nation, not the nation-state, which is ruled through institutions and not persons, or that the logic behind such a prohibition in the established juridical Sunni Schools was based on an assumption that the justice/fairness of non-Muslims cannot be verified. For this see the same references.

2 Egypt: Surviving autocratic regimes

1 The term 'coup' mostly refers to a violent ousting of a regime/government through the military or with its help. For this definition, see: Robertson, David (2002), *A Dictionary of Modern Politics*, 3rd edn, London: Europa Publications, 125.

2 Khurshid, 'I'timād (1988), *Shāhida 'alā 'Inḥirāfāt Ṣalāḥ Naṣr* (A Witness on Salah Nasr's Perversions), Cairo: 'Amūn Institution for Print and Publication.

3 The demonstrations broke out in Cairo and Alexandria in support of the worker's movement. Although the student movement erupted across the world in the 1960s, there is reason to believe that the 1967 military defeat played a role in giving ride to the student demonstrations. For this, see Dirlik, Arif (1998), 'The Third World in 1968', in Carole Fink, Philipp Gassert and Detlef Junker (eds) (1968), *The World*

Transformed, Cambridge: Cambridge University Press, 295–318. doi:10.1017/CBO9781139052658.

4 For a fairly good account on the Suez Canal Nationalization, see Varble, Derek (2003), *The 1956 Suez Crisis (Essential Histories)*, Oxford: Osprey Publishing.

5 The attack was triggered by al-Sanhuri's opposition to the Law on political isolation against pre-republican politicians in Egypt. There was frequent gossip that Nasser was behind these attacks. For a brief account on this incident, see al-Ruqaʿī, Salīm Naṣr (2013), Qānun al-ʿAzl al-Siyāsī lan Yuḥaqqiq al-Murād (The Law on Political Isolation Will Not Achieve the Goal), *al-Ḥiwār al-Mutamaddin* (the Civilized Dialogue), 10 April 2013, at: http://m.ahewar.org/s.asp?aid=353714&r=0&cid=179&u=&i=0&q=.

6 Linguistically, Waqf is prevention or impediment, there is no juristic consensus on what the term means though, but in Sunni discourse, it is generally taken to connote that the kind should be held after it turns into an endowment (Waqf), and its revenue is used for philanthropic purposes. For an account on this definition, see ʾImām, Muḥammad Kamāl al-Dīn (1996), *al-Waṣāiyā wa-l-ʾAWqāf fī-l-Fiqh al-ʾIslāmi*, Beirut: al-Muassasa al-Jaamiʿiyya li-l-Dirasat wa-l-Nashr wa-l-Tawziʿ, 170–2.

7 This was after an alleged attempt on Nasser's life. For a good account on his persecution of the MB, see Mitchell, Richard (1993), *The Society of the Muslim Brotherhood*, New York: Oxford University Press, 123–41.

8 Abaza worked back then in *al-Musawir* Magazine, issued by al-Hilal Press, where he wrote a sarcastic column, titled '*al-Jasusa al-Hasnaa*' (The Pretty Female Spy).

9 The indirect message al-Banna wanted to make through his book was clearest at the end of his book when he wrote that this book 'came at the right time'. See al-Bannā, Jamāl (1963), *al-Qaḍāʾ wa-l-Qānūn fī-l-Mujtamaʿ al-ʾIshtirākī* (Law and Judiciary in the Socialist Society), Cairo: author Copy rights.

10 Al-Bishri gave a detailed account on his writings in an interview with me in his house in greater Cairo on 8 January 2011, where he clarified several points, like possible duplications in publications, several editions, with alterations in the content as well as publications that are not easily found in bookstores that he offered help with finding or giving copies to me.

11 Although the first edition of this book was published in 1972, under Sadat, he mentioned in its introduction that he finished writing it in January 1970, under Nasser. The publication process was delayed for granting permissions to publish it. al-Bishrī, Ṭāriq (2002a), *al-Ḥaraka al-Siyāsiyya fī Miṣr 1945/1953* (The Political Movement in Egypt 1945/1953) (new), 2nd edn, Cairo: Dar El Shorouk.

12 For a good account on the move away from populist socialism towards Infitah policy, see Matzke, Torsten, "Das Ende des Post-Populismus: Soziale und Ökonomische Entwicklungstrends im "Arabischen Frühling"' (The End of

Post-Populism: Social and Economic Development Trends in the 'Arab Spring'), in Peter Pawelka et al. (2012), *Der Bürger im Staat: Proteste und Potentaten-Die Arabische Welt im Wandel* (The Citizen in the State: Protests and Potentates – The Arab World in Change), Baden-Württemberg: Landeszentrale für Politische Bildung, 56–63, at: https://www.buergerundstaat.de/1_2_12/proteste_potentaten.pdf.

13 The 1971 Constitution was amended more than once.

14 Plurality in political systems usually refers to the existence of several centres of power and authority rather than the state controlling every aspect of state and society. See Robertson, David (2002), *A Dictionary of Modern Politics*, 3rd edn, London: Europa Publications, 380.

15 The vast presidential prerogatives stipulated in the 1971 Constitution were an extension of the broad presidential powers, stipulated in the constitutions of 1956 and 1958 under Nasser.

16 Large-scale detention of political activists was not a practice initiated by Mubarak; it was widely used under Nasser against the MB. See for this, Zahid, Mohammed (2010), *The Muslim Brotherhood and Egypt's Succession Crisis: The Politics of Liberalization and Reform in the Middle East*, New York: I.B. Tauris, 79–80.

17 Article 167 of the 1971 Constitution of Egypt.

18 Article 171 of the 1971 Constitution of Egypt.

19 See 'Egypt: Margins of Repression, state Limits on Nongovernmental Organization Activism', *Human Rights Watch*, Vol. 17, No. 8(E), http://www.hrw.org/sites/default/files/reports/egypt0705.pdf.

20 For the evolution of non-state media and zoomed-in analysis on red lines in the public sphere under Mubarak, see: Hussein, Ebtisam (2018), 'Rationalizing Public Repression: Mubarak's Self-Toppling Regime', *Middle East Policy*, Vol. 25, No. 1, 124–35, https://doi.org/10.1111/mepo.12329.

21 After the 25 January revolution, 'Izz faced charges of using his position in the former dissolved NDP to make illegitimate gains of five billion Egyptian pounds. On this, see Awad, Marwa (2013), 'Egypt Steel Tycoon Gets 37 Years for Profiteering', *Reuters*, 6 March, https://www.reuters.com/article/uk-egypt-ezz-jail-idUKBRE9250RW20130306.

22 See for cases where journalists were persecuted, 'Egypt Attacks on the Press: 1999', *Community to Protect Journalists*, http://cpj.org/reports/1999/05/egyptattacks.php.

23 For instance, *al-Masry al-Yum* newspaper published several articles on government corruption under Mubarak and the newspaper was not closed. See for examples of these articles, Blaydes, Lisa (2011), *Elections and Distributive Politics in Mubarak's Egypt*, New York: Cambridge University Press, 210–11.

24 Starting the 2000s, al-Banna's involvement in newspaper article writing and media appearance was on the rise; still, the profile presented through both did not collide with the regime fixed red lines. TV appearances in particular were highly focused

on his 'liberal profile' and not on government critique. See Shehata, Dina (Principal Researcher) (2012), *Mapping Islamic Actors in Egypt*, Netherlands Flemish Institute in Cairo and al-Ahram Center for Political and Strategic Studies, 131.

25 Al-Qaradawi published a whole book on the issue of usury in Islam, maintaining bank interest contradicts Islamic Shari'a. See: al-Qaraḍāwī, Yūsuf (1994), *Fawā'id al-Bunūk Hiyya al-Ribā al-Ḥarām* (Bank Interests Are the Illicit Usury), Cairo: Dar al-Sahwa for Publications.

26 This point will become clear in tackling his intellectual production in Chapter 4.

27 Al-Azhar center for Islamic Research called for a ban on his book (*Rab Hadhā al-Zamān*) or God of this Age. See for this: Suleiman, Mustafa (2009), 'Egyptians Protest Award to Controversial Writer',' *al-Arabiyya News*, 13 July, http://www.alarabiya.net/articles/2009/07/13/78580.html.

28 Al-Banna published three main books: Al-Banna (2011), *al-Ta'bi'a al-Fikriyya li-l-Thawra wa Mā ba'd al-Thawra* (The Intellectual Mobilization for the Revolution and After the Revolution), Cairo: Dar al-Fikr al-Islami; Al-Banna (2012), *Lābud min Mujāwazat al-Salafiyya* (Salafism Must be Surpassed), Cairo: Dar al-Fikr al-Islami; Al-Banna (2012), *'Ilhāmāt Qur'āniyya* (Qur'anic Inspirations), Cairo: Dar al-Fikr al-Islami. Al-Bishri published more books, including: Al-Bishri (2011), *al-Dawla wa-l-Kanīsa* (The State and the Church), 1st edn, Cairo: Dar El Shorouk; Al-Bishri (2011), *al-Siyāq al-Tārikhī wa-l-Thaqāfī li-Taqnīn al-Sharī'a al-'Islāmiyya* (The Historical and Cultural Context of codifying Islamic Shari'a), 1st edn, Cairo: Shorouk International Bookshop; Al-Bishri (2012), *Sa'd Zaghlūl Yufāwiḍ al-'Isti'mār* (Sa'd Zaghlul Negotiates with Colonialism), 1st edn, Cairo: Dar El Shorouk; Al-Bishri (2012), *Min 'Awrāq Thawrat 25 Yanāyir* (From the 25th of January Revolution Papers), Cairo: Dar El Shorouk. See Bibliography for more on their publications after the 2011 uprising.

29 see 'Khaled Said, the Face which Launched a Revolution', *Ahram Online*, 6 June 2012, http://english.ahram.org.eg/NewsContent/1/0/43995/Egypt/0/Khaled-Said-The-face-that-launched-a-revolution.aspx.

30 See 'Egypt Has Failed to Meet January 25 Revolution Demands: Amnesty', *Ahram Online*,4 December 2013, http://english.ahram.org.eg/NewsContent/1/64/88281/Egypt/Politics-/Egypt-has-failed-to-meet-January--Revolution-deman.aspx.

31 For a good account on the founding and core principles of the party, see: 'The Free Egyptians', *Ahram Online*, 18 November 2011, https://english.ahram.org.eg/NewsContent/33/104/24944/Elections-/Political-Parties/The-Free-Egyptians.aspx.

32 See 'Egypt Draft Constitution Approved by Islamist-Dominated Assembly', *The Guardian*, 30 November 2012, http://www.theguardian.com/world/2012/nov/30/egypt-draft-constitution-islamist-assembly.

33 See 'Washington Tattahim Miṣr bi-l-Taḍiyyīq 'alā Ḥurriyyat al-Ta'bīr Ba'd al-Taḥqīq ma'a Bāsim Yūsuf' (Washington Accuses Egypt of Limiting Freedom of Expression

after Interrogating Basim Yusuf), *BBC Arabic*, 1 April 2013, http://www.bbc.co.uk/arabic/middleeast/2013/04/130401_us_freedom_bassem.shtml.

34 This book was first published in 1981. The 2004 edition used in this research is the fourth, updated, version.

35 For the Diaspora conditionality theme, see 'Minority at Risk: Coptic Christians in Egypt' (22 July 2011) Hearing before the Commission on Security and Cooperation in Europe, esp. pp. 20–9, Washington, DC: US Government Printing Office, https://www.csce.gov/international-impact/events/minority-risk-coptic-christians-egypt.

3 Jamal al-Banna on CIPT

1 The term dictator was originally associated with the Roman Empire. Although, today, the coercive nature of dictatorial rule cannot be disputed, it was first presented in Lenin's work, especially after the October Revolution of 1917. It was, at the latest, after 1933, used to describe the coercive rule of both fascist and national socialist regimes of Hitler and Mussolini. For more on the term, see Merkel, Wolfgang (2007), 'Diktatur' (Dictator), in Dieter Fuchs and Edeltraud Roller (eds), *Lexikon Politik: Hunderte Grundbegriffe* (Lexicon of Politics: Hundreds of Basic Terms), Stuttgart: Phillip Reclam jun., 47–9.

2 Despotism is a term referring to absolutist rule. In history, monarchies with no limitations on their powers were regarded as absolutist. It may also be viewed as an ancient form of authoritarianism. See for this, Bealey, Frank (1999), *The Blackwell Dictionary of Political Science: A User's Guide to its Terms*, Oxford: Blackwell, 1.

3 See also al-Bannā, Jamāl (1995), *al-Mashrūʿ al-Ḥaḍārī bi-Ṣarāḥa* (The Civilizational Project, Frankly), Cairo: Dar al-Fikr al-Islami, 19–20.

4 In addition to the forms listed here, he also mentioned fascist and single/party forms of rule as authoritarian regimes in an interview on his writings on 22 May 2011, conducted in his Cairo office.

5 See al-Bannā, Jamāl (1999), *al-'Islām wa Ḥurriyyat al-Fikr* (Islam and Freedom of Thought), Cairo: Dar al-Fikr al-Islami, see, particularly, 185–209.

6 The impossibility of exchanging justice for freedom was also addressed in al-Bannā, Jamāl (1979), *al-'Uṣūl al-Fikriyya li-l-Dawla al-'Islāmiyya* (The Intellectual Origins of the Islamic State), Cairo: Dar al-Tiba'a al-Haditha, 76.

7 These were violent protests launched by central security forces in and around the Egyptian capital, demanding better economic conditions, see for this: Weaver, Mary Ann (2000), *A Portrait of Egypt: A Journey Through the World of Militant Islam*, New York: Farrar, Straus and Giroux, 104

8 The liberal phase stretched from the conclusion of the year 1923 to 1948. For a good account on press freedom and party press during the liberal phase, see Talhami,

Ghada Hashem (2007), *Palestine in the Egyptian Press: From al-Ahram to al-Ahli*, Plymouth: Lexington Books, 57–101.

9 Literature in English on the 1952 Revolution used the word coup in referring to the ousting of King Faruq by Free Officers. For instance, see, Botman, Selma (1991), *Egypt from Independence to Revolution, 1919–1952*, New York: Syracuse University Press, 54, 180. See also: Goldschmidt, Arthur and Amy Johnson (eds) (2005), *Re-Envisioning Egypt: 1919–1952*, Cairo: American University in Cairo Press, 7, 85

10 He also blamed the military rule established by Nasser for resisting religion. (al-Bannā, interview, 1 November 2010).

11 For a thorough account on the revolution, see King, Mary Elizabeth (2007), *A Quiet Revolution: The First Palestinian Intifada and Nonviolent Resistance*, New York: Nations Books, 49–54.

12 Though very supportive of non-violent engagement, he criticized the MB running in 1987 elections not for opposing electoral politics but rather because the movement, to him, failed to read the scene and lacked electoral experience. See: al-Bannā, Jamāl (1996), *Mā Ba'd al-'Ikhwān al-Mūslimīn???* (What after the Muslim Brotherhood???), Cairo: Dar al-Fikr al-Islami, 87.

13 The notion of human progress was historically associated with European Enlightenment; however, with the advent of the First World War and later the Holocaust in Germany, among other human tragedies, the validity of the term progress was questioned. See, for this, Mazlish, Bruce, and Marx, Leo (eds) (1999), 'Introduction', in *Progress: Fact or Illusion*?, Ann Arbor: University of Michigan.

14 Capitalism, for him, does not include norms or ideals, above those of profit and material happiness. For a complete account on his critique, see al-Bannā, Jamāl (1984a), *Wūjūh al-'I'itilāf wa-l-'Ikhtilāf Baiyn al-Ra'smāliyya wa-l-Shiyū'iyya wa-l-'Islām* (Aspects of Similarity and Difference between Capitalism, Socialism and Islam), Cairo: Dar al-Fikr al-Islami, 27–35.

15 A similar reference – where he claimed that democracies' strength, that is freedom, is in itself its weakness, because it allows its enemies of communists, or fascists to penetrate it and spoil it (p. 91) – can be seen in his book, al-Bannā, Jamāl (1986), al-Ḥukm bi-l-Qur'ān wa Qaḍiyyat Taṭbīq al-Sharī'a (Rule of Qur'an and the Issue of Applying Shari'a), Cairo: Dar al-Fikr al-Islami.

16 The same reference to Abi Bakr's election was in his book (1952/199b), *Mas'ūliyyat al-'Inḥilāl Baiyn al-Shu'ūb wa-l-Qāda kamā Yuqadimuhā al-Qur'ān al-Karīm* (The Responsibility for Dissolution between the Masses and the Leaders as Presented by the Holy Qur'an), Cairo: Dar al-Fikr al-Islami, 54.

17 Here, he quoted the Qur'anic verse of Sūrat el-Nisā', no. 97.

18 For him, political rule of the early Islamic history, till the end of 'Umar b. al-Khattab's time was a role model; it is meant to show the conditions and give guidance to how rule should be. See al-Bannā, Jamāl (2004), *al-'Islām kamā*

Tuqaddimuhu Da'wat al-'Iḥiyā' al-'Islamī (Islam, as Presented by the Islamic Revival Call), Cairo: Dar al-Fikr al-Islami, 142.

19 see also al-Bannā, Jamāl (2003), *al-'Islām Dīn wa 'Umma wa laiysa Dīn wa Dawla* (Islam is Religion and Nation and not Religion and State), Cairo: Dar al-Fikr al-Islam, 30–1.

20 It is a jurisprudence theme pertaining to verifying Hadith. For this and the larger debate on how reliable Hadith-telling is, see al-Sa'd, Muḥammad (2003), *'Ishkāliyyāt al-Khiṭāb al-Dīnī* (Problematics of Religious Discourse), Book No. 3, Cairo: Press Houses of al-Dar al-Handasiyya.

21 For a good account on the juridical and intellectual debate associated with the concept of justice in Islam, see Krämer, Gudrun (2007), 'Justice in Modern Islamic Thought', in Abbas Ammanat and Frank Griffel (eds), *Shari'a: Islamic Law in the Contemporary Context*, 45–76, Stanford, CA: Stanford University Press.

22 see also al-Bannā, Jamāl (2002), *al-Jihād* (Jihad), Cairo: Dar al-Fikr al-Islami, 8.

23 Although Islamic futūḥāt deteriorated significantly later on, during the time of Umayyads and Abbasids, it never reached the cruelty of Roman invasions. For this view, see al-Bannā, Jamāl (2003), *al-'Islām Dīn wa-'Umma wa laiysa Dīn wa Dawla* (Islam Is Religion and Nation and Not Religion and State), Cairo: Dar al-Fikr al-Islami, 59–68.

24 see also al-Bannā, Jamāl (2005), *Tajdīd al-'Islām wa 'I'ādat Ta'sīs Manẓūmat al-Ma'rifa al-'Islāmiyya* (Renewing Islam and Re-establishing the System of Islamic Knowledge), Cairo: Dar al-Fikr al-Islami, 80, 119, 138–9.

25 Although, he argued that religion is quite central and indispensable in societies of the East, including countries like Egypt (al-Bannā, interview, 1 November 2010).

26 The quote here is from the 1999 edition, the introduction of which was originally written in 1952, on 26 August. See al-Bannā, Jamāl (1952/1999) *Mas'ūliyyat al-'Inḥilāl Baiyna al-Shu'ūb wa-l-Qāda kamā Yuqadimuhā al-Qur'ān al-Karīm* (The Responsibility for Dissolution between the Masses and the Leaders as Presented by the Holy Qur'an), Cairo: Dar al-Fikr al-Islami, 170–2.

27 Once outside Europe, this sense loses its discipline and limits, whereas, the Islamic ethics are principle-based, applied by Muslims wherever they are, against all people. See al-Bannā, Jamāl (1984), *Siyādat al-Qānūn: Ru'iya li-Maḍmūn al-Ḥukm bi-l-Qur'ān* (Sovereignty of Law: A Vision to the Content of Rule by Qur'an), Cairo: Dar al-Fikr al-Islami, 59–63.

28 Usually referred to as 'Constitution of Madīna', this was some sort of legal document that regulated rights and duties of its different tribes. Madīna was a city where the Prophet of Islam, Muhammad, first established an Islamic community. For more on Wathīqat al-Madīna, see: Emon, Anver M. (2012), *Religious Pluralism and Islamic Law: Dhimmis and Others in the Empire of Law*, Oxford: Oxford University Press, 48.

29 Based on Qur'anic verses, such as Sūrat al-Mā'ida, verse 48, or Sūrat Hūd verse 119.

30 This practice was, in his analysis, rare and progressive compared to Europe, which rejected pluralism; Europeans excluded Islam from all the regions they dominated and suppressed pluralism even within Christianity. Wars between Catholics and Protestants prevailed throughout the medieval history and some of them are still found in Ireland. See al-Bannā, Jamāl (2003), *Mawqifunā Min al-'Almāniyya, al-Qawmiyya, al-'Ishtrākiyya* (Our Position towards Secularism, Nationalism, Socialism), Cairo: Dar al-Fikr al-Islami.

31 For a detailed account on these incidents and their sectarian context, see: Labīb, Hānī (2012), *al-Kanīsa al-Miṣriyya: Tawāzunāt al-Dīn wa-l-Dawla* (The Egyptian Church: The Balances of Religion and the State), Cairo: Dār Nahḍat Miṣr for Publications, 28–34.

32 *The Middle East Times* was ordered by the Ministry of Information to remove two articles from its September 19th edition, one of them was about the Coptic diaspora accusations to the government on allegations of persecuting Copts in 1998. See Community for Protecting Journalists, http://cpj.org/reports/1999/05/egyptattacks.php.

4 Tariq al-Bishri on CIPT

1 Al-Wafd Party is one of the biggest political parties in Egypt's modern history. It won parliamentary majorities and formed the cabinet more than once and was strongly viewed as a counter/balancing force against the monarchy in Egypt. For more on the party, see al-Quraishi, Zāhīr Mas'ud (1967), *Liberal Nationalism in Egypt: Rise and Fall of University of the Wafd Party*, Ithaca, MI: Kitab Mahal.

2 This was a treaty concluded between Great Britain and Egypt, towards revising some of the provision of prior treaties, concluded in 1920 and 1930, respectively. In 1936, the British side sought a revision of the military terms already settled in the two former treaties. For more on the 1936 treaty and its reception in Egypt, see: Sayyid-Marsot, Afaf Lutfi (1977), Egypt's *Liberal Experiment: 1922–1936*, University of California, 181–3.

3 For a detailed account on the juristic term necessity, see Qāsim, Yūsuf (1993), *Nazariyyat al-Ḍarūra fī-l-Fiqh al-Jinā'ī al-'Islāmī wa-l-Qānūn al-Jinā'ī al-Waḍ'ii* (Theory of Necessity in Islamic and Positive Criminal Jurisprudence), Cairo, Dār al-Nahāa al-'Arabiyya.

Bibliography

'Abd al-'Azīz, Jum'a 'Amīn (2001), *al-Farīḍa al-Muftarā 'Alaihā; al-Jihād fī Sabīl 'Illāh* (The Religious Duty Done Injustice: Jihad for the Sake of God), Cairo: Dar al-Da'wa.

'Abd al-'Azīz, Jum'a 'Amīn (2003), *Qirā'a fī Rakā'iz al-Mashrū' al-Ḥaḍārī al-'Islāmī* (A Reading into the Pillars of the Islamic Civilizational Project), Cairo: Dar al-Da'wa.

'Abd al-Fattāḥ, Fatḥī (1975), *Shiyū'iyūn wa-Nāṣiriyūn* (Communists and Nasserists), Cairo: Rūz al-Yūsuf.

'Abd al-Fattāḥ, Saif al-Dīn (2008), 'Ru'iyā fī-l-'Illāqa Baiyn al-Dīnī wa-l-Madanī wa-l-Siyāsī: Muqadimāt Minhājiyya' (A Perspective on the Relation between the Religious, the Civil and the Political: Methodological Introductions). In Midḥat Māhir (ed.), *al-'Ilāqa Baiyn al-Dīnī wa-l-Siyāsī: Miṣr wa-l-'Ālam; Ru'ā Mutanawwi'a wa-Khibrāt Muta'addida* (The Relation between the Religious and the Political: Egypt and the World: Various Visions and Multiple Experiences), Cairo: Shorouk Intl. Library.

'Abd al-Ghanii, Muṣṭafā (1993), *al-Muthaqqaf wa 'Abd al-Nāṣir* (The Intellectual and Abd al-Nasser), Kuwait: Dar Su'ad al-Sabbah.

'Abd al-Hādī, Fāṭima (2011), *Riḥlatī Ma'a al-'Akhawāt al-Muslimāt: Min al-'Imām Ḥasan al-Bannā 'Ilā Sujūn 'Abd al-Nāṣir* (My Journey with the Muslim Sisters: From Imam Hasan al-Banna to Abd al-Nasser's Prisons), Cairo: Dar El Shorouk.

'Abd al-Ḥalīm, Hishām (2008), 'al-Mufakkir al-'Islāmī Jamal al-Bannā …' (The Islamic Thinker Jamal al-Banna...), *al-Miṣrī al-Youm*, 14 June, http://today.almasryalyoum.com/article2.aspx?ArticleID=109171.

'Abd al-Majīd, Waḥīd (2010), *al-'Ikhwān al-Muslimūn: baiyn al-Tārīkh wa-l-Mustaqbal: Kaiyfa Kānat al-Jamā'a wa Kaiyfa Takūn?* (The Muslim Brotherhood between History and Future: How Was the Group and How Would It Be?), 1st edition, Cairo: al-Ahram Center for Publication, Translation and Distribution.

'Abd al-Mun'im, 'Intiṣār (2011), *Mudhakkirāt 'Ukht Sābiqa: Ḥikāiyatī Ma'a al-'Ikhwān* (The Diary of a Former Sister: My Story with the Brothers), Cairo: al-Hayaa al-Misriyya al-'Amma li-l-Kitab.

Abdel Kouddous, Sharief (2011), 'After Mubarak: Fighting for Press Freedom in Egypt', *The Nation*, 20 June, http://www.thenation.com/article/161555/after-mubarak-fighting-press-freedom-egypt.

Abdelhadi, Magdi (2012), 'Egypt's Army in Charge of a Vast Business Empire', *BBC News: Middle East*, 23 June, http://www.bbc.co.uk/news/world-middle-east-18548659.

Abdel-Malek, Anouar (1971), *Ägypten, Militärgesellschaft. Das Arrmeeregime, die Linke und der Soziale Wandel unter Nasser* (Egypt, Military Society. The Army Regime, the Leftists and Social Change under Nasser), translated to German by Richard Kruse, Frankfurt am Main: Suhrkampf Verlag.

Abdel Meguid, Nivine, Sanaa El Banna, Rana Korayem and Hoda Salah Eldin (2011), *The Economic Causes of the Egyptian Revolution 'January 25, 2011'*, American University in Cairo, Digital Archive and Research Repository, 29 December, https://fount.aucegypt.edu/studenttxt/29.

Abdel-Rahman, Islam (2013), 'Morsi as Symbol', *Open Democracy*, 12 December, https://www.opendemocracy.net/en/north-africa-west-asia/morsi-as-symbol/.

Abou Bakr, Thoraia (2013), 'Cutlure and Lifestyle during Morsi's Reign', *Egypt Daily News*, 30 June, http://www.dailynewsegypt.com/2013/06/30/culture-and-lifestyle-during-morsis-reign/.

Abou El-Magd, Nadia (2000), 'The Meanings of al-Kosheh', *al-Ahram Weekly Online*, 3–9 February, Issue no. 467, http://weekly.ahram.org.eg/2000/467/eg7.htm.

Abdulla, Rasha (2014), *Egypt's Media in the Midst of Revolution*, Carnegie Endowment for International Peace, 16 July, https://carnegieendowment.org/2014/07/16/egypt-s-media-in-midst-of-revolution-pub-56164.

Abul-Magd, Zeinab (2011), 'The Army and the Economy in Egypt', *Jadaliyya*, 23 December, http://www.jadaliyya.com/pages/index/3732/the-army-and-the-economy-in-egypt.

'Aḥmad, 'Abd al-'Āṭī Muḥammad (2012), *al-Fikr al-Siyāsī li-l-'Imām Muḥammad 'Abdū* (The Political Thought of Imam Muhammad 'Abdu), Cairo: al-Haiy'a al-Misriyya al-'Amma li-l-Kitab.

Ajijola, al-Haj A. D. (2007), *What Is Shariah*, New Delhi: Adam Publishers and Distributors.

Akouri, Mouna A. (2005), *L'Enseignement de Gamal al-Banna* (The Education of Jamal al-Banna), 2nd edition, Cairo: Dar al-Fikr al-Islami.

Ali, Mostafa (2011), 'Finally, Egypt's Parties Set to Begin the Battle for Post-Mubarak Parliament', *Ahram Online*, 25 November, http://english.ahram.org.eg/News/25030.aspx.

'Allām, Muḥammad 'Abd al-Hādī (2012), *'Isqāṭ Niẓām Māiyū 1971 wa-l-Mashrū' al-'Amrīkī al-Ṣahiyūnī: Thawrat 25 Yanāiyir, al-Thawra Mustamirra* (Toppling the 1971 Regime and the American-Zionist Project: the 25th of January Revolution: The Revolution Continues), Cairo: Dar al-'Aiyn li-l-Nashr.

Alt, Ernst (1980), *Ägyptens Kopten-Eine Einsame Minderheit: zum Verhältnis von Christen und Moslems in Ägypten in Vergangenheit und Gegenwart* (Egypt's Copts-A Lonely Minority: On the Relationship between Christians and Muslims in Egypt in the Past and the Present), Heft 51, Saarbrücken: Verlag Breitenbach.

Amer, Pakinam (2010), 'Chronology: Egypt's Sectarian Violence', *Egypt Independent*, 12 January, https://egyptindependent.com/chronology-egypts-sectarian-violence/.

'Amīn, Jalāl (1989), *Naḥw Tafsīr Jadīd li-'Azmat al-'Iqtiṣād wa-l-Mujtama' fī Miṣr* (Towards a New Interpretation of the Crisis of the Economy and Society in Egypt), Cairo: Madbouly Library.

'Amīn, Jalāl (2009), *Miṣr wa-l-Miṣriyūn fī 'Ahd Mubārak (1981–2008)* (Egypt and Egyptians in the Mubarak Era (1981–2008), Cairo: Dar Merit.

'Anān, Muḥammed 'Abd 'Allah (1969), *Miṣr al-'Islāmiyya: wa Tārīkh al-Khiṭaṭ al-Miṣriyya* (The Islamic Egypt: and the History of Egyptian Maps), Cairo: al-Khanji Library.

Anderson, Jon W. (1999), 'The Internet and Islam's New Interpretations'. In Dale F. Eickelmann and Jon W. Anderson (eds), *New Media in the Muslim World: The Emerging Public Sphere*, 45–60, Bloomington: Indiana University Press.

Arabi, Oussama (2001), *Studies in Modern Islamic Law and Jurisprudence*, Arab and Islamic Law Series, London: Kluwer Law International.

Arafat, Alaa ad-Din (2009), *The Mubarak Leadership and Future of Democracy in Egypt*, New York: Palgrave Macmillan.

Aravamudan, Srinivas (2012), *Enlightenment Orientalism: Resisting the Rise of the Novel*, Chicago: University of Chicago Press.

'Arkūn, Muḥammad (1992), *al-Fikr al-'Islāmī: Naqd wa 'Ijtihād* (Islamic Thought: Critique and Ijtihad), trans. Ṣāliḥ, Hāshim, Beirut: Dar al-Saqi.

'Arkūn, Muḥammad (1995), *al-'Islām, 'Ūrūba, al-Gharab: Rihānāt al-Ma'nā wa 'Irādāt al-Haiymana* (Islam, Arabism, the West: Bets on Meaning and Wills to Hegemony), trans. Hāshim Ṣāliḥ, Beirut: Dar al-Saqi.

Armanios, Febe (2013), 'Egypt's Copts between Morsi and the Military', *AUC, The Cairo Review of Global Affairs*, 2 September, https://www.thecairoreview.com/tahrir-forum/egypts-copts-between-morsi-and-the-military/.

Arnason, Johann P., Armando Salvatore and Georg Stauth (eds) (2006), 'Introduction'. In *Islam in Process: Historical Civilizational Perspectives*, Yearbook of the Sociology of Islam, Vol. 7, 8–22, Piscataway, NJ: Transaction Publishers.

Attia, Jamal El-Din (2008), *Towards a Realization of the Higher Intents of Islamic Law: Maqasid al-Shari'ah, a Functional Approach*, London: Cromwell Press.

Awad, Sherif (2013), 'Straight Talk: Dina Abd al-Rahman on Being off the Air', *Egypt Today*, 26 September, https://www.egypttoday.com/Article/10/439/Straight-Talk-Dina-Abdel-Rahman-on-being-off-the-air.

'Ayūb, Ḥasan (2005), *Fiqh al-Jihād fi-l-'Islām* (Jihad Jurisprudence in Islam), Cairo: Dar al-Salam.

Ayubi, Nazih N. (1991a), *Political Islam: Religion and Politics in the Arab World*, New York: Routledge.

Ayubi, Nazih N. (1991b), *The State and Public Policies in Egypt since Sadat*, Ithaca, NY: Ithaca Press.

Ayubi, Nazih N. (1995), *Over-Stating the Arab State: Politics and Society in the Middle East*, New York: I.B. Tauris.

al-'Abiīrī, al-Sayyid (2007), *al-Firaq al-'Islāmiyya Baiyn al-Qadīm wa-l-Ḥadīth* (Islamic Groups between the Old and the Modern), Cairo: Dār al-Ḥadīth.

al-'Ajūz, 'Aḥmad (2011), *'Ikhwānī: Out of the Box* (A Brother: Out of the Box), Cairo: Dar Dawwana li-l-Nashr wa-l-Tawzi'.

al-Anani, Khalil (2014), 'The Return of the Repressive State in Egypt', *Ahram Online*, 11 January, http://english.ahram.org.eg/NewsContentPrint/4/0/90488/Opinion/0/The-return-of-the-repressive-state-in-Egypt.aspx.

al-Anani, Khalil (2015), 'Upended Path: The Rise and Fall of Egypt's Muslim Brotherhood', *Middle East Journal* 69 (4): 527–43.

Al-Arabiya News (2009), 'Egypt Court Rejects Ex-Muslim Convert's Case: Christian Wanted New Religion Recorded on Egypt ID, 14 June, https://english.alarabiya.net/articles/2009/06/14/75916.

al-'Arawī, 'Abd 'Allāh (1984), *Mafhūm al-Dawla* (The Concept of the State), Beirut: Dar al-Tanwir.

al-Ashmawy, Muhammad Saiid (1987), *L'Islamisme Contre l'Islame* (Islamism Against Islam), Cairo: Edition al-Fikr.

al-Ashmawy, Muhammad Saiid (1994), *Islam and the Political Order*, Washington, DC: Council for Research in Values and Philosophy.

al-'Āṣī, al-Sayyid Aḥmad 'Abd al-Maqṣūd (2009), *'Aqīdat al-'Ikhwān al-Muslimīn fī Mizān al-Kitāb wa-l-Sunna min Khilāl Mu'assisihā* (Creed of the Muslim Brotherhood on the Scale on the Holy Qur'an and Sunna, through its Founder), al-Mansoura: Dar al-Wafa'.

al-'Awwā, Muḥammad Salīm (2003), *al-Ḥaq fī-l-Ta'bīr* (Freedom of Expression), 2nd edition, Cairo: Dar El Shorouk.

Al-Azm, Sadik Jalal (1981), 'Orientalism and Orientalism in Reverse'. Reprinted in A. L. Macfie (ed.), *Orientalism: A Reader*, 217–38, Edinburgh: Edinburgh University Press.

Al-Azm, Sadik Jalal (2011), 'Orientalism and Conspiracy'. In Arndt Graf, Fathi Schirin and Paul Ludwig (eds), *Orientalism & Conspiracy: Politics and Conspiracy Theory in the Islamic World*, 3–28, New York: I.B. Tauris.

Al-Azmeh, Aziz (ed.) (1988), 'Islamic Legal Theory and the Appropriation of Reality'. In *Islamic Law: Social and Historical Contexts*, London: Routledge.

El Amrani, Issander (2006), 'The Emergence of Coptic Question in Egypt', *MERIP*, 28 April, http://www.merip.org/mero/mero042806.

Baker, Raymond, William (1990), *Sadat and After: Struggles for Egypt's Political Soul*, Cambridge, MA: Harvard University Press.

Balnaves, Mark, and Mitchelle Willson (2011), *A New Theory of Information and the Internet: Public Sphere Meets Protocol*, New York: Peter Lang.

Bar-Joseph, Uri (2005), *The Watchman Fell Asleep: The Surprise of Yom Kippur and Its Sources*, New York: State University of New York Press.

Barnett, Michael N. (1992), *Confronting the Costs of War: Military Power, State, and Society in Egypt and Israel*, Princeton, NJ: Princeton University Press.

Barsamian, David (1994), *The Pen and the Sword: Conversations with Edward Said*, Chicago: Haymarket Books.

Barthes, Roland (1998), 'The Death of the Author'. In Eric Dayton (ed.), *Art and Interpretation: An Anthology of Readings in Aesthetics and the Philosophy of Art*, 383–6, Peterborough, Ontario: Broadview.

Bassiouni, Cherif (2012), 'Schools of Thought in Islam', *Middle East Institute*, 24 January, https://www.mei.edu/publications/schools-thought-islam.

Bayat, Asef (2007), *Making Islam Democratic*, Stanford, CA: Stanford University Press.

Bayat, Asef (2010), *Life as Politics: How Ordinary Citizens Change the Middle East*, Netherlands: Amsterdam University Press.

Bayat, Asef (ed.) (2013a), 'Introduction: Post-Islamism at Large'. In *Post-Islamism: The Changing Faces of Political Islam*, 3–34, New York: Oxford University Press.

Bayat, Asef (ed.) (2013b), 'Egypt and Its Unsettled Islamism'. In *Post-Islamism: The Changing Faces of Political Islam*, 185–239, New York: Oxford University Press.

Bayoumy, Alaa (2010), 'The Battle for al-Azhar', *al-Jazeera*, 17 March, http://www.aljazeera.com/focus/2010/03/201031763554123901.html.

Bayyoumi, Alaa (2011), 'A Reading of "the Church and the State", Book Reviews', *Doha Institute*, Arab center for Research and Policy Studies, https://www.dohainstitute.org/en/lists/ACRPS-PDFDocumentLibrary/A_Reading_of_The_Church_and_The_State.pdf.

Bealey, Frank (1999), *The Blackwell Dictionary of Political Science: A User's Guide to Its Terms*, Oxford: Blackwell Publishers.

Beattie, Kirk J. (1994), *Egypt during the Nasser Years*, Boulder, CO: Westview Press.

Beattie, Kirk J. (2000), *Egypt during the Sadat Years*, New York: Palgrave.

Beinin, Joel (2013), 'Egyptian Workers after June 30', *Middle East Research and Information Project*, 23 August, http://www.merip.org/mero/mero082313.

Ben Jelloun, Tahar (2011), *Arabischer Frühling: Vom Wiedererlangen der Arabischen Würde* (Arab Spring: From Restoring Arab Dignity), Bonn: Bundeszentrale für Politische Bildung.

Bhaba, Homi K. (1996), 'The Other Question'. In Padmini Mongia (ed.), *Contemporary Postcolonial Theory: A Reader*, London: Arnold.

Bielfeldt, Heiner (2004), 'Political Secularism and European Islam: A Challenge to Muslims and Non-Muslims'. In Jamal Malik (ed.), *Muslims in Europe: From the Margin to the Centre*, Münster: Lit Verlag.

Bilāl, 'Abd 'Allāh (1974), *Ta'ammulāt fī-l-Nāṣiriyya* (Insights into Nasserism), 2nd edition, Tarablus: Dār Maktabat al-Fikr.

Black, Antony (2008), *The West and Islam: Religion and Political Thought in World History*, Oxford: Oxford University Press.

Blaydes, Lisa (2011), *Elections and Distributive Politics in Mubarak's Egypt*, New York: Cambridge University Press.

Bourdieu, Pierre (1984), *Distinction: A Social Critique of the Judgement of Taste*, Cambridge, MA: Harvard University Press.

Bourdieu, Pierre (2001), *Contre-feux 2: Pour un Mouvement Social Européen* (Against-Fires 2: For a European Social Movement), Paris: Editions Raisons d'Agir.

Bradely, John R. (2008), *Inside Egypt: The Land of the Pharaohs on the Brink of a Revolution*, New York: Palgrave Macmillan.

Bradley, Matt (2012), 'Egypt's Military Seeks to Preserve Powers', *Wall Street Journal*, 18 May, http://online.wsj.com/news/articles/SB10001424052702303879604577412442090000020.

Brooks, Risa (2021), 'Civil-Military Relations in Sisi's Egypt', *Carnegie Middle East Center*, 17 March, https://carnegie-mec.org/2021/03/17/civil-military-relations-in-sisi-s-egypt-pub-84074.

Brown, Nathan J. (2011), *Egypt's Constitutional Ghosts*, originally published in Foreign Affairs, Carnegie Endowment for International Peace, 15 February, http://carnegieendowment.org/2011/02/15/egypt-s-constitutional-ghosts/930?reloadFlag=1.

Brown, Nathan J., and Amr Hamzawy (2010), *Between Religion and Politics*, Washington, DC: Carnegie Endowment for International Peace.

Brown, Nathan J., and Michele Dunne (2014), 'Egypt's Judges Join In: The Crackdown on the Muslimbrotherhood Enters a New Phase', *Foreign Affairs*, 1 April, http://www.foreignaffairs.com/articles/141088/nathan-j-brown-and-michele-dunne/egypts-judges-join-in.

Brownlee, Jaso (2002), 'Democratization in the Arab World? The Decline of Pluralism in Mubarak's Egypt?', *Journal of Democracy* 13 (4): 6–14.

Brunner, Rainer (2004), *Islamic Ecumenism in the 20th Century: The Azhar and Shiism between Rapprochement and Restraint*, trans. Joseph Greenman, Leiden: Brill.

Burgat, Francois (1997), 'Ballot Boxes, Militaries and Islamic Movements'. In Martin Kramer (ed.), *The Islamism Debate*, Tel Aviv: Tel Aviv University Press.

Burney, Shehla (2012), *Pedagogy of the Other: Edward Said, Postcolonial Theory, and Strategies for Critique*, New York: Peter Lang Press.

al-Bahii, Muḥammad (1991), *al-Fikr al-'Islāmī al-Ḥadīth wa Ṣilatihi bī-l-'Isti'mār al-Gharbī* (Modern Islamic Thought and its Connection to Western Colonialism), Cairo: Maktabat Wahba.

al-Banhāwī, Nādia (2009), *Jamāl al-Bannā: Mufakkiran wa Dāi'yan* (Jamal al-Banna: a Thinker and a Preacher), Cairo: Dar al-Fikr al-Islami.

al-Bannā, Jamāl (1946), *Dīmūqrāṭiyya Jadīda* (New Democracy), 2nd edition, Cairo: Dar al-Fikr al-Islami.

al-Bannā, Jamāl (1957), *al-'Azma wa-l-Batāla fi-l-Ra'smāliyya* (Crisis and Unemployment in Capitalism), Cairo: Dar al-Muhaiyid al-'Arabi.

al-Bannā, Jamāl (1963), *al-Qanūn wa-l-Qaḍā' fi-l-Mujtama' al-'Ishtirākī* (Law and Judiciary in the Socialist Society), Author Copy rights.

al-Bannā, Jamāl (1967), *al-Tārīkh al-Niqābī al-Muqāran* (Comparative Syndical History), Cairo: al-Ittihad al-'Am li-Niqabaat 'Ummal Misr.

al-Bannā, Jamāl (1972), *Rūḥ al-'Islām* (Spirit of Islam), Cairo: Dar al-Fikr al-Islami.

al-Bannā, Jamāl (1973), *Qaḍiyyat al-'Intāj baiyn al-Niqābāt wa-l-'Idārāt wa-l-Sulṭāt* (The Issue of Production between Syndicates, Administrations and Authorities), Cairo: Hassaan Press.

al-Bannā, Jamāl (1977), *Ẓuhūr wa Suqūṭ Jumhūrriyyat Vaimār* (The Rise and the Fall of the Weimar Republic), Cairo: Hassaan Press.

al-Bannā, Jamāl (1978), *al-Da'awāt al-'Islāmiyya Mā lahā wa Mā 'Alaihā* (Islamic Calls, Their Virtues and Vices), Cairo: Hassaan Press.

al-Bannā, Jamāl (1979a), *al-'Uṣūl al-Fikriyya li-l-Dawla al-'Islāmiyya* (The Intellectual Origins of the Islamic State), Cairo: Dar al-Tiba'a al-Haditha.

al-Bannā, Jamāl (1979b), *Baiyān Ramaḍān* (Ramadan Declaration), Cairo: Dar al-Fikr al-Islami.

al-Bannā, Jamāl (1979c), *al-Jāmi'a al-'Ummāliyya* (The Labor University), Cairo: Dar al-Tiba'a al-Ḥaditha.

al-Bannā, Jamāl (1981a), *'Azmat al-Niqābiyyah* (Syndical Crisis), Cairo: Dar al-Fikr al-Islami.

al-Bannā, Jamāl (1981b), *al-'Islām wa-l-Ḥaraka al-Niqābiyya* (Islam and the Syndical Movement), Cairo: Dar al-Fikr al-Islami.

al-Bannā, Jamāl (1982), *al-Dawla al-'Aṣriyya* (The Contemporary State), Cairo: Dar al-Fikr al-Islami.

al-Bannā, Jamāl (1983), *al-'Awda li-l-Qur'ān* (The Return to Qur'an), Cairo: al-Ittihad al-Islami al-Dawli li-l-'Amal.

al-Bannā, Jamāl (1984), *Siyādat al-Qānūn: Ru'iya li-Maḍmūn al-Ḥukm bi-l-Qur'ān* (Sovereignty of Law: A Vision to the Content of Rule by Qur'an), Cairo: Dar al-Fikr al-Islami.

al-Bannā, Jamāl (1984a), *Wūjūh al-'I'itilāf wa-l-'Ikhtilāf Baiyna al-Ra'smāliyya wa-l-Shiyū'iyya wa-l-'Islām* (Aspects of Similarity and Difference between Capitalism, Socialism and Islam), Cairo: Dar al-Fikr al-Islami.

al-Bannā, Jamāl (1985), *Qaḍiyyat al-Ḥurriyya fī-l-'Islām* (The Issue of Freedom in Islam), Cairo: Dar al-Fikr al-Islami.

al-Bannā, Jamāl (1986a), *al-Ḥukm bi-l-Qur'ān wa Qaḍiyyat Taṭbīq al-Sharī'a* (Rule of Qur'an and the Issue of Applying Shari'a), Cairo: Dar al-Fikr al-Islami.

al-Bannā, Jamāl (1986b), *al-Shūrā fī-l-'Idāra* (Shura in Management), Cairo: al-Ittihad al-Islami al-Dawli li-l-'Amal.

al-Bannā, Jamāl (1987a), *Tārīkh al-Thaqāfa al-'Ummāliyya fī Miṣr* (History of the Labor Culture in Egypt), Cairo: Dar al-Fikr al-Islami.

al-Bannā, Jamāl (1987b), *Mashrū' li-'Iṣlāḥ al-Ḥaraka al-Niqābiyya al-Miṣriyya* (A Project to Reform the Egyptian Syndical Movement), Cairo: Dar al-Fikr al-Islami.

al-Bannā, Jamāl (1988), *al-'Islām Huwa al-Ḥal* (Islam is the Solution), Cairo: Dar al-Fikr al-Islami.

al-Bannā, Jamāl (1989), *al-Ḥurriyya al-Niqābiyya* (Syndical Freedom), in three parts, Cairo: Dar al-Fikr al-Islami.

al-Bannā, Jamāl (1990), *Naḥwa Ḥaraka Niqābiyya Muthaqqafa* (Towards a Cultivated Syndical Movement), Cairo: Dar al-Fikr al-Islami.

al-Bannā, Jamāl (1991a), *al-Birnāmij al-'Islāmī* (The Islamic Program), Cairo: Dar al-Fikr al-Islami.

al-Bannā, Jamāl (1991b), *al-'Islām wa-l-'Aqlāniyya* (Islam and Rationality), Cairo: Dar al-Fikr al-Islami.

al-Bannā, Jamāl (1992), *al-Ḥaraka al-Niqābiyya Ḥaraka 'Insāniyya* (The Syndical Movement Is a Human Movement), Cairo: Dar al-Fikr al-Islami.

al-Bannā, Jamāl (1993), *Limādhā yajib 'an Takūn li-l-Ḥaraka al-Niqābiyya 'Aqīda?* (Why Should the Syndical Movement Have a Creed?), Cairo: Dar al-Fikr al-Islami.

al-Bannā, Jamāl (1994a), *Mas'ūliyyat Fashal al-Dawla al-'Islāmiyya fī-l-'Aṣr al-Ḥadīth wa-Buḥūth 'Ukhrā* (The Responsibility for Failure of the Islamic State and Other Research), Cairo: Dar al-Fikr al-Islami.

al-Bannā, Jamāl (1994b), *Naḥwa Ta'adudiyya Niqābiyya bi-lā Tafattut wa lā 'Iḥtikār* (Towards Syndical Pluralism without Fragmentation or Monopoly), Cairo: Dar al-Fikr al-Islami.

al-Bannā, Jamāl (1994c), *Kallā Thum Kallā: Kallā li-fuqahā' al-Taqlīd, Kallā li-'Ad'iyā' al-Tanwīr* (No, Then No: No to Imitation Jurists, No to Enlightenment Claimers), Cairo: Dar al-Fikr al-Islami.

al-Bannā, Jamāl (1995a), *al-Mashrū' al-Ḥaḍārī bi-Ṣarāḥa* (The Civilizational Project, Frankly), Cairo: Dar al-Fikr al-Islami.

al-Bannā, Jamāl(1995b), *Ḥurriyyat al-Fikr wa-l-'I'tiqād fī-l-'Islām* (Freedom of Thought and Belief in Islam), Cairo: Dar al-Fikr al-'Islāmī.

al-Bannā, Jamāl (1995c), *Naẓriyyat al-'Adl fī-l-Fikr al-'Urūbbī wa-l-Fikr al-'Islāmī* (Justice Theory in European and Islamic Thought), Cairo: Dar al-Fikr al-Islami.

al-Bannā, Jamāl (1995d), *al-Niqābāt al-Mihaniyya al-Miṣriyya fī Ma'rakat al-Baqāa'* (Professional Syndicates in Egypt in the Survival Battle), Cairo: Dar al-Fikr al-Islami.

al-Bannā, Jamāl (1995e), *Naḥwa Fiqh Jadīd* (Towards New Jurisprudence), Cairo: Dar al-Fikr al-Islami.

al-Bannā, Jamāl (1996a), *Khamsat Ma'āīr li–Miṣdāqiyyit al-Ḥukm al-'Islāmī* (Five Criteria for the Credibility of Islamic Rule), Cairo: Dar al-Fikr al-Islami.

al-Bannā, Jamāl (1996b), *Mā Ba'd al-'Ikhwān al-Mūslimīn???* (What after the Muslim Brotherhood???), Cairo: Dar al-Fikr al-Islami.

al-Bannā, Jamāl (1997), *Takuīn wa 'Amal al-Jam'iyya al-Miṣriyya li-Ri'āyyat al-Masjūnīn* (The Forming and Work of the Egyptian Association for Prisoners Care), Cairo: Dar al-Fikr al-Islami.

al-Bannā, Jamāl (1998), *Qaḍiyyat Taṭbīq al-Sharī'a* (The Issue of Applying Shari'a), Cairo: Dar al-Fikr al-Islami.

al-Bannā, Jamāl (1999a), *al-'Islām wa Ḥurriyyat al-Fikr* (Islam and Freedom of Thought), Cairo: Dar al-Fikr al-Islami.

al-Bannā, Jamāl (1952/1999b), *Mas'ūliyyat al-'Inḥilāl Baiyn al-Shu'ūb wa-l-Qāda kamā Yuqadimuhā al-Qur'ān al-Karīm* (The Responsibility for Dissolution beween the Masses and the Leaders as Presented by the Holy Qur'an), Cairo: Dar al-Fikr al-Islami.

al-Bannā, Jamāl (2000), *'Istrātījiyyat al-Da'wa al-'Islāmiyya fī-l-Qarn al-21* (The Strategy for the Call in the 21st Century), Cairo: Dār al-Fikr al-Islami.

al-Bannā, Jamāl (2001a), *al-Ta'adudiyya fī Mujtama' 'Islāmī* (Plurality in an Islamic Society), Cairo: Dar al-Fikr al-Islami.

al-Bannā, Jamāl (2002a), *al-Ḥijāb* (The Veil), Cairo: Dar al-Fikr al-Islami.

al-Bannā, Jamāl (2002b), *al-Jihād* (Jihad), Cairo: Dar al-Fikr al-Islami.

al-Bannā, Jamāl (2002c), *al-Mar'a al-Muslima Baiyn Taḥrīr al-Qur'ān wa-Taqīīd al-Fuqahā'* (The Muslim Woman between Emancipation of Qur'an and Restriction of the Jurists), Cairo: Dar al-Fikr al-Islami.

al-Bannā, Jamāl (2003a), *al-'Islām Dīn wa'Umma wa laiysa Dīn wa Dawla* (Islam Is Religion and Nation and Not Religion and State), Cairo: Dar al-Fikr al-Islami.

al-Bannā, Jamāl (2003b), *Mawqifunā Min al-'Almāniyya, al-Qawmiyya, al-'Ishtrākiyya* (Our Position towards Secularism, Nationalism, Socialism), Cairo: Dar al-Fikr al-Islami.

al-Bannā, Jamāl (2004), *al-'Islām kamā Tuqaddimuhu Da'wat al-'Iḥiyā' al-'Islāmī* (Islam, as Presented by the Islamic Revival Call), Cairo: Dar al-Fikr al-Islami.

al-Bannā, Jamāl (2005a), *Jawāz 'Imāmit al-Mar'a al-Rijāl* (The Permissibility of Women Leading Men), Cairo: Dar al-Fikr al-Islami.

al-Bannā, Jamāl (2005b), *Khitān al-Banāt, Laisa Sunna wa-lā Makrama wa Lākin Jarīma* (Female Circumcision, not a Sunna, nor Honor, Rather a Crime), Cairo: Dar al-Fikr al-Islami.

al-Bannā, Jamāl (2005c), *Tajdīd al-'Islām wa 'Iādat Ta'sīs Manẓūmat al-Ma'rifa al-'Islāmiyya* (Renewing Islam and Re-establishing the System of Islamic Knowledge), Cairo: Dar al-Fikr al-Islami.

al-Bannā, Jamāl (2006a), *Tafnīd Da'wa Ḥad al-Ridda* (Refuting the Claim for the Apostasy Penalty), Cairo: Dar al-Fikr al-Islami.

al-Bannā, Jamāl (2006b), *'Ikhwānī al-'Aqbāṭ* (My Brothers, the Copts), Cairo: Dar al-Fikr al-Islami.

al-Bannā, Jamāl (2006c), *al-Rad 'Alā al-Bābā: Malaf Tawthīqī wa 'Ibdā'ī* (The Reply to the Pope: An Educational and Creative File), Cairo: Dar al-Fikr al-Islami.

al-Bannā, Jamāl (2007a), *al-Mukhtār* (The Selected), Part 3, Cairo: Dar al-Fikr al-Islami.

al-Bannā, Jamāl (2008a), *al-Mukhtār* (The Selected), Part 9 Cairo: Dar Fikr al-Islami.

al-Bannā, Jamāl (2008b), "Aṣr al-'Aql wa-l-Ḥurriyya lā-bud 'an Yaḥkum, Nadwat al-Hilāl' (The Age of Mind and Freedom Must Rule-, al-Hilal Seminar), *al-Hilāl*, August, Cairo: al-Mu'assasa al-'Arabiyya al-Ḥaditha li-l-Tab' wa-l-Nashr.

al-Bannā, Jamāl (2008c), *Tajrīd al-Bukhārī wa Muslim min al-'Aḥādīth 'Allatī lā Talzam* (Stripping Bukari and Muslim from Unnecessary Hadith Tradition), Cairo: Dar al-Fikr al-Islami.

al-Bannā, Jamāl (2008d), *al-'Islām wa Ḥurriyyat al-Fikr* (Islam and Freedom of Thought), Cairo: Dar al-Fikr al-Islami.

al-Bannā, Jamāl (2008e), *Qaḍaiyyat al-Qubulāt wa Baqiyyat al-'Ijtihādāt* (The Issue of Kisses and the Rest of Ijtihads), Cairo: Dar al-Fikr al-Islami.

al-Bannā, Jamāl (2009), *Man Huwa Jamāl al-Bannā? Wa Mā Hiyya Da'wat al-'Iḥiyā'?* (Who Is Jamal al-Banna? And What Is the Revival Call?), Cairo: Dar al-Fikr al-Islami.

al-Bannā, Jamāl (commentator) (2009a), *Dhikraiyāt Fawziyya al-Bannā bī-Qalamihā* (Memoirs of Fawziyya al-Banna with Her Pen), Cairo: Dar al-Fikr al-Islami.

al-Bannā, Jamāl (2010a), *al-Mukhtār* (The Selected), Part 16, Cairo: Dar al-Fikr al-Islami.

al-Bannā, Jamāl (2010b), *al-'Ikhwān al-Muslimūn 'Alā Muftaraq al-Ṭuruq* (The Muslim Brotherhood at the Crossroads), Cairo: Dar al-Fikr al-Islami.

al-Bannā, Jamāl (2010c) *Jināyat Qabīlat Ḥaddathanā* (The Crime of the Told Us Tribe), Cairo: Dār al-Fikr al-Islami.

al-Bannā, Jamāl (2011), *al-Ta'bi'a al-Fikriyya li-l-Thawra wa Mā ba'd al-Thawra* (The Intellectual Mobilization for the Revolution and after the Revolution), Cairo: Dar al-Fikr al-Islami.

al-Bāz, Muḥammad (1998), *al-Sha'rāwī wa-l-Sādāt* (al-Sha'rawi and al-Sadat), Cairo: Junior Madbouly Library.

al-Bāz, Muḥammad (2011), *Suqūṭ al-'Āliha: Kaiyfa 'Inhār Mubārak wa-Rijāluh?* (The Fall of the Gods: How Mubarak and His Men Went Down?), Cairo: Jazirat al-Ward Library.

al-Bishrī, Ṭāriq (1977), 'Thawrat 23 Yūliū wa Qaḍiyyat al-Dīmūqrāṭiyya' (The 23rd of July Revolution and the Issue of democracy). In Mar'ī, Sayyid, and others, *al-Dīmūqrāṭiyya fī Miṣr: Rub' Qarn Ba'd Thawrat 23 Yūliyū* (Democracy in Egypt: A Quarter of a Century after the 23rd of July Revolution), 17–25, Cairo: al-Ahram Centre for Political and Strategic Studies.

al-Bishrī, Ṭāriq (1978), 'Miṣr fī 'Iṭār al-Ḥaraka al-'Arabiyya' (Egypt in the Frame of the Arab Movement). In Sa'ad Eddīn 'Ibrāhīm and others (eds, 1983), *Miṣr wa-l-'Urūba wa Thawrit Yūliyū* (Egypt, Arabism and the July Revolution), *al-Mustaqbal al-'Arabī*, 27–42, Cairo: Dar al-Mustaqbal al-'Arabi.

al-Bishrī, Ṭāriq (1987a), *Dirāsāt fī-l-Dīmūqrāṭiyya al-Miṣriyya* (Studies in Egyptian Democracy), 1st edition, Cairo: Dar El Shorouk.

al-Bishrī, Ṭāriq (1987b), 'al-Mas'ala al-Qānūniyya baiyn al-Sharī'a al-'Islāmiyya wa-l-Qānūn al-Waḍ'ī' (The Legal Issue Between Islamic Shari'a and Positive Law). In al-Sayyid Yāsīn and others (eds), *al-Turāth wa-Taḥadiyyāt al-'Aṣr fī-l-Waṭan al-'Arabī* (Heritage and Challenges of the Age in the Arab World), 617–44, Beirut: Center for Arab Unity Studies.

al-Bishrī, Ṭāriq (1988), 'al-Khulf Baiyn al-Nukhba wa-l-Jamāhīr 'Izā' al-'Ilāqa Baiyn al-Qawmiyya al-'Arabiyya wa-l-'Islām' (The Disagreement between the Elite and the Masses Regarding the Relation between Arab Nationalism and Islam). In Muḥammad Aḥmad Khalaf 'Allāh and others (eds), *al-Qawmiyya al-'Arabiyya wa-l-'Islām* (Arab Nationalism and Islam), 2nd edition, 275–360, Beirut: Centre for Arab Unity Studies.

al-Bishrī, Ṭāriq (1988a), *Baiyn al-'Islām wa-l-'Urūba* (Between Islam and Arabism), Part 1, 1st edition, Kuwait: al-Qalam Press House.

al-Bishrī, Ṭāriq (1989), ''Awalan: Ḥawl al-'Urūba wa-l-'Islām' (First: On Arabism and Islam). In Ṭāriq al-Bishrī and others (eds), *al-Ḥiwār al-Qawmī al-Dīnī* (The National-Religious Dialogue), 31–41, Beirut: Centre for Arab Unity Studies.

al-Bishrī, Ṭāriq (1991a), *al-Dīmūqrāṭiyya wa-Niẓām 23 Yūliyū 1952–1970* (Democracy and the 23rd of July System, 1952–1970), al-Hilāl Book, Vol. 492, al-Hilal Press House, Cairo: Modern Arab Institution for Publication.

al-Bishrī, Ṭāriq (1991b), 'Muqaddima' (Introduction). In *al-'Umma fī-'Ām* (The Nation in a Year), an Annual Report on Egypt's Political and Economic Affairs, for the year 1990–1, 5–21, Cairo: Centre for Arab Consultants.

al-Bishrī, Ṭāriq (1991c), 'Naḥw Ṭaqqabul Mutabādal baiyn al-'Urūba wa-l-'Islām (Towards Mutual Acceptance between Arabism and Islam). In 'Abd al-Ḥalīm Qandīl (ed.), *'An al-Nāṣiriyya wa-l-'Islām* (About Nasserism and Islam), 1st edition, 273–86, Egypt: Center for Arab Nation Media.

al-Bishrī, Ṭāriq (1992), *Mushkilatān wa Qirā'a Fīhimā* (Two Problems and a Reading in Them), Silsilat 'Islāmiyyat al-Ma'rifa (9) (Islamic knowledge Series "9"), Virginia: International Institute for Islamic Thought.

al-Bishrī, Ṭāriq (1996a), *al-Ḥiwār al-'Islāmī al-'Almānī* (The Islamic Secular Dialogue), 1st edition, Cairo: Dar El Shorouk.

al-Bishrī, Ṭāriq (1996b), *Shakhṣiyyāt Tārīkhiyya* (Historical Personalities), Vol. 552, al-Hilāl Book, al-Hilal Press House, Cairo: Modern Arab Institution for Publication.

al-Bishrī, Ṭāriq (1996c), *al-Malāmiḥ al-'Āmma li-l-Fikr al-Siyāsī al-'Islāmī fī-l-Tārīkh al-Mu'āṣir* (General Features of Islamic Political Thought in Contemporary History), 1st edition, Cairo: Dar El Shorouk.

al-Bishrī, Ṭāriq (1998), *Baiyn al-Jāmi'a al-Dīnniyya wa-l-Jāmi'a al-Waṭanniyya fī-l-Fikr al-Siyāsī* (Between the Religious and the National Bond in Islamic Thought), Silsilat fī-l-Mas'ala al-'Islāmiyya al-Mu'āṣira (In the Contemporary Islamic Issue Series), 1st edition, Cairo: Dar El Shorouk.

al-Bishrī, Ṭāriq (2000), Taqdīm (Preface), *'Ummatī fī-l-'Ālam* (My Nation in the World), Cairo: Civilization Centre for Political Studies.

al-Bishrī, Ṭāriq (2001), *Naql al-'A'ḍā' fī Ḍū' al-Sharī'a wa-l-Qānūn* (Organs' Transplantation in the Light of Shari'a and Law), Cairo: Nahdat Misr Publishers.

al-Bishrī, Ṭāriq (2002a), *al-Ḥaraka al-Siyāsiyya fī Miṣr 1945/1953* (The Political Movement in Egypt 1945/1953), (new) 2nd edition, Cairo: Dar El Shorouk, 1st edition published 1972.

al-Bishrī, Ṭāriq (2002b), *Shakhṣiyyāṭ wa-Qaḍāiyyā Mu'āṣira* (Contemporary Personalities and Issues), al-Hilāl Book, Vol. 617, Cairo: al-Hilal Press House, Modern Arab Institution for Publication.

al-Bishrī, Ṭāriq (2002c), *al-'Arab fī Muwājahat al-'Idwān* (Arabs in the Face of Aggression), 1st edition, Cairo: Dar El Shorouk.

al-Bishrī, Ṭāriq (2003a), 'Tajrubat Tanẓīm al-Ḥukm fī Miṣr fī Siyāq al-Tārīkh al-Miṣrī al-Mu'āṣir' (The Experience of Rule Organization in Egypt in the Context of Contemporary Egyptian History). In Muḥammad al-Sa'īd 'Idrīs (ed.), *Thawrat 23 Yūliū 1952: Dirāsāt fī-l-Ḥiqbat al-Nāṣiriyya* (The 23rd of July Revolution: Studies in the Nasserist Period), 177–212, Cairo: Ahram Center for Political and Strategic Studies.

al-Bishrī, Ṭāriq (2003b), *Fī Dhikrā 'Intiṣār al-'Āshir min Ramaḍān, Miṣr fī Mwājahat 'Isrā'īl Baiyn al-Tārīkh wa-l-Ḥāḍir wa-l-Mustaqbal* (On the Anniversary of the 10th of Ramadan Victory, Egypt in the Face of Israel between the Past, the Present and the Future), Cairo: Cairo University, Club of Academics, Committee for Public affairs and Media.

al-Bishrī, Ṭāriq ([1980] 2004), *al-Muslimūn wa-l-'Aqbāṭ fī-'Iṭār al-Jamā'a al-Waṭaniyya* (Muslims and Copts within the Framework of National Community), 4th edition (refined), Cairo: Dar El Shorouk.

al-Bishrī, Ṭāriq (2005a), *al-Waḍ' al-Qānūnī Baiyn al-Sharī'a al-'Islāmiyya wa-l-Qānūn al-Waḍ'ī* (The Legal Situation between Islamic Shari'a and Positive Law), 2nd edition, Cairo: Dar El Shorouk.

al-Bishrī, Ṭāriq (2005b), *al-Ḥiwār al-'Islāmī al-'Almānī* (The Islamic Secular Dialogue), 2nd edition, Cairo: Dar El Shorouk.

al-Bishrī, Ṭāriq (2005c), ''Aiyn al-Miḥna 'Allatī Tuwājih al-'Umma?' (Where Is the Crisis Facing the Nation?). In *'Ummatī fī-l-'Ālam* (My Nation in the World), Part 1, 7–16, Cairo: Civilization Centre for Political Studies.

al-Bishrī, Ṭāriq (2005d), *al-Jamā'a al–Waṭaniyya Baiyn al-'Uzla wa-l-'Indimāj* (The National Community between Isolation and Integration), al-Hilāl Book, Cairo: al-Hilal Press House, Modern Arab Institution for Publication.

al-Bishrī, Ṭāriq (2006a), *Miṣr Baiyn al-'Iṣiyān wa-l-Tafakkuk* (Egypt between Disobedience and Disintegration), 1st edition, Cairo: Dar El Shorouk.

al-Bishrī, Ṭāriq (2006b), *al-Qaḍā' al-Miṣrī Baiyn al-'Istiqlāl wa-l-'Iḥtiwā'* (Egyptian Judiciary between Autonomy and Co-optation), 2nd edition, Cairo: Shorouk International Bokshop.

al-Bishrī, Ṭāriq (2006c), "An al-Quds wa Falasṭīn: Wi'ā'uhā al-Jughrāfī' (On Jerusalem and Palestine: Its Geographical Vessel). In Saif al-Dīn 'Abd al-Fattāḥ and Riyāḍ Jarjūr (eds), *'Istishrāf Qaḍiyyat al-Quds fī Ḍū' al-Taṭawūrāt al-Rāhina* (Exploring the Future of Jerusalem Issue in the Light of Current Developments), Works of the 22nd of March 2005 Meeting, 15–22, Cairo: Faculty of Economics and Political Science, Cairo University and Arab Group for Christian-Muslim Dialogue.

al-Bishrī, Ṭāriq (2007a), *Manhaj al-Naẓar fī-l-Nuẓum al-Siyāsiyya li-Buldān al-'Ālam al-'Islāmī* (The Methodology for Studying Political Systems of Islamic World Countries), 2nd edition, Cairo: Dar El Shorouk.

al-Bishrī, Ṭāriq (2007b), *Mā-Hiyyat al-Mu'āṣara* (What Is Contemporaneity), 3rd. edition, Cairo: Dar El Shorouk.

al-Bishrī, Ṭāriq (2007c), ‘al-Ta‘dīlāt al-Dustūriyya fī-Miṣr: Taḥlīl li-l-’Iṭār al-Siyāsī’ (Constitutional Amendments: Analysis of the Political Framework). In Muṣṭafā Kāmil al-Sayyid (ed.), *al-Ta‘dīlāt al-Dustūriyya: Ru’ā Mustaqilla* (Constitutional Amendments: Independent Perspectives), Forum for Constitutional Reform Discussions (November 2006–March 2007), 15–22, Cairo: Partners for Development.

al-Bishrī, Ṭāriq (2008), *Naḥw Ṭaiyyār ’Asāsī li-l-’Umma* (Towards a Main Stream of the Nation), 1st edition, al-Jazīra papers (8), Qatar: al-Jazīra Center for Studies.

al-Bishrī, Ṭāriq (2011a), *al-Dawla wa-l-Kanīsa* (The State and the Church), 1st edition, Cairo: Dar El Shorouk.

al-Bishrī, Ṭāriq (2011b), *al-Siyāq al-Tārikhī wa-l-Thaqāfī li-Taqnīn al-Sharī‘a al-’Islāmiyya* (The Historical and Cultural Context of Codifying Islamic Shari‘a), 1st edition, Cairo: Shorouk International Bookshop.

al-Bishrī, Ṭāriq (2012a), *Sa‘d Zaghlūl Yufāwiḍ al-’Isti‘mār* (Sa‘d Zaghlul Negotiates with Colonialism), 1st edition, Cairo: Dar El Shorouk.

al-Bishrī, Ṭāriq (2012b), *Min ’Awrāq Thawrat 25 Yanāyir* (From the 25th of January Revolution Papers), Cairo: Dar El Shorouk.

al-Bishrī, Ṭāriq (2013), “Ilāqat al-Dīn bi-l-Dawala: Ḥālat Miṣr ba‘d al-Thawra’ (The Relation between Religion and the State: The Case of Egypt after the Revolution), *al-Mustaqbal al-‘Arabī*, Vol. 3, Iss. 407, January: 80–100.

al-Bishrī, Ṭāriq (2014), *Thawrat 25 Yanāyir wa-l-Ṣirā‘ ḥawl al-Sulṭa* (The 25th of January Revolution and the Struggle for Authority), Cairo: Dar El Bashir.

al-Bishrī, Ṭāriq (2015), *Qirā’āt Fikriyya wa-Humūm Miṣriyya* (Intellectual Readings and Egyptian Concerns), Cairo: Dar El Bashir.

al-Bishrī, Ṭāriq (2019), *Naḥw ’Islāmiyyat al-Ma‘rifa fī-l-Fikr al-Siyāsī al-Mu‘āṣir* (Towards Islamic Knowledge in Contemporary Political Thought), Cairo: Mufakkiroun al-Dawliyya li-l- Nashr wa-l-Tawzi‘.

Burman, E., and I. Parker (1993), ‘Against Discursive Imperialism, Empiricism and Constructionism: Thirty-Two Problems with Discourse Analysis’. In E. Burman and I. Parker (eds), *Discourse Analytic Research: Repertoires and Readings of Texts in Action*, London: Routledge.

El-Bendary, Mohamed (2010), *The Egyptian Press and Coverage of Local and International Events*, Plymouth: Lexington books.

Camus, Albert (2012), ‘Realismus’ (Realism). In Werner Pfennig (ed.), *Definitionen Moderne Politikwissenschaft: Die Sammlung Pfennig* (Definitions of Modern Political Science: the Pfennig Collections, Shwalbach: Wochen Schau Verlag.

Carr, Mathew (2011), ‘The Moriscos: A Lesson from History?’, *Arches Quarterly*, 4(8): 10–17.

Caso, Frank (2008), *Global Issues: Censorship*, New York: Infobase Publishing.

Casper, Gretchen (1995), *Fragile Democracies: The Legacies of Authoritarian Rule*, Pittsburgh: University of Pittsburgh Press.

Chilton, Paul (2004), *Analyzing Political Discourse: Theory and Practice*, London: Routledge.

Ching, Erik (2014), *Authoritarian El Salvador: Politics and the Origins of the Military Regime, 1880–1940*, Notre Dame, IN: Notre Dame Press.

Clark, Janine A. (2004), *Islam, Charity and Activism: Middle-class Networks and Social Welfare in Egypt, Jordan and Yemen*, Bloomington: Indiana University Press.

Cleveland, William L. (2000), *A History of the Modern Middle East*, 2nd edition, Oxford: Westview Press.

Cook, Steven A. (2007), *Ruling but Not Governing: The Military and Political Development in Egypt, Algeria and Turkey*, Baltimore: John Hopkins University Press.

Dalton, Russell J. (1988), *Citizen Politics in Western Democracies: Public Opinion and Political Parties in the United States, Great Britain, West Germany, and France*, New Jersey: Chatham House Publishers.

Das, Rahul Peter (2005), *Eurocentrism and the Falsification of Perception: An Analysis with Special Reference to South East Asia*, Südasienwissenschaftliche Arbeitsblätter, South Asia Scholarly Working Papers, Band 7, Halle (Saale).

Davidson, Donald (2001), *Subjective, Intersubjective, Objective*, Oxford: Clarendon Press.

Dekmejian, Richard Hrair (1972), *Egypt under Nasir: A Study in Political Dynamics*, London: University of London Press.

Demirovic, Alex (2007), 'Politische Gesellschat-Zivile Gesellschaft: Zur Theorie des integralen Staates bei Antonio Gramsci' (Political Society-Civil society: On the Theory of the Integral State of Antonio Gramsci). In Sonja Buckel and Andreas Fischer-Lescano (eds), *Hegemonie gepanzert mit Zwang: Zivilgesellschaft und Politik im Staatsverstaendnis Antonio Gramsci* (Hegemony Shielded with Coercion: Civil Society and Politics in the Conception of the State of Antonio Gramsci), Baden/Baden: Nomos Press.

Djaiit, Hichem (1978), *L'Europe et l'Islam* (Europe and Islam), Paris: Editions du Seuil.

Dodwell, Henry (2011), *The Founder of Modern Egypt: A Study of Muhammad 'Ali*, first printed in 1931, New York: Cambridge University Press.

Doorn-Harder, Pieternella Van (2005), 'Copts: Fully Egyptian, but for a Tattoo?'. In Maya Shatzmiller (ed.), *Nationalism and Minority Identities in Islamic Societies*, Canada, Ontario: McGill-Queen's University.

Dunne, Michele D., and Tarek Radwan (2014), 'Egypt: Why Liberalism Still Matters'. In Larry Diamond and Marc F. Plattner (eds), *Democratization and Authoritarianism in The Arab World*, Baltimore: John Hopkins University Press.

Dunne, Michele D., and Amr Hamzawy (2017), 'Egypt's Secular Parties: Struggle for Identity and Independence', Carnegie Endowment for International Peace, 31 March, https://carnegieendowment.org/2017/03/31/egypt-s-secular-political-parties-strug gle-for-identity-and-independence-pub-68482.

Dunne, Michele D., and Amr Hamzawy (2019), *Egypt's Political Exiles: Going Anywhere but Home*, Carnegie Endowment for International Peace, 29 March, https://carnegieendowment.org/2019/03/29/egypt-s-political-exiles-going-anywh ere-but-home-pub-78728.

Elgindy, Khaled (2011), 'Army Might Be the Real Winner in Egypt', *CNN*, 13 December, https://edit ion.cnn.com/2011/12/13/opin ion/elgi ndy-egypt-electi ons/index.html.

Eltahawy, Mona (2000), Kosheh Clashes Egypt in Shock after Sectarian Violence, *The Guardian*, 17 January, at: https://www.theguardian.com/world/2000/jan/17/4.

(Enayat) 'Ināyit, Ḥāmid (1984), *al-Fikr al-Siyāsī al-'Islāmī al-Mu'āṣir* (Contemporary Islamic Political Thought), trans. 'Ibrāhīm al-Disūkī Shitā, Cairo: Madbouly Library.

England, Andrew (2023), Egypt Vows to Cut Military's Outsized Role in Economy under IMF Bailout, *Financial Times*, 10 January, https://www.ft.com/content/0ab59 ecb-da0b-42d9-a5da-35674c001e28.

Esposito, John L. (1992), *The Islamic Threat: Myth or Reality?* New York: Oxford University Press.

Esposito, John L. (ed.) (1999), *The Oxford History of Islam*, New York: Oxford University Press.

Esposito, John L. (2010), *The Future of Islam*, New York: Oxford University Press.

Esposito, John L., and Dalia Mogahed (2007), *Who Speaks for Islam: What a Billion Muslims Really Think*, New York: Gallup Press.

Essam El-Din, Gamal (2011), 'The Coincidental Rise and Momentous Fall of Hosni Mubarak', *Ahram Online*, 17 April, https://english.ahram.org.eg/News Content/1/64/10190/Egypt/Politics-/The-coincidental-rise-and-moment ous-fall-of-Hosni-.aspx.

Ettmueller, Eliane (2008), 'Religion, Reform and Progress Critical Voices from Egypt', *Konrad-Adenauer-Stiftung*, https://www.kas.de/documents/252038/253252/7_d okument_dok_pdf_14769_1.pdf/ba1c6d38-99c5-aabb-f82a-d926e1db184f?vers ion=1.0&t=1539670231923.

Ezzat, Heba (1995), *Woman and Political Activity: An Islamic Vision* (al- Maraa wa-l-'Amal al-Siyasi: Ruyaa Islamiyya), Virginia: Internayional Institute for Islamic Thought.

Ezzeldeen, Nahed (2010), 'Protest Movements in Egypt: The Case of Kefaya'. In Dimitar Bechev and Isabel Schäfer (ed.), *Agents of Change in the Mediterranean*, Ramses Working paper, 14 May, https://t.ly/YmbE.

Faḍl 'Allāh, Mahdī (1995), *al-'Aql wa-l-Sharī'a: Mabāḥith fī-l-'Ipistomoljiya al-'Arabiyya al-'Islāmiyya* (Intellect and Shari'a: Research in Arab and Islamic Epistemology), Beirut: Dar al-Tali'a.

Faḍl 'Allāh, Mahdī (2004), *al-'Islām wa-l-Ḥaḍāra* (Islam and Civilization), Beirut: Dar al-Hadi.

Fairfield, Paul (2011), *Philosophical Hermeneutics Reinterpreted: Dialogues with Existentialism, Pragmatism, Critical Theory and Postmodernism*, London: Continuum International Publishing group.

Farrūkh, 'Umar (1986), *Tajdīd fi-l-Muslimīn, lā fi-l-'Islām* (Renewal in Muslims, Not in Islam), Beirut: Dar al-Kitab al-'Arabi.

Farrūkh, 'Abd al-Khāliq (2011), *al-'Usus al-Dustūriyya wa-l-Qānūniyya li Muḥākamit Mubārak* (The Constitutional and Legal Grounds of Trying Mubarak), Giza: al-Markaz al-'Arabi al-Dawli li-l-Islam.

Fattah, Moataz A. (2006), *Democratic Values in the Muslim World*, Boulder, CO: Lynne Rienner Publishers.

Fawzī, Maḥmūd (2001), *Mā Baiyn al-Ru'sā' wa-l-Kuttāb Mā Ṣana' al-Ḥaddād* (Between Presidents and Writers: What the Ironsmith Did), Cairo: Dar al-Fikr al-'Arabi.

Faye, Jan (2012), *After Postmodernism: A Naturalistic Construction of the Humanities*, New York: Palgrave Macmillan.

Fāyid, Maḥmūd 'Abd al-Wahhāb (1976), *'Ālim 'Azharī Ḥur Yuwājih al-Sulṭān al-Jā'ir Bi-Qalamih, wa Qalbih wa Lisānih* (A Free Azhari Scholar Facing the Unjust Sultan, with his pen, Heart and Tongue), Cairo: Dar al-Nasr li-l-Tiba'a wa-l-Nashr.

Ferris, Jesse (2012), *Nasser's Gamble: How Intervention in Yemen Caused the Six-Day War and the Decline of Egyptian Power*, Princeton, NJ: Princeton University Press.

Foucault, Michael (1969), 'What Is an Author?'. In Donald F. Bouchard (ed.) (1977), *Language, Counter-Memory, Practice: Selected Essays and Interviews by Michell Foucault*, Ithaca, NY: Cornell University Press.

Foucault, Michael (1970), 'The Order of Discourse, Inaugural Lecture at the College de France'. In Robert Young (ed.) (1981), *Untying the Text: A Post-Structuralist Reader*, Boston: Routledge.

Foucault, Michael (2008), *Le Gouvernement de Soi et des Autres* (Government of the Self and the Other). In Frederic Gros (ed.), *Lectures of College de France* (1982–3), an edition prepared under the supervision of Francois Ewald et al. Gallimard: Seuil.

Foucault, Michael (2011), *Leçons sur la Volonté de Savoir* (Lessons on the Desire to Know), Lectures of College de France (1970–1), an edition prepared under the supervision of Francois Ewald et al. Gallimard: Seuil.

Fuchs, Dieter (2007), 'Legitimität' (Legitimacy). In Dieter Fuchs and Edeltraud Roller (eds), *Lexikon Politik: Hunderte Grundbegriffe* (Lexicon of Politics: Hundreds of Basic Terms), 158–61, Stuttgart: Phillip Reclam jun.

Fudge, Bruce (2011), *Qur'ānic Hermeneutics: al-Ṭabrisī and the Craft of Commentary*, New York: Routledge.

Fukuyama, Francis (1992), *The End of History and the Last Man*, New York: Macmillan.

Fyzee, Asaf A. (1963), *A Modern Approach to Islam*, India: Asia Publishing House.

al-Fiqī, Muḥammad 'Alī 'Uthmān (1986), *Fiqh al-Mu'āmalāt: Dirāsa Muqārana* (Mu'amalat Jurisprudence: a Comparative Study), Riyad: Dar al-Marrikh.

Gadamer, Hans-Georg (1960), *Wahrheit und Methode, Grundzüge einer Philosophischen Hermeneutik* (Truth and Method, Basics of a Hermeneutic Philosophy), 5th edition, 1986, Tübingen: JCB Mhr, Paul Siebeck.

Gamal El-Din, El-Sayed (2013), 'Egypt's Prosecutor-General Appeals Court Verdict Ordering His Removal', *Ahram Online*, 25 April, http://english.ahram.org.eg/News

Content/1/64/70142/Egypt/Politics-/Egypts-prosecutorgeneral-appeals-court-verdict-ord.aspx.
Gartman, David (2013), *Culture, Class, and Critical Theory: Between Bourdieu and the Frankfurt School*, New York: Routledge.
Gat, Moshe (2012), *In Search of a Peace Settlement: Egypt and Israel between the Wars 1967–1973*, New York: Palgrave Macmillan.
Ghānim, ʾIbrāhīm al-Bayūmī (1992), *al-Fikr al-Siyāsī li-l-ʾImām Ḥasan al-Bannā* (The Political Thought of Imam Hasan al-Banna), Cairo: Dar al-Tawziʿ wa-l-Nashr al-Islamiyya.
Ghānim, ʾIbrāhīm al-Bayūmī (ed.) (1999), *Ṭāriq al-Bishrī: al-Qāḍī wa-l-Mufakkir* (Tariq al-Bishri: The Judge and the Thinker), Cairo: Dar El Shorouk.
Ghuliyūn, Burhān (2007), *Naqd al-Siyāsa: al-Dawla wa-l-Dīn* (Criticizing Politics: The State and Religion), 4th edition, Beirut: al-Markaz al-Thaqafi al-ʿArabi.
Goldschmidt, Arthur (2013), *Historical Dictionary of Egypt*, 4th edition, Lanham, MD: Scarecrow Press.
Gordon, Joel (1992), *Nasser's Blessed Movement: Egypt's Free Officers and the July Revolution*, Oxford: Oxford University Press.
Gordon, Joel (2006), *Nasser: Hero of the Arab Nation*, Oxford: Oneworld Publications.
Görgün, Hilal (1997), *Die Politische Rolle der Azhar in der Sadat-Ära (1970–1981)* (The Political Role of al-Azhar in the Sadat Era), Istanbul: Türkiye Diyanet Vakfi: Islam Arastrmalari Merkezi.
Gothoni, Rene (2011), *Words Matter: Hermeneutics in the Study of Religions*, Bern: Peter Lang.
Gramsci, Antonio (1986), *Zu Politik, Geschichte und Kultur: ausgewählte Schriften* (On Politics, History and Culture: Selected Writings), Leipzig: Philipp Recalm jun Press.
Grant, Kevin Douglas (2011), 'Samira Victorious: Egyptian Military to End "Virginity Tests"', *Global Post*, 27 December, https://theworld.org/stories/2011-12-27/samira-victorious-egyptian-military-end-virginity-tests.
Griffel, Frank (2007), 'Introduction'. In Abbas Ammanat and Frank Griffel (eds), *Shari'a: Islamic Law in the Contemporary Context*, 10–44, Stanford, CA: Stanford University Press.
Gruber, Mark (2003), *Sacrifice in the Desert: A Study of an Egyptian Minority through the Prism of Coptic Monasticism*, Lanham, MD: University Press of America.
al-Ghazālī, Muḥammad (1987), *Jihād al-Daʿwa: Baiyn ʿAjz al-Dākhil wa Qaiyd al-Khārij* (Jihad of the Call: Between Domestic Inability and External Limitation), Cairo: Dar al-Sahwa.
Habermas Jürgen (1996), *Between Facts and Norms: Contributions to a Discourse Theory of Law and Democracy*, trans. W. Rehg, Cambridge: Polity Press.
Ḥabīb, Rafīq (2012), *al-Dawlatān: al-ʾIslāmiyūn wa-l-Dawla al-Qawmiyya* (The Two States: Islamists and the Nation State), Cairo: al-Madani Print house.

Hakeem, Farrukh B., M. R. Haberfeld and Arvind Verma (2012), *Policing Muslim Communities: Comparative International Context*, New York: Springer.

Halverson, Jeffry R. (2010), *Theology and Creed in Sunni Islam: The Muslim Brotherhood, Ash'arism and Political Sunnism*, New York: Palgrave Macmillan.

Ḥanafī, Ḥasan (1983), *Qadāiyā Mu'āṣira fī Fikrina al-Mu'āṣir (1)* (Contemporary Issues in Our Contemporary Thought), Beirut: Dar al-Tanwir.

Ḥanafī, Ḥasan (1990), 'al-'Almāniyya wa-l-Islam: al-'Islām lā Yaḥtāj 'ilā 'Almāniyya Gharbiyya' (Secularism and Islam: Islam Does Not Need Western Secularism). In Ḥasan Ḥanafī and Muḥammad 'Ābid al-Jābrī (eds), *Ḥiwār al-Mashriq wa-l-Maghrib* (The East and West Dialogue), 34–8, Cairo: Madbouly library.

Hanna, Michael W. (2013), 'With Friends Like These: Coptic Activism in the Diaspora', *MERIP* 267, Vol. 43, Summer, http://www.merip.org/mer/mer267/friends-these.

Harders, Cilja (1998), 'Die Furcht der Reichen und Die Hoffnungen der Armen – Ägyptens Schwieriger Weg zur Demokratie' (The Fear of the Rich and the Hopes of the Poor – Egypt's Difficult Route to Democracy). In Gunter Schubert and Rainer Tetzlaff (eds), *Blockierte Demokratien in der Dritten Welt* (Blocked Democracies in the Third World), 267–95, Opladen, Germany: Leke & Budrich.

Harders, Cilja (2009), 'Politik von Unten – Perspektiven auf den autoritären Staat in Ägypten' (Politics from Below – Perspectives on the Authoritarian State in Egypt). In Martin Beck, Annette Jünemann and Stephan Stetter (eds), *Der Nahe Osten im Umbruch: Zwischen Transformation und Autoritarismus* (The Middle East in Radical Change: Between Transformation and Authoritarianism), 299–323, Wiesbaden: VS Verlag für Sozialwissenschaften.

Hardy, C. (2001), 'Researching Organizational Discourse', *International Studies in Management and Organization* 31 (3): 25–47.

Hardy, C., N. Phillips and B. Harley (2004), 'Discourse Analysis and Content Analysis: Two Solitudes?', *Qualitative Methods*, Spring: 19–22, https://doi.org/10.5281/zenodo.998649.

Hardy, Roger (2010), 'Was Egypt's Sheikh Tantawi a Liberal or a Stooge?', *BBC News*, 10 March, http://news.bbc.co.uk/2/hi/middle_east/8560149.stm.

Hartmann, Jürgen (2011), *Staat und Regime im Orient und im Afrika: Regionenporträts und Länderstudien* (State and Regime in the Orient and in Africa: Regions' Portraits and Country Studies), Wiesbaden: Verlag für Sozialwissenschaften.

Ḥasan, 'Ammār 'Alī (2012), *al-Ṭarīq 'ilā al-Thawra: al-Tabāshīr wa-l-Nubū'a…al-'Inṭilāq wa-l-Ta'aththur* (The Road to Revolution: The Annunciations and the Prophecy… The Launch and the Stumble), Cairo: Dar Merit.

Hashim, A. S. (n.d.), 'al-Hadith, Analysis and Overview', *al-Islam.org*, https://www.al-islam.org/articles/al-hadith-analysis-and-overview-hashim.

Hassan, Hamdy A. (2010), 'State versus Society in Egypt: Consolidating Democracy or Upgrading Autocracy', *African Journal of Political Science and International Relations* 4 (9): 319–29.

Hassan, Hamdy A. (2011), 'Civil Society in Egypt under the Mubarak Regime', *Afro Asian Journal of Social Sciences* 2 (2.2) Quarter II, http://onlineresearchjournals.com/aajoss/art/61.pdf.

Hatina, Meir (2000), 'On the Margins of Consensus: The Call to Separate Religion and State in Modern Egypt', *Middle Eastern Studies* 36 (1): 35–67.

Ḥawwā, Sa'īd (1994), *Fuṣūl fi-l-'Imra wa-l-'Imāra* (Chapters on Command and Emirate), 2nd edition, Cairo: Dar al-Salam

Helfont, Samuel (2009), *The Sunni Divide: Understanding Politics and Terrorism in the Arab Middle East*, Philadelphia: Center on Terrorism and Counterterrorism at the Foreign Policy Research Institute, November, https://www.fpri.org/docs/media/Helfont.SunniDivide.pdf.

Ḥilmī, Muṣṭafā (2005), *'Ulamā' al-Ḥadīth wa-l-Sunna fī 'Uṣūl al-Dīn* (The Hadith and Tradition Scholars in Basics of Religion), Beirut: Dar al-Kutub al-'Ilmiyya.

Hodgson, Marshall G. S. (1974), *The Venture of Islam, Conscience and History in a World Civilization*, Vol. 1, The Classical Age of Islam, Chicago: University of Chicago Press.

Hofstadter, Dan (ed.) (1973), *Egypt & Nasser, Military Defeat, Death and Aftermath, 1967–72*, Vol. 3, New York: Library of Congress Catalog, Facts on File, INC.

Human Rights Watch (1994), 'Egypt: Violations of Freedom of Religious Belief and Expression of the Christian Minority', 1 November, https://www.refworld.org/docid/3ae6a7ec0.html.

Hussein, Abdel-Rahman (2012), 'Egypt Swears in First Post-Revolution Cabinet with Plenty of Old Guard', *The Guardian*, 2 August, https://www.theguardian.com/world/2012/aug/02/egypt-middleeast.

Hussein, Ebtisam (2012), 'Participation in Contemporary Islamic Discourse'. In *Non-Violent Protests and the Future of Moderate Islamic Reformers Post-Arab Spring*, 46–8, Conference Report, EU Parliament, Brussels, 26 April.

Hussein, Ebtisam (2018), 'Rationalizing Public Repression: Mubarak's Self-Toppling Regime', *Middle East Policy* 25 (1): 124–35, https://doi.org/10.1111/mepo.12329.

Hussein, Tam (2012), 'Suez: The Psychological Victory and the Military Defeat', *Egypt Today*, 27 June, https://www.egypttoday.com/Article/10/528/Suez-The-Psychological-Victory-and-Military-Defeat.

Hūwaidī, Fahmī (1987), *Taziyyīf al-Wa'ī* (Forging the Conscience), Cairo: Dar El Shorouk.

Hūwaidī, Fahmī (1999), *Mūwāṭinūn lā Dhimmiyyūn: Mawqi' Ghaiyr al-Muslimīn fī Mujtama' al-Muslimīn* (Citizens Not Dhimmis: Position of Non-Muslims in Muslim Society), 3rd edition, Cairo: Dar El Shorouk.

al-Ḥafiyān, Faiṣal (2006), 'al-'Ilāqa Baiyn al-Lugha wa-l-Hawiyya' (The Relation between Language and Identity). In Aḥmad Jibrīl (ed.), *al-Lugha, al-Hawiyya wa Ḥiwār al-Ḥaḍārāt* (Language, Identity and Civilizations Dialogue), Cairo University: Program for Dialogue of Civilizations.

Hoyle, Charlie (2020), 'Savior or Dictator: Copts in Sisi's Egypt Trapped by a Strongman's Balancing Act', *New Arab*, 4 February, https://www.newarab.com/analysis/copts-egypt-trapped-between-strongman-and-saviour.

al-Hawwārī, 'Abd al-Qādir (2012), *Ḥarb al-lā 'Unf wa 'Ilāqatuhā bi-l-Fawḍā al-khallāqa* (The War of No-Violence and Its Relation to Constructive Chaos), Cairo: Supreme Council for Culture.

El-Hennawy, Noha (2013), 'Gamal al-Banna Leaves behind a Controversial Legacy of Controversial Views on Islam', *Egypt Independent*, 17 February, http://www.egyptindependent.com/news/gamal-al-banna-leaves-behind-legacy-controversial-views-islam.

al-Hibri, Azizah Y. (1999a), 'Islamic Constitutionalism and the Concept of Democracy'. In Fred Dallmayr (ed.), *Border Crossings: Toward a Comparative Political Theory*, 61–88, New York: Lexington Books.

al-Hibri, Azizah Y. (1999b), 'Islamic and American Constitutional Law: Borrowing Possibilities or a History of Borrowing?', *Journal of Constitutional Law* 1 (3): 492–527.

al-Hilālī, Sa'd al-Dīn (2014), 'Tawliyyat al-Mar'a 'Aw Ghaiyr al-Muslim al-Qaḍā' 'Alā al-Muslimīn' (Allowing a Woman or a Non-Muslim Judicial Positions over Muslims), *al-Yūm al-Sābi'*, http://www1.youm7.com/News.asp?NewsID=1500126.

al-Ḥirānī, al-Saiyyid (2014), 'Mudhakkirāt Jamāl al-Bannā: al-Mutamarrid 'alldhī Faḍaḥ al-'Ālam al-Sirrī li-l-('Ikhwān) (al-Ḥalaqa al-'Akhīra)' (Memoirs of Jamal al-Banna: The Rebel Who Disclosed the Secret World of (The Brotherhood) (The Last Episode)), *al-Maṣrī al-Yūm*, 1 March, https://www.almasryalyoum.com/news/details/402682.

'Ibn Taiymiyya (1951), *Naqd al-Manṭiq li-'Ibn Tayimiyya* (Criticizing Logic by b. Taiymiyya), verified by Muḥammad 'Abd al-Rāziq Ḥamza and Sulaimān 'Abd al-Raḥmān al-Ṣāni', Cairo: al-Sunna al-Muḥammadiyya.

'Ibn Taiymiyya (1993), *Thalāth Rasā'il fi-l-Jihād lī-Shaikh al-'Islām 'Ibn Taiymiyya* (Three Letters on Jihad by Islam's Sheikh b. Taiymiyya), verified by Muḥammad 'Abū Ṣu'iliq and 'Ibrāhīm al-'ALī, Jordan: Dar al-Nafais.

Ibrahim, Saad Eddin, Marylin Tadros, Mohammed El-Fiki and Soliman S. Soliman (1996), *The Copts of Egypt*, Ibn Khaldoun Center for Development Studies, UK: British library Catalogue, http://www.refworld.org/pdfid/469cbf8ed.pdf.

Ibrahim, Solava (2021), 'The Dynamics of the Egyptian Social Contract: How the Political Changes Affected the Poor', *World Development* 138, https://doi.org/10.1016/j.worlddev.2020.105254.

'Imāra, Muḥammad (1972), *al-'Islām wa 'Uṣūl al-Ḥukm li-'Alī 'Abd al-Rāziq* (Islam and Origins of Rule of 'Ali 'Abd al-Raziq), Beirut: Arabic Institute for Studies and Publication.

'Imāra, Muḥammad (1985), *Taiyyārāt al-Fikr al-'Islāmī* (Streams of Islamic Thought), Beirut: Dar al-Wihda.

ʿImāra, Muḥammad (1988), *al-Dawla al-ʾIslāmiyya baiyn al-ʿAlmāniyya wa-l-Sulṭa al-Dīniyya* (The Islamic State between Secularism and Religious Authority), Cairo: Dar El Shorouk.

ʿImāra, Muḥammad (1989a), *al-ʾIslām wa Ḥuqūq al-ʾInsān: Ḍarūrāt .. lā Ḥuqūq* (Islam and Human Rights: Necessities: Not Rights), Cairo: Dar El Shorouk.

ʿImāra, Muḥammad (1989b), *al-ʾIslām wa Falsafit al-Ḥukm* (Islam and the Philosophy of Rule), Cairo: Dar El Shorouk.

ʿImāra, Muḥammad (1997), *Jamāl al-Dīn al-ʾAfghānī: baiyn Haqāʾiq al-Tārīkh wa ʾAkādhīb Liwīs ʿAwaḍ* (Jamal al-Din al-Afghani: Between Realities of History and LewisʿAwad Lies), 2nd edition, Cairo, Dar al-Rushd.

ʿImāra, Muḥammad (2006), *al-ʾAʿmāl al-Kāmila lī-l-ʾImām al-Shaikh Mūḥammad ʿAbdū* (The Complete Works of Imam Sheikh Muhammad ʿAbdu), Cairo: Dar El Shorouk.

ʿĪsā, ʾIbrāhīm (2008), *Kitābī ʿan Mubārak, ʿAṣrih wa Miṣrih* (My Book on Mubarak, His Time and His Egypt), Cairo: Madbouly Library.

Iskandar, Nadine A. (2014), *Les Mobilisations Sociales en Egypte Entre les Revendications Economiques et Opposition Du Regime (2005–2009)* (Social Mobilization between Economic Demands and Regime Opposition (2005–2009), PhD thesis, Grenoble University, France.

Iskander, Elizabeth (2012), *Sectarian Conflict in Egypt: Coptic Media, Identity and Representation*, New York: Routledge Press.

ʾIqbāl, Muḥammad (2010), *Tajdīd al-Fikr al-Dīnī fi-l-ʾIslām* (Renewing Religious Thought in Islam), trans. ʿAbbās Maḥmūd, Cairo: al-Hayaa al-Misriyya al-ʿAmma li-l-Kitab.

al-ʿIrāqī, ʿĀṭif (superv) (1995), *al-Shaikh Muḥammad ʿAbdū (1849–1905)* (Sheikh Muhammad ʿAbdu), Cairo: Supreme Council of Culture.

al-Jābrī, Muḥammad ʿĀbid (1990a), ʿal-ʿAlmāniyya wa-l-ʾIslām: al-ʾIslām laiysa Kanīsa Kay Nafṣilahu ʿan al-Dawlaʾ (Secularism and Islam: Islam Is not a Church to Separate from the State). In Ḥasan Ḥanafī and Muḥammad ʿĀbid al-Jābrī (eds), *Ḥiwār al-Mashriq wa-l-Maghrib* (The East and West Dialogue), 39–44, Cairo: Madbouly Library.

al-Jābrī, Muḥammad ʿĀbid (1990b), *ʾIshkāliyyāt al-Fikr al-ʿArabī al-Muʿāṣir* (The Problematics of Contemporary Arab Thought), Beirut: Center for Arab Unity Studies.

al-Jābrī, Muḥammad ʿĀbid (1992), *Wijhat Naẓar…Naḥw ʾIʿādat Bināʾ Qaḍāiya al-Fikr al-ʿArabī al-Muʿāṣir* (A Perspective: Towards Reconstructing the Issues of Contemporary Arab Thought), Casablanca: el Markaz al-Thaqafi al-ʿArabi.

al-Jabri, Mohammad Abed (2009), *Democracy, Human Rights and Law in Islamic Thought*, London: I.B. Tauris.

James, Laura M. (2006), *Nasser at War: Arab Images of the Enemy*, New York: Palgrave Macmillan.

Jāmiʿ, Maḥmūd (1998), *ʿAraft al-Sādāt: Niṣf Qarn min Khafāiya al-Sādāt wa-l-ʾIkhwān* (I Knew Sadat: Half a Century of Sadat and Brotherhood Secrets), Cairo: al-Maktab al-Misri al-Hadith.

Jid'ān, Fahmī (1988), *'Usus al-Taqaddum 'ind Mufakkirī al-'Islām* (Foundations of Progress of Islam Thinkers), Amman, Jordan: Dar El Shorouk.

Johnson, Amy J. (2004), *Reconstructing Rural Egypt*, New York: Syracuse University Press.

Jung, Dietrich (2011), *Orientalists, Islamists and the Global Public Sphere: A Genealogy of the Modern Essentialist Image of Islam*, Oakville: Equinox.

al-Juhainī, Aḥmad, and Muḥammad Muṣṭafā (2005), *al-'Islām wa-l-'Ākhar* (Islam and the Other), Cairo, al-Haiyaa al-Misriyya al-'Amma li-l-Kitab.

Kahn-Paycha, Daniele (2000), Popular Jewish Literature and Its Role in the Making of an Identity, *Jewish Studies*, Vol. 21, New York: Edwin Mellen Press.

Kalmar, Ivan (2012), *Early Orientalism: Imagined Islam and the Notion of Sublime Power*, New York: Routledge.

Kamali, Mohammad Hashim (2008), *Shari'ah Law: An Introduction*, Oxford: One World Publications.

Kamrava, Mehran (2006), 'Introduction: Reformist Islam in Comparative Perspective'. In Mehran Kamrava (ed.), *The New Voices of Islam Reforming Politics and Modernity-A Reader*, 1–27, New York: I.B. Tauris.

Karlsson, Johan (2008), *Democrats without Borders: A Critique of Transnational Democracy*, Sweden: University of Gothenburg.

Karūm, Ḥasan (2012), *al-Taḥarrukāt al-Siyāsiyya lī-l-'Ikhwān al-Muslimīn* (The Political Moves of the Muslim Brotherhood), Cairo: International Media Arab Center.

Kassab, Beesan (2018), 'Egypt's History of Privatization', *Ahram Online*, 28 June, https://english.ahram.org.eg/NewsContent/3/12/305720/Business/Economy/Egypts-history-of-privatisation-.aspx.

Kassem, May (2004), *Egyptian Politics: The Dynamics of Authoritarian Rule*, Colorado: Lynne Rienner Publishers.

Katsumori, Makoto (2011), *Niels Bohr's Complementarity: Its Structure, History, and Intersections with Hermeneutics and Deconstruction*, New York: Springer.

Kenez, Peter (2006), *A History of the Soviet Union from the Beginning to the End*, 2nd edition, New York: Cambridge University Press.

Khalaf 'Allāh, 'Aḥmad Ṭāha (2010), *Taraddī al-Fikr al-'Islāmī al-Mu'āṣir: Bayn al-'Uṣūliyya al-Mustabidda wa-l-'Almāniyya al-Mustafizza* (Deterioration of Contemporary Islamic Thought between Despotic Fundamentalism and Provocative Secularism), Cairo: Madbouly.

Khalil, Ashraf (2001), 'Paper's Sex Expose Stirs Egypt Furor', *Chicago Tribune*, 20 June, https://www.chicagotribune.com/news/ct-xpm-2001-06-20-0106200212-story.html.

Khamīs, Muḥammad 'Aḥmad, and 'Ibrāhīm Mukhtār (2011), *Thawra bi-lā Qā'id: 'Asrār wa Waqā'i' Thawrat 25 Yanāiyir 2011* (A Revolution with No Leader: Secrets and Facts of the 25th of January Revolution), Cairo: Dar al-Tiba'a al-Ḥaditha.

Khazbak, Rana (2011), 'Military Questions Journalists over Allegations of Abuse by Military Police', *Egypt Independent*, 31 May, http://www.egyptindependent.com/news/military-questions-journalists-over-allegations-abuse-military-police.

Khurshid, 'I'timād (1988), *Shāhida 'alā 'Inḥirāfāt Ṣalāḥ Naṣr* (A Witness on Salah Nasr's Perversions), Cairo: 'Amūn Institution for Print and Publication

Kienle, Eberhand (2000), *A Grand Delusion: Democracy and Economic Reform in Egypt*, New York: I.B. Tauris.

Kilpatrick, Hilary (2006), 'Socializing'. In Joseph W. Meri (ed.), *Medieval Islamic Civilization: Encyclopedia*, Vol. 2, 762–3, New York: Taylor and Francis.

Kirkpatrick, David D. (2011), 'Egypt Military Aims to Cement Muscular Role in Government', *New York Times*, 16 July, http://www.nytimes.com/2011/07/17/world/middleeast/17egypt.html?pagewanted=all&_r=0.

Kirkpatrick, David D., and Kareem Fahim (2011), 'In Egypt, a Panel of Jurists Is Given the Task of Revising the Constitution', *New York Times*, 15 February, https://www.nytimes.com/2011/02/16/world/middleeast/16egypt.html?referringSource=articleShare.

Kogelmann, Franz (1994), *Die Islamisten Aegyptens In der Regierungszeit Von Anwar As-Sadat (1970–1981)* (Egypt's Islamists during the Rule of Anwar al-Sadat), Berlin, Klaus Schwarz Verlag.

Krämer, Gudrun (1986), *Ägypten unter Mubarak: Identität und nationales Interesse* (Egypt under Mubarak: Identity and National Interest), Baden-Baden: Nomos Verlagsgesellschaft.

Krämer, Gudrun (1994), *Politischer Islam. 3. Elemente einer 'Islamischen Ordnung'* (Political Islam. 3. Elements of an 'Islamic Order'), Hagen: Fern University.

Krämer, Gudrun (2000a), *Gottes Staat als Republik: Reflexionen Zeitgenössischer Muslime zu Islam, Menschen Rechte und Demokratie* (God's State as a Republic: Reflections of Contemporary Muslims on Islam, Human Rights and Democracy), Baden. Baden: Nomos Verlaggesellschaft.

Krämer, Gudrun (2000b), *Responsabilité, Égalité, Pluralisme: Reflexions sur Quelques Notions-Clés d'un Ordre Islamique Moderne* (Responsibility, Equality and Pluralism: Reflections on Some Key-Notions in a Modern Islamic Order), Casablanca: Editions Le Fennec.

Krämer, Gudrun, and Sabine Schmidtke (eds.) (2006), 'Introduction: Religious Authority and Religious Authorities in Muslim Societies: A Critical Overview'. In *Speaking for Islam: Religious Authorities in Muslim Societies*, Leiden: Brill.

Krämer, Gudrun (2007), 'Justice in Modern Islamic Thought'. In Abbas Ammanat and Frank Griffel (eds), *Shari'a: Islamic Law in the Contemporary Context*, 45–76, Stanford, CA: Stanford University Press.

Krämer, Gudrun (2010), *Hassan al-Banna*, Oxford: One World.

Krämer, Gudrun (2011), *Demokratie im Islam: Der Kampf für Toleranz und Freiheit in der Arabischen Welt* (Democracy in Islam: The Struggle for Tolerance and Freedom in the Arab World), München: Verlag C.H. Beck.

Krämer, Gudrun (2013), *Geschichte des Islam* (History of Islam), 3rd edition, München: Deutsche Taschenbuch Verlag.

Kuraiyyma, Aḥmad Muḥammad (2003), *al-Jihād fī-l-'Islām: Dirāsa Fiqhiyya Muqārana* (Jihad in Islam: A Comparative Juridical Study), Cairo: Matabiʿ al-Dar al-Handasiyya.

al-Khaiyyāṭ, ʿAbd al-ʿAzīz (1989), *Huqūq al-'Insān wa-l-Tamyyīz al-ʿUnṣurī fī-l-'Islām* (Human Rights and Racial Discrimination in Islam), Cairo: Dar al-Salam.

al-Khaiyyāṭ, Muḥammad Haiytham (2006), 'Kaiyf Yaḥduth al-Taghaiyyur fī-l-Lugha al-ʿArabiyya? Wa-Mādhā Ḥadath?' (How Does Change in the Arabic Language Take Place? And What Happenend?). In Aḥmad Jibrīl (ed.), *al-Lugha, al-Hawiyya wa Ḥiwār al-Ḥaḍārāt* (Language, Identity and Civilizations Dialogue), Cairo: Cairo University, Program for Dialogue of Civilizations.

al-Khaṭīb, ʿAbd al-Karīm (1982), *al-Ḥudūd fī-l-'Islām: Ḥikmatuhā .. wa 'Atharuhā fī-l-'Afrād wa-l-Jamāʿāt wa-l-'Umam* (Hudud in Islam: Its Wisdom and its Impact on Individuals and Communities and Nations), Cairo: Dar al-Fikr al-ʿArabi.

al-Kinānī, ʿAbd al-Ḥalīm (1998), *'Ahdāfunā: 'Akhṭar Qaḍāiyā al-Muslimīn* (Our Goals: Most Serious Muslim Issues), 1st edition, Daqahliyya, Egypt: Dar al-Wafaa.

Labīb, Hānī (2012), *al-Kanīsa al-Miṣriyya: Tawāzunāt al-Dīn wa-l-Dawla* (The Egyptian Church: The Balances of Religion and the State), Cairo: Dar Nahdat Misr for Publications.

Lambton, Ann K. S. (1981), *State and Government in Medieval Islam: an Introduction to the Study of Islamic Political Theory: The Jurists*, Oxford: Oxford University Press.

Lane, Jan-Erik, and Hamadi Redissi (2004), *Religion and Politics: Islam and Muslim Civilization*, England: Ashgate.

Lavi, L. (2012), 'People's Assembly Elections in Egypt Yield Victory for Muslim Brotherhood, Salafis: Downfall of Liberals, Left and Revolutionary Youth', *Middle East Media Research Institute*, 3 February, http://www.memri.org/report/en/print6052.htm.

Lemon, Robert (2011), *Imperial Messages: Orientalism as Self-Critique in the Habsburg Fin de Siecle*, New York: Camden House.

Lewis, Bernard (1993), *Islam and the West*, New York: Oxford University Press.

Lindroos-Hovinhemo, Susanna (2012), *Justice and the Ethics of Legal Interpretation*, New York: Routledge.

Lippman, Thomas W. (1989), *Egypt after Nasser*, New York: Paragon House.

Lippman, Thomas W. (2016), *Hero of the Crossing: How Anwar Sadat and the 1973 War Changed the World*, Lincoln, NE: Potomac Books, 264.

Little, D. P. (1979), 'Three Arab Critiques of Orientalism', *Muslim World* 69 (2): 110–31.

Longman Active Study Dictionary of English (2010), 5th revised edn, London: Pearson Longman.

Lynch, Mark (2006), *Voices of the New Arab Republic: Iraq; al-Jazeera and Middle East Politics Today*, New York: Columbia University Press.

Maʿhad al-ʿArabiyya lil-Dirāsāt (al-Arabiya Institute for Studies) (2012), 'Al-'Azhar wa Ṯhawrat 25 Yanāyyer: Raṣd Tawthīqī wa Qrā'a Mawḍūʿiyya' (al-Azhar and the 25 January Revolution: Documentary Monitoring and an Objective Reading), 15

October, https://www.alarabiya.net/2012/10/15/الأزهر-وثورة-25-يناير-رصد-توثيقي-وقراءة-موضوعية.

Maḥmūd, ʻAbd al-Ḥalīm (1994), *Fihm ʼUṣūl al-ʼIslām* (Understanding the Origins of Islam), Cairo, Dar al-Tawziʻ wa-l-Nashr al-Islamiyya.

Māher Midḥat (2019), *Ḥwārāt maʻa Ṭāriq al-Bishrī: Sīra Maʻrifiyya Baiyn al-ḏāt wal-ʼUmma* (Dialogues with Tariq al-Bishri: A Knowledge Biography between the Self and the Nation), Cairo: Civilizational Center for Studies and Research.

Makar, Johannes (2016), 'How Egypt's Copts Fell Out of Love with President Sisi?', *Foreign Policy*, 9 December, https://foreignpolicy.com/2016/12/09/how-egypts-copts-fell-out-of-love-with-president-sisi/.

Makari, Peter E. (2007), *Conflict and Cooperation: Christian-Muslim Relations in Contemporary Egypt*, New York: Syracuse University Press.

Mandour, Maged (2018), *The Military's Immunity in Egypt*, Carnegie Endowment for International Peace, 2 July, https://carnegieendowment.org/sada/76904.

Mansour, Sherif (2013), 'Two Years on, Mubarak's Tactics still Haunt Egypt Media', *Committee to Protect Journalists CPJ Blog*, 24 January, http://cpj.org/blog/2013/01/two-years-on-mubaraks-tactics-still-haunt-egypt-me.php.

Margolis, Joseph (1995), *Historied Thought, Constructed World. A Conceptual Primer of the Turn of the Millennium*, Berkley: University of California Press.

Marshall, Paul (2004), 'Egypt's Endangered Christians'. In Martyn Thomas (ed. in chief) (2006), *Copts in Egypt, a Christian Minority under Siege*, Zürich, September 23–25, 2004, papers presented at the first international Coptic Symposium, Zürich: Vandenheock & Reprecht GMbH.

Mashhūr, Muṣṭafā (2004), *Durūs ʻAlā al-Ṭarīq* (Lessons on the Road), Cairo: Dar al-Tawziʻ wa-l-Nashr al-Islamiyya.

Mayo, Peter (2006), *Politische Bildung bei Antonio Gramsci und Paulo Freire: Perspektiven einer veränderten Praxis* (Political Education of Antonio Gramsci und Paulo Freire: Perspectives of a Changed Practice), Hamburg: Argument Verlag.

McDermott, Anthony (1988), *Egypt from Nasser to Mubarak: A Flawed Revolution*, Australia: Croom Helm.

McLean, Iain (ed.) (1996), *Oxford Concise Dictionary of Politics*, Oxford: Oxford University Press.

Mehrez, Samia (2008), *Egypt's Cultural Wars: Politics and Practice*, New York: Routledge.

Mikhail, Kyriakos (1911), *Copts and Moslems under British Control: A Collection of Facts and a Resume of Authoritative Opinions on the Coptic Question*, London: Smith, Elder.

Milner, Alfred ([1892] 1970), *England in Egypt*, New York: Howard Fertig. Reprint of the 1920, 13th edition, London: Edward Arnold.

Mitchell, Richard (1993), *The Society of the Muslim Brotherhood*, New York: Oxford University Press.

Mitwallī, ʻAbd al-Ḥamīd (1985), *Āzmat al-Fikr al-Siyāsī al-'Islāmī fī-l-ʻAṣr al-Ḥadīth: Maẓāhirhā, 'Asbābhā-'Ilājhā* (Crisis of Islamic Political Thought in the Modern Age: Its Manifestations, Causes and Remedies), Cairo: al-Haiyaa al-Misriyya al-ʻAmma li-l-Kitab.

Morshedy, Youssef Esmat (2014), 'Constructing an Islamist Vision: A Discourse Analysis of Egyptian Islamist Websites', *American University in Cairo, Digital Archive and Research Repository*, 23 January, https://fount.aucegypt.edu/cgi/viewcontent.cgi?article=2003&context=etds.

Morsy, Ahmed, and Nathan Brown (2013), *Egypt's al-Azhar Steps Forward*, Carnegie Endowment for International Peace, 7 November, https://carnegieendowment.org/2013/11/07/egypt-s-al-azhar-steps-forward-pub-53536.

Mostyn, Trevor (2010), 'Sheikh Mohammed Tantawi Obituary', *The Guardian*, 10 March, http://www.theguardian.com/world/2010/mar/10/sheikh-mohammed-tantawi-obituary.

Moustafa, Tamir (2008), 'Law and Resistance in Authoritarian States: The Judicialisation of Politics in Egypt'. In Tom Ginsburg and Tamir Moustafa (eds), *Rule by Law: The Politics of Courts in Authoritarian Regimes*, 132–55, New York: Cambridge University Press.

Moustafa, Tamir, and Tom Ginsburg (2008), 'The Functions of Courts in Authoritarian Politics'. In Tom Ginsburg and Tamir Moustafa (eds), *Rule by Law: The Politics of Courts in Authoritarian Regimes*, 1–22, New York: Cambridge University Press.

Muḥammad, ʻAlā' Muḥammad Saʻīd (2007), *Muḥāwalāt al-'Iṣlāḥ wa-l-Taghyyīr fī-l-ʻĀlam al-ʻArabī al-Muʻāṣir wa Mawqif al-Daʻwa al-'Islāmiyya Minhā* (Attempts at Reform and Change in Contemporary Arab World and Islamic Daʻwa Position on it), al-Mansoura: Shorouk.

Muḥī al-Dīn, Khālid (1995), *Memoires of a Revolution: Egypt 1952*, Cairo: American University in Cairo Press.

Muntaṣir, Ṣalāḥ (2011), *al-Ṣuʻūd wa-l-Suqūṭ: min al-Manaṣṣa 'ilā al-Maḥkama* (The Rise and the Fall from the Podium to the Court), 1st edition, Cairo: Muassasat al-Misri li-l-Sahafa wa-l-Tibaʻa.

Mūrū, Muḥammad (1991), *Ṭāriq al-Bishrī: Shāhid ʻalā Suqūṭ al-ʻAlmāniyya* (Tariq al-Bishri: Witness to the Fall of Secularism), Cairo: Dar al-Mukhtar al-Islami.

Muṣṭafā, 'Aḥmad, and 'Aḥmad Raḥīm (2011), 'Miṣr: al-Majlis al-ʻAskarī Maṣdūm min Ḥajm al-Fasād… wa Ḥamlat "Taṭhīr" fī-l-Dākhiliyya' (Egypt: The Military Council Is Shocked from the Size of Corruption…and a 'Purging' Campaign in the Interior Ministry), *al-Ḥaiyāt*, 16 February, no. 17484.

Muzikar, Joseph (1989), 'Gamal Abdel Nasser and His Attitude to Islam'. In Martin Robbe and Jürgen Hösel (eds), *Egypt: The Revolution of July 1952 and Gamal Abdel Nasser*, Asia Africa Latin America Special Issue 23, Berlin: Akademie-Verlag.

al-Mīlād, Zakī (1999), *al-Fikr al-'Islāmī: Qirā'āt wa Murājaʻāt* (Islamic Thought: Readings and Revisions), Beirut: Muassasat al-Intishar al-ʻArabi.

al-Misīrī, 'Abd al-Wahhāb (2002), *al-Falsafa al-Mādiyya wa Tafkīk al-'Insān* (Materialist Philosophy and the Deconstruction of the Human Being), Beirut: Dar al-Fikr al-Mu'asir.

Nordland, Rod, and Mayy El Sheikh (2012), 'Egyptian President Names Minister in Interim Cabinet as Premier', *New York Times*, 24 July, http://www.nytimes.com/2012/07/25/world/middleeast/egyptian-president-names-prime-minister.html?_r=0.

Nyang, Sulayman, Mumtaz Ahmad and Zahid Bukhari (2012), 'Introduction'. In Mumtaz Ahmad, Zahid Bukhari, and Sulayman Nyang (eds), *Observing the Observer: The State of Islamic Studies in American Universities*, IX–XXVII, Washington, DC: International Institute of Islamic Thought, https://doi.org/10.2307/j.ctvkc672v.

An-Na'im, Abdullahi Ahmed (2008), 'Shari'a in the Secular State: A Paradox of Separation and Conflation'. In Peri Bearman, Wohlfahrt Heinrichs and Bernard Weiss (eds), *The Law Applied: Contextualizing the Islamic Shari'a*, New York: I.B. Tauris.

Oweidat, Nadia et al. (2008), *The Kefaya Movement: A Case Study of a Grassroots Reform Initiative*, Pittsburgh: Rand Corporation.

Pace, Eric (1981), 'Anwar el-Sadat, the Daring Arab Pioneer of Peace with Israel', Obituary, *New York Times on the Web*, 7 October, https://www.nytimes.com/1981/10/07/obituaries/anwar-el-sadat-daring-arab-pioneer-peace-with-israel-sadat-s-innovations-sprang.html.

Pargeter, Alison (2010), *The Muslim Brotherhood: The Burden of Tradition*, India: Thomas Press.

Peters, Rudolph (2005), *Punishment in Islamic Law: Theory and Practice from the Sixteenth to the Twenty-first Century*, New York: Cambridge University Press.

Podeh, Elie, and Onn Winckler (eds) (2004), 'Introduction'. In *Rethinking Nasserism: Revolution and Historical Memory in Modern Egypt*, 1–44, Gainesville: University Press of Florida.

Puolakka, Kalle (2011), *Relativism and Internationalism in Interpretation: Davidson, Hermeneutics, and Pragmatism*, Lanham, MD: Lexington Books.

Qandīl, 'Abd al-Ḥalīm (2010), *al-Ra'īs al-Badīl* (The Alternative President), 1st edition, Cairo: Dār al-Thaqāfa al-Jadīda.

al-Qaraḍāwī, Yūsuf (1985), *Sharī'at al-'Islām: Ṣāliḥa li-l-Taṭbīq fī kul Zamān wa Makān* (Islam's Shari'a: Applicable in Every Time and Place), Cairo: Dar al-Sahwa.

al-Qaraḍāwī, Yūsuf (1997a), *Mustaqbal al-'Uṣūliyya al-'Islāmiyya* (Future of Islamic Fundamentalism), Cairo: Wahba Library.

al-Qaraḍāwī, Yūsuf (1997b), *al-'Islām wa-l-'Almāniyya Wajhan li-Wajh* (Islam and Secularism: Face-to-Face), Cairo: Wahba Library.

al-Qaraḍāwī, Yūsuf (1997c), *Min Fiqh al-Dawla fī-l-'Islām* (From the State Jurisprudence in Islam), Cairo: Dar El Shorouk.

al-Qaraḍāwī, Yūsuf (2001), *Fī Fiqh al-'Aqalliyyāt al-Muslima* (On Muslim Minority Jurisprudence), Cairo: Dār El Shorouk.

al-Qaraḍāwī, Yūsuf (2004), *Khiṭābunā al-'Islāmī fī 'Aṣr al-'Awlama* (Our Islamic Discourse in the Age of Globalization), Cairo: Dar El Shorouk.

al-Qimnī, al-Sayyid (2006), 'al-'Istibdād bi-Musānadat al-Samā'' (Despotism with the Backing of Heaven), *The Website for al-Quimny Works*, 4 December, http://quemny.blog.com/tag.

al-Qimnī, al-Sayyid (2022), "al-Kahanūt al-'Islāmī Yasriq al-Dīn" (Islamic Priesthood Steals Religion), *al-Ḥiwār al-Mutamaddin* (Civilized Dialogue), 10 February, https://www.ahewar.org/debat/show.art.asp?aid=331679.

Raiyyān, Muḥammad Sayyid (2011), *Kaiyf Tafajjarat al-Thawra fī 25 Yanāyir?! al-'Facebook' wa 'Adwāt al-Tuknulūjiya al-Ḥadītha* (How the 25th of January Revolution broke out? The 'Facebook' and Modern Technological Tools), 1st edition, Dar al-Kutub li-l-Nashr wa-l-Tawzi'.

Ramaḍān, 'Abd al-'Aẓīm (1986), *Miṣr fī 'Aṣr al-Sādāt* (Egypt at the Time of Sadat), 1st edition, Cairo: Madbouly Library.

Ramaḍān, Sa'īd (1987), *Ma'ālim al-Ṭarīq: al-Fikra '1'* (Landmarks of the Road: The Idea '1'), Cairo Dar at-Tawzi' wal-Nashr al-Islamiyya.

Rashwan, Nada H. (2012), 'Morsi's Coup against the SCAF: The Hows and the Whys', *Ahram Online*, 14 August, http://english.ahram.org.eg/NewsContent/1/140/50324/Egypt/First--days/Morsis-coup-against-SCAF-The-hows-and-the-whys.aspx.

Rejwan, Nissim (1974), *The Nasserist Ideology: Its Exponents and Critics*, Tel Aviv: Tel Aviv University, Shiloah Center for Middle Eastern and African Studies.

Ricoeur, Paul (1970), *Freud and Philosophy: An Essay on Interpretation*, trans. D. Savage, New Haven, CT: Yale University Press.

Rizq, Yāsir (2012), *Thawrat Yanāyir wa Mā Ba'dahā: Haikal Yatakallam* (The January Revolution and After: Haikal Speaks), Egypt: Akhbar al-Yum Press.

Rogers, Karl (2012), *On Foucault's Discourse*, 2nd edition, Los Angeles: Trebol Press.

Roll, Stephan (2013), *Egypt's Business Elite after Mubarak: A Powerful Player between Generals and Brotherhood*, SWP, Berlin, https://www.swp-berlin.org/publications/products/research_papers/2013_RP08_rll.pdf.

Rowberry, Ryan, and John Khalil (2013), 'A Brief History of Coptic Personal Law', *Berkeley Journal for Middle Eastern and Islamic Law* 3 (1), Article 2, https://rb.gy/e1jd4.

Rutherford, Bruce K. (2008), *Egypt after Mubarak: Liberalism, Islam, and Democracy in the Arab World*, Princeton, NJ: Princeton University Press.

Saeed, Abdullah, and Hassan Saeed (2004), *Freedom of Religion, Apostasy and Islam*, Burlington, VT: Ashgate.

Said, Edward W. (1978), *Orientalism*, New York: Pantheon Books

Said, Edward W. (1981), *Covering Islam: How the Media and the Experts Determine How we See the Rest of the World*, New York: Pantheon Books.

Said, Edward W. (1983), *The World, the Text, and the Critic*, Cambridge, MA: Harvard University Press.

Said, Edward W. (1994), *Culture and Imperialism*, New York: Alfred A. Knopf.

Said, Mohamed Sayed (2008), 'A Political Analysis of the Egyptian Judges' Revolt'. In Nathalie Bernard-Maugiron (ed.), *Judges and Political Reform in Egypt*, 19–26, Cairo: American University in Cairo Press.

Saif al-Dawla, 'Iṣmat (1977), *Hal Kān 'Abd al-Nāṣir Diktātūran?* (Was 'Abd al-Nasser a Dictator?), 1st edition, Beirut: Dar al-Masira.

Salama, Ingy (2018), 'The Role of Egypt's Armed Forces: A Military Empire', *Qantara*, 13 February, https://en.qantara.de/content/the-role-of-egypts-armed-forces-a-military-empire.

Saleh, Heba (2017), 'Egypt Fights Inflation after Its Currency Devaluation', *Financial Times*, 12 Deceber, https://www.ft.com/content/dc2871fe-d4f9-11e7-8c9a-d9c0a5c8d5c9.

Ṣāliḥ, Farḥān (1983), *Jadaliyyat al-'Ilāqa baiyn al-Fikr al-'Arabī wa-l-Turāth* (The Dialictic of the Relation between Arabic Thought and Heritage), Beirut: Dar al-Hadatha.

Salvatore, Armando (2000), 'The Islamic Reform Project in the Emerging Public Sphere: the (Meta-) Normative Redefinition of Shari'a'. In Almut Höfert and Armando Salvatore (eds), *Between Europe and Islam: Shaping Modernity in a Transcultural Space*, Brussels: P.I.E Peter Lang.

Salvatore, Armando (2007), *The Public Sphere, Liberal Modernity, Catholicism, Islam*, New York: Palgrave Macmillan.

Salvatore, Armando (ed.) (2011), 'Before (and After) the "Arab Spring": From Connectedness to Mobilization in the Public Sphere'. In *Between Everyday Life and Political Revolution: The Social Web in the Middle East*, 5–12, Rome: Istituto per l'Oriente.

Salvatore, Armando, and Dale Eickelmann (2004), 'Preface: Public Islam and the Common Good'. In Armando Salvatore and Dale Eickelmann (eds), xi–xxv, *Public Islam and the Common Good*, Leiden: Brill.

Sardar, Ziauddin (1999), *Orientalism*, Philadelphia, PA: Open University Press.

Sayah, Reza, and Amir Ahmed (2012), 'Egypt's High Court Suspends Sessions after Protestors Block Judges Way', *CNN*, 3 December, http://edition.cnn.com/2012/12/02/world/meast/egypt-protests.

Sayigh, Yezid (2019), *Egypt's Military Now Controls Much of its Economy. Is This Wise?*, Carnegie Middle East Center, 25 November, https://carnegie-mec.org/2019/11/25/egypt-s-military-now-controls-much-of-its-economy.-is-this-wise-pub-80281.

Scruton, Roger (2007), *The Palgrave Macmillan Dictionary of Political Thought*, 3rd edition, New York: Palgrave Macmillan.

Sīdā, 'Abd al-Bāsiṭ (1990), *al-Wad'iyya al-Manṭiqiyya wa-l-Turāth al-'Arabī* (Logical Positivism and The Arab Heritage), Beirut: Dār al-Farābī.

Sisk, Timothy D. (2000), *Islam and Democracy: Religion, Politics and Power in the Middle East*, 3rd edition, Washington, DC: United States Institute of Peace

Shaker, Hossam (2010), 'Will Europe Surrender to Selective Racism? An Interpretive Model of a Worsening Phenomenon'. In Abdullah Faliq (ed.), *Islamophobia and Anti-Muslim Hatred: Causes and Remedies, Arches Quarterly*, vol. 4, 7th edition: 84–8.

Shalabī, 'Abd al-Wadūd (1998), *Min Shaikh 'Azharī 'ilā Shaikh al-'Azhar: al-'Azhar 'Ilā 'Aiyn?* (From an Azhari Sheikh to al-Azhar Sheikh: Al-Azhar, Where to?), Cairo: Dar el I'tisam.

Shāma, Muḥammad (2012), *al-'Islām fī 'Arwiqat al-Mustashriqīn* (Islam in the Hallways of Orientalists), Egypt, Giza: al-Iman Library.

Shama, Nael (2010), 'Decoding Egypt: 1967, 2010: The Annals of Defeat', *Daily News, Egypt*, 18 August, http://www.dailynewsegypt.com/2010/08/18/decoding-egypt-1967-2010-the-annals-of-defeat/.

Shammākh, 'Amīr (2012), *al-'Ikhwān al-Muslimūn fī Sujūn wa Mu'taqalāt Mubārak* (The Muslim Brotherhood in Mubarak's Prisons and Jails), Cairo: Muassasat Iqraa.

Sharaf, Muḥammad Jalāl (1982), *Nash'at al-Fikr al-Siyāsī wa Tatwūruh fī-l-'Islām* (The Origin of Political Thought and Its Evolution in Islam), Beirut: Dar al-Nahda al-'Arabiyya.

Sharp, Jeremy M (2014), *Egypt: Background and US Relations*, Congressional Research Service, 10 January, http://www.fas.org/sgp/crs/mideast/RL33003.pdf.

Shenker, Jack (2011a), 'Egypt Election Results Put Muslim Brotherhood Ahead', *The Guardian*, 30 November, http://www.theguardian.com/world/2011/nov/30/egypt-election-results-muslim-brotherhood.

Shenker, Jack (2011b), 'Egypt's Military Will Have Final Say on Country's New Constitution', *The Guardian*, 7 December, http://www.guardian.co.uk/world/2011/dec/07/egypt-military-final-say-constitution.

Shlaim, Iva, and William Roger Louis (eds) (2012), *The 1967 Arab-Israeli War: Origins and Consequences*, New York: Cambridge University Press.

Sirrs, Owen L. (2010), *A History of the Egyptian Intelligence Service*, New York: Routledge.

Slackman, Michael (2006), 'A Voice for "New Understanding of Islam" – International Herald Tribune', *New York Times*, 20 October, http://www.nytimes.com/2006/10/20/world/africa/20iht-profile.3237674.html?pagewanted=all&_r=0.

Soffar, Mohamed (2004), *The Political Theory of Sayyid Qutb: A Genealogy of Discourse*, Berlin, Verlag Dr. Köster.

Soliman, Hany (2022), 'Why Do Egypt's Christians Support Sisi?', *Middle East Monitor*, 17 January, https://www.middleeastmonitor.com/20220117-why-do-egypts-christians-support-sisi/.

Soliman, Samer (2004), 'The Rise and Decline of Islamic Banking Model in Egypt'. In Clement M. Henry and Rodney Wilson (eds), *The Politics of Islamic Finance*, Edinburgh: Edinburgh University Press.

Soueif, Ahdaf (2011), 'Image of Unknown Woman Beaten by Egypt's Military Echoes around the World', *The Guardian*, 18 December, http://www.guardian.co.uk/commentisfree/2011/dec/18/egypt-military-beating-female-protester-tahrir-square.

Spector, Regine A. (2007), 'Authoritarianism as a Style of Rule'. In Mark Bevir (ed.), *Encyclopedia of Governance II*, California: Sage Publication.

Springborg, Robert (2013), 'The Nasser Playbook: The Future US-Egyptian Relations is in the Past', *Foreign Affairs*, 5 November, http://www.foreignaffairs.com/articles/140242/robert-springborg/the-nasser-playbook.

Stacher, Joshua A. (2004), 'Parties Over: The Demise of Egypt's Opposition Parties', *British Journal of Middle Eastern Studies* 31 (2): 215–33.

Stagh, Marina (1993), *The Limits of Freedom of Speech: Prose Literature and Prose Writers in Egypt Under Nasser and Sadat*, Stockholm: Almqvist & Wiksell International.

Stolze, Radegundis (2010), *The Translator's Approach-Introduction to Translational Hermeneutics: Theory and Examples from Practice*, Berlin: Frank & Timme Verlag für Wissenschaftliche Literatur.

Svolik, Milan W. (2012), *The Politics of Authoritarian Rule*, New York: Cambridge University Press.

El Saadawi, Nawal (2011), *The Day Mubarak was Tried/der Tag in dem Mubarak der Prozess gemacht wurde*, 100 Notes-100 Thoughts/100 Notizen-100 Gedanken, No. 048, Ostfildern: Hatje Cantz Verlag.

al-Ṣādiq, Ja'far (2012), *Islamic Law: According to Ja'fari School of Jurisprudence: Transactions*, Vol. 2, Oakland, CA: CreateSpace Independent Publishing Platform.

al-Sa'īd, Rif'at (2004), *al-Mut'aslimūn, Mādhā Fa'alū bi-l-'Islām wa ..binā?* (Islam Pretenders, What They Did to Islam and .. to Us?), Cairo, al-Haiyaa al-Misriyya al-'Amma li-l-Kitab.

al-Shāmī, 'Imān Muḥammad (2012), *al-Tarbiyya wa Ba'ḍ Qaḍāiyā al-Mar'a baiyn al-Fikr al-'Islāmī wa-l-Fikr al-Gharbī* (Socialization and Some Women Issues between Islamic and Western Thought), Dissouq: Dar el-'Ilm wa-l-Iman for Publishing.

al-Sharīf, Muḥammad (1984), *Ṣalāḥ al-'Umma 'alā Hadi al-Sunna* (Good of the Nation on the Sunna Path), Cairo: Dar al-Sahwa.

al-Shihābī, 'Ibrāhīm Yiḥiyā (1992), *Mafhūm al-Ḥarb wa-l-Salām fī-l-'Islām: Ṣirā'āt wa Ḥurūb..'am Tafā'ul wa Salām?* (The Concept of War and Peace in Islam: Struggles and Wars or Interaction and Peace?), Libya, Tripoli: kulliyyat al-Da'wa al-Islamiyya.

al-Shirbīnī, Maḥmūd (1999), *Ta'āmulāt fī-l-Sharī'a al-'Islāmiyya* (Insights on Islamic Shari'a), 2nd edition, Cairo: al-Haiyaa al-Misriyya al-'Amma li-l-Kitab.

al-Shūbāshī, Sharīf (2013), *Li-mādhā Takhallafnā? wa Li-mādhā Taqaddam al-'Ākharūn?* (Why We Retarded? and Why Others Progressed?), Cairo: Dar al'Aiyn.

Ṭabliyya, Muḥammad al-Quṭb (2000), *Ruwwād al-Fikr al-'Islāmī fī-l-'Aṣr al-Ḥadīth* (Pioneers of Islamic Thought in the Modern Age), Cairo: Dar al-Fikr al-'Arabi.

Tadros, Mariz (2013), *Copts under Morsi: Defiance in the Face of Denial, MERIP*, Middle East Report 267, https://merip.org/2013/06/copts-under-mursi/.

Tamura, Aira (1985) 'Ethnic Consciousness and Its Transformation in the Course of Nation-Building: The Muslim and the Copt in Egypt, 1906–1919', *Muslim World* 75 (2): 102–14.

Tarek, Sherif (2012), 'Morsi Declared Egypt's First Civilian President, but Military Stays in Control', *al-Ahram Online*, 24 June, http://english.ahram.org.eg/NewsContent/36/122/46061/Presidential-elections-/Presidential-elections-news/Morsi-declared-Egypts-first-civilian-president,-bu.aspx.

Ternisien, Xavier (2010), *Les Freres Musulmans* (The Muslim Brotherhood), new edition, Paris: Librairie Artheme Fayard, Pluriel.

Tibawi, A. L. (1976), *Arabic and Islamic Themes: Historical, Educational and Literary Studies*, London: Luzac.

Timm, Christian (2010), 'Jenseits von Demokratiehoffnung und Autoritarismus-Verdacht: eine Herrschaftssoziologie Analyse post-transformatorischer Regime' (Beyond Hope for Democracy, and Suspicion of Authoritarianism: A Sociology of Domination Analysis of Post-Transformational Regimes). In Holger Albrecht and Rolf Frankenberger (eds), *Autoritarismus Reloaded: Neuer Ansätze und Erkenntnisse der Autokratieforschung* (Authoritarianism Reloaded: New Approaches and Findings of the Autocracy Research), Baden-Baden: Nomos Verlagsgesellschaft.

al-Tiftizānī, 'Abū al-Wafā al-Ghunīmī (1997), 'Madrasat Muṣṭafā 'Abd al-Rāziq' (The School of Mustafa 'Abd al-Raziq). In 'Āṭif al-'Irāqī et al. (eds), *al-Shaikh al-'Akbar Muṣṭafā 'Abd al-Rāziq: Mufakkiran, wa 'Adīban, wa Muṣliḥan* (The Grand Sheikh Mustafa 'Abd al-Raziq: Thinker, Worshiper and Reformer), Cairo: al-Majlis al-A'la li-l-Thaqafa.

al-Turābī, Ḥasan 'Abd 'Allāh (1988), *Naẓarāt fi-l-Fiqh al-Siyāsī* (Looks at Political Thought), al-Khartoum: al-Sharika al-'Alamiyya li-khadamat al-I'lam.

El Tantawy, Nadia, and Jullie B. Wiest (2011), 'Social Media in the Egyptian Revolution: Reconsidering Resource Mobilisation Theory', *International Journal of Communication*, No. 5, http://ijoc.org/index.php/ijoc/article/viewFile/1242/597.

U.S. Senate (2001). Egypt, *Annual Report on International Religious Freedom 2001*. Report Submitted to the Committee on International Relations, U.S. House of Representatives and the Committee on Foreign Relations, 420–8, Washington, DC: Government Printing Office.

'Uwaiys, Saiyyd (2002), *Lā li-l-'Unf: Dirāsa 'Ilmiyya fī Takwīn al-Ḍamīr al-'Insānī* (No to Violence: A Scientific Study on the Formation of the Human Conscience), Cairo: al-Haiyaa al-Misriyya al-'Amma li-l-Kitab.

al-'Ulwānī, Ṭāha Jābir (2002), 'Madkhal 'lā Fiqh al-'Aqalliyyāt al-Muslima' (An Introduction to Muslim Minorities Jurisprudence), *al-Masār Magazine* 2: 5–26.

al-'Ulwānī, Ṭāha Jābir (2006), *lā 'Ikrāh fī-l-Dīn: 'Ishkāliyyat al-Ridda wa-l-Murtaddīn min Ṣadr al-'Islām 'lā al-Yawm* (No Coercion in Religion: Apostasy and Apostates Problematic from Early Islam til Today), Cairo: International Shorouk Library.

al-'Ulwānī, Ṭāha Jābir (2008), *Naḥw al-Tajdīd wa-l-'Ijtihād* (Towards Renewal and Ijtihad), Cairo: Tanwir Press.

al-'Ulwānī, Ṭāha Jābir (2010), *al-'Imām Fakhr al-Dīn al-Rāzī wa Muṣanafātuh* (Imam Fakhr al-Din al-Razi and His Writings), Cairo: Dar al-Salam.

al-'Umrī, 'Ādil (2009), *al-Yasār..wa-l-Nāṣiriyya..wa-l-Thawra al-Muḍāḍa..: Naẓra Jadīda fī Mallafāt Qadīma* (The Left..and Nasserism..and the Counter-Revolution: A New Look in Old files), Cairo: al-Maḥrusa Press.

Valkenberg, Pim (2011), 'Sifting the Qur'an: Two Forms of Interreligious Hermeneutics in Nicholas of Cusa'. In David Cheetham et al. (eds), *Interreligious Hermeneutics in Pluralistic Europe: Between Texts and People*, New York: Rodopi B.V.

Vishanoff, David R. (2011), *The Formation of Islamic Hermeneutics: How Sunni Legal Theorists Imagined a Revealed Law*, Ann Arbor, MI: American Oriental Society.

Warde, Ibrahim (2000), *Islamic Finance in the Global Economy*, Edinburgh: Edinburgh University Press.

Waterbury, John (1983), *The Egypt of Nasser and Sadat: The Political Economy of Two Regimes*, Princeton, NJ: Princeton University Press.

Weaver, Mathew (2012), 'Muslim Brotherhood's Mohamed Morsi Win Egypt's Presidential Race', *The Guardian*, 2 June, http://www.theguardian.com/world/middle-east-live/2012/jun/24/egypt-election-results-live.

Wickham, Carrie R. (2002), *Mobilizing Islam: Religion, Activism, and Political Change in Egypt*, New York: Columbia University Press.

Wilson, Rodney (2003), 'Arab Government Responses to Islamic Finance'. In B. A. Roberson (ed.), *Shaping the Current Islamic Reformation*, London: Frank Cass Publishers.

Wittgenstein, L. (1958), *Philosophical Investigations*, 2nd edition, Oxford: Basil Blackwell.

Wolf, Eric R. (1984), 'Introduction'. In Eric R. Wolf (ed.), *Religion, Power and Protest*, Berlin: Mouton Publishers.

Wood, Philip (2013), *History and Identity in the Late Antique Near East*, New York: Oxford University Press.

Woodward, Peter (1992), *Nasser*, Essex: Longman House.

Yerkes, Sarah (2016), 'What Egypt Is Really Like under Sisi for Coptic Christians', *Brookings*, 20 June, https://www.brookings.edu/articles/what-egypt-under-sissi-is-really-like-for-coptic-christians/.

Yūnis, Sharīf (2012), *Nidā' al-Sha'b: Tārīkh Naqdī li-l-'Aidūlūjiyya al-Nāṣiriyya* (The Call of the People: A Critical History of the Nasserist Ideology), 1st edition, Cairo: El Shorouk Press.

Zahid, Mohammed (2010), *The Muslim Brotherhood and Egypt's Succession Crisis: The Politics of Liberalization and Reform in the Middle East*, New York: I.B. Tauris.

Zahran, Farid (2013), 'What Are the Chances of Mergers and Alliances inside the Democratic Movement?(2–2)', *Daily News Egypt*, 30 October, http://www.dailyne

wsegypt.com/2013/10/30/what-are-the-chances-of-mergers-and-alliances-inside-the-democratic-movement-2-2/.
Zakaria, Fareed (1997), 'The Rise of Illiberal Democracy', *Foreign Affairs* 76 (6): 22–43.
Zaman, Muhammad Qasim (2002), *The Ulama in Contemporary Islam: Custodians of Change*, Princeton, NJ: Princeton University Press.
Zaman, Muhammad Qasim (2004), 'The 'Ulama of Contemporary Islam and Their Conceptions of the Common Good'. In Armando Salvatore and Dale F. Eickelman (eds), *Public Islam and the Common Good*, Leiden: Brill.
Zaqzūq, Maḥmūd Ḥamdī (2012), *al-Fikr al-Dīnī wa Qaḍāiyā al-'Aṣr* (Religious Thought and Issues of the Age), Cairo: al-Haiyaa al-Misriyya al-'Amma li-l-Kitab.
Zarnūqa, Ṣalāḥ Salīm (2002), *al-Sharikāt al-Dawliyya wa-l-Tanmiya: al-Jawānib al-Siyāsiyya* (International Companies and Development: The Political Aspects), Cairo: Center for the Study of Developing Countries.
Zulkifli (2013), *The Struggle of the Shi'Is in Indonesia: Islam in Southeast Asia*, Canberra: Australian National University, ANU E Presse.
al-Zuḥīlī, Wahbā (2006), *Qaḍāiyā al-Fiqh wa-l-Fikr al-Mu'āṣir* (Issues of Jurisprudence and Contemporary Thought), Damascus: Dar al-Fikr.

Interviews

18 October 2010, al-Banna, Cairo.
27 October 2010, al-Banna, Cairo.
29 October 2010, al-Banna, Cairo.
1 November 2010, al-Banna, Cairo.
3 November 2010, al-Banna, Cairo.
5 November 2010, al-Banna, Cairo.
10 November 2010, al-Banna, Cairo.
15 November 2010, al-Banna, Cairo.
22 May 2011, al-Banna, Cairo.
25 October 2010, al-Bishri, Cairo.
8 January 2011, al-Bishri, Cairo.
2 June 2011, al-Bishri, Cairo.
6 September 2011, al-Bishri, Cairo.
16 July 2011, al-Bishri, Cairo.
15 August 2011, al-Bishri, Cairo.
23 December 2010, Dr Maḥmūd Jāmi', Tanta, Egypt.
2 December 2010, Dr 'Amr al-Shūbakī, political expert in the Ahram Center of Political and Strategic Studies and head of the Badael Forum.
9 December 2010, Aḥmad Rā'if, ex-MB member with wide juridical knowledge, Cairo.

14 December 2010, Dr Dīna Shiḥāta, PhD holder and senior expert in the Ahram Center for Political and Strategic Studies.

15 December 2010, Dr Muḥammad Farīd 'Abd al-Khāliq, former leading figure in the MB and PhD holder.

7 November 2010, Dr Waḥīd 'Abd al-Majīd, head of the Ahram Center for Publication and Translation.

28 December 2010, Dr Pakīnām al-Sharqāwī, former professor of Political Science Dept, Cairo University.

30 December 2010, Dr Nājiḥ 'Ibrāhīm, intellectual leader of the Islamic group al-Jama'a al-Islamiyya.

9 January 2011, Dr Kamāl al-Munūfī, Professor of Political Science, Cairo University.

9 January 2011, Dr Nūrā Midḥat, Lecturer of Political Science, Cairo University.

2 August 2011, Dr 'Abd al-Mun'im 'Abū al-Futūḥ, leading Islamic figure and ex-MB top-ranking member.

3 August 2011, Dr Muḥammad Salīm al-'Awwa, a renowned lawyer and Islamic intellectual, Cairo.

10 August 2011, Dr 'Ammār 'Alī Ḥasan, journalist in *al-sharaq al-Awsat* newspaper.

16 August 2011, Dr Nādia Muṣṭafā, Professor of Political Science, Cairo University.

15 September 2011, Dr Muḥammad 'Imāra, PhD holder and renowned Islamic intellectual.

Index

'Abd al-Raziq, A. 16, 27–8, 82, 132, 135
'Abdu, M. 16–17, 21–3
Abi bakr 30, 93, 102–3
abidance 33, 68
abundance/abundant 9, 130, 163
activism 53–4, 61, 67, 89–90, 101, 108, 120
political 48, 144, 146
violent 149, 161
activist/s 46–9, 60, 63–6
'Ahl al-Dhimma 37–8, 99, 110, 117, 151, 164
al-Afghani 17, 21–3
al-Azhar 10, 42–3, 46–9, 55, 57, 65–70, 77–8, 98, 139, 146, 167
al-Banna, H. 9, 11, 16, 51, 90, 104, 106, 108–9
al-Ma'mun (Caliph) 30, 83
al-Nabaa 118, 150
al-Qaradawi (Sheikh) 24, 38, 66, 139
al-Qimni, S. 15, 25, 68
al-Sanhuri, 'A. 45, 70, 149
al-Shafi'i (Imam) 31, 146
al-Sisi, A. 71, 73, 77, 87–8, 119–30, 131
al-Wafd Party 51, 55–6, 73, 124–5, 129, 144–6, 149–60, 160
'Ali, M. 31, 88, 113, 117
alliance 20, 60, 64, 67, 71–2, 86
amendment/s 54, 77, 107–8, 132
apostasy 21, 30, 38, 103, 105
authority
absolute 45, 125
religious 13, 28
state 25, 136, 139–40, 146
authoritarianism 92, 94

b. al-Khattab, 'U 92, 100
Bible/biblical 11, 139, 162
b. Khaldun 21, 23
b. Taimiyya 21, 23

cabinet/s 54, 86, 152
caliphate 26–7, 39, 82, 117, 123, 132, 149, 155, 164, 177
Camp David 52, 55, 58–9, 78
censorship 47, 64, 77, 85
charisma 43–5, 51, 53, 77
chauvinism 115, 122, 169
collective decision-making 125–6, 135, 154, 161
colonizer/s 2, 37, 91, 110, 112, 126, 128, 137–8, 162, 170
common ground 56, 115, 164, 169
communal 4, 37–8, 118–20, 150, 160
conqueror/s 34, 37, 40, 102, 110, 148, 151, 155
conquests 33–5, 50, 101–3, 121, 164
constant/s (*Thawābit*) 6, 17, 19, 41, 78, 99, 141, 148, 161
Constitution
1923 58, 111, 113, 129
1971 53, 55, 59–60
contextuality 1, 7, 8
convergence 19, 22, 26, 36, 133, 139–40, 144, 146, 155
conversion/s 37–8, 40, 110, 118, 151, 159
convert/s 37–8, 40, 83, 102, 117–18
Coptic Church 79, 119–20, 159–60, 162, 167
Coptic diaspora 75, 119, 120, 159–60, 185
counterargument 137, 162
counter-force 51, 143, 154

Dār al-'Islām/Dār al-Ḥarb 37, 110, 151
defence 45, 73, 87, 102, 105
despotic rule 82–4, 93, 128, 138, 161
despotism 84, 126, 161, 170

education 5–6, 11, 24, 46, 105
effective/ness 114, 133, 144–5, 147, 161, 170
evade 42, 67, 69, 77
equality 38, 102, 120, 147, 160, 164
equality and participation 141–2, 157–8

exclusion 7–8, 27, 108, 114, 122, 134, 142, 155, 160, 167
exclusionary 6, 76
practices of 17, 39
extremism/extremist 35, 60, 120

fascist/s 57, 182–3
Foucault, M. 3, 20, 27, 163
freedom
of expression 54, 64, 147
and justice 83–4, 95, 138, 169
and rights 10, 20, 146, 170
futūḥāt 33–4, 101–3, 121, 144, 164
and apostasy 103, 105
history of 37, 102

Hadith 5, 7, 18–21, 31, 67–8, 85, 95, 100, 140, 157, 168–9
Hanafi, H. 3, 5, 21, 25
hermeneutic/al circle 11–12, 31, 163
human rights 52, 61, 72

Ibn Hanbal (Imam) 20, 84
identity circle/s 151–3, 158, 170
identity
counter- 153, 158
inter- 110, 158
intra- 36, 40, 110, 150
'Illa 32, 40, 100, 121, 168
Imam 9, 20, 31, 65, 146
inclusion 29, 41, 114, 166
individual rule 85, 88, 125–8, 146, 161, 170
infitah 51, 53, 56, 107, 179
intelligence 43, 45–6, 60, 69, 77, 130
Islamist business/es 66, 105–7, 134, 139
Israel 35, 44, 51–4, 58–9, 78, 112
Israeli/s 52, 58, 76, 78, 104, 109, 112

jail (*see also* prison) 9, 62–3, 69, 88, 105–6, 109
jeopardize 42, 45, 47, 62, 114, 128, 152, 158, 165
Jihad 26, 33–6, 39–50, 101, 103–5, 112, 144, 148–50, 156, 162, 164, 167, 170
Jiziya 34, 3–8, 99, 102, 110, 117, 151, 164
judiciary 50, 54, 65, 70, 108, 155, 160
juristic 17, 21, 37, 49, 67, 110, 132, 140, 144, 151

Kifaya 11, 64, 71
King Faruq 57, 68, 88, 129, 166

legacy 52, 66, 166
liberal/s/ism 10, 17, 42, 49, 67, 88–90, 98, 103, 111, 121, 126, 129, 144

Malik 20, 146
Marxism/t 10, 145
meta-language 8, 15–6, 21, 25–6, 81, 122, 163–4, 168
militancy 35, 40, 66, 101, 103–4, 110, 144, 161
minorities 38, 110, 142, 151, 161, 168
minority 38, 110, 113, 118, 121, 151, 167
monitor 63, 77, 167
morality 37, 112
Mursi, M. 72–7, 78, 87, 108, 119, 134–5
Muslim community 34–6, 38

Nasser 41–71, 65–80, 77–8, 85–6, 88
National Assembly 73, 118, 131
nationalism 91, 115–16, 122, 129, 169
Nazi/sm 57, 104
new media 8, 25, 59, 63, 78, 165
1952 coup 43, 46, 49–50, 56, 58, 65, 77, 88, 10, 130–1, 134, 159, 166
1967 defeat 10, 44–5, 50–1, 66, 69, 77, 106, 112, 116

orient/alist 1–2, 91, 105, 111, 126, 153–4
Orientalism (Said, E.) 1–2, 4, 29, 36, 91, 110–11, 122, 124, 138, 161, 164, 170
Ottoman/s 27, 31, 35, 43, 149, 152, 155–6
ouster
Mubarak 41, 71–2, 79, 87, 108, 131, 134
Mursi 72, 75–6, 79, 87, 119, 131, 134

Palestine 58, 104, 134
parliamentary 29, 39, 54, 58–9, 73, 90, 108, 123, 166
Parliament/s 54, 59, 73, 82, 87, 108, 120, 123, 146, 152, 160
peace treaty 51–7, 66, 78
persecution 41–2, 48, 71, 75, 77–9, 105, 107–8, 131, 134, 139, 166
Pope
Coptic 79, 139, 159, 167
Roman 120–1

popularity 44–5, 56
praise 70, 76, 89–91, 95–6, 109, 126–7, 137, 149, 154, 162, 169–70
predecessor 52, 55, 58, 65, 166
prison/s (*see also* jail) 45, 60, 95–7, 103–4, 107, 149
prisoner/s 60, 62, 69, 103, 107
propagate 5, 32, 40, 49, 66–7, 99, 121, 128, 147, 156

red lines 13, 41–2, 48, 56, 59, 62–3, 65, 69–71, 77, 149, 165–6, 170
revolution
  1919 51, 149
  1952 43, 45, 57–8, 130
revolutionary/ies 73, 75, 113, 124, 166
Revolution Command Council (RCC) 43, 106, 130
rivalry 13, 54–5, 63, 66, 86–7, 88, 109, 139
rivals 50, 60, 63, 66, 77, 166

Salvatore, A. 8, 15, 163
SCAF (Supreme Council of Armed Forces) 71–4, 76, 78, 87, 119, 131
scripture/s 17–18, 33
secret apparatus (al-Nizam al-Khas) 35, 51, 104, 106, 134, 166
secularism 91, 134, 145, 154, 156–7, 162
sentiment/s 36, 106–7, 115–16, 120, 156, 159, 167
Shiite/s 21, 37, 110, 117, 151
Siraj al-Din 56, 58, 65, 88
social justice 72, 126
socialism 10, 44, 46, 49, 99–1, 122, 166–7, 172
state security 45, 69, 62–3, 69
strike/s 60, 62, 63, 74, 90, 145
Sudan 89, 100, 106
Sunna 16, 18–9, 57, 95, 164
syndicate/s 10, 56, 61, 68–9, 90, 107, 140
syndicalism 56–8, 68–9, 89, 104

Tahrir square 74, 87
terrorism 35, 60, 86, 148
trial/s 21, 25, 52–3, 60, 62, 70, 74, 87
  levels 154, 170
truth 3, 8, 12, 20, 26–7, 94, 163–4
  religious 15, 21, 23–5, 27, 48, 68–9, 96, 164, 167, 170

2011 uprising 66, 71–9, 86–7, 108, 119, 130–1, 134, 150, 159–60, 166–7, 181
'Umma 18, 36–7, 94
United States 52, 75, 103, 111
unity 36, 44, 61, 77, 102, 121, 129, 142, 152, 155–7
  Arab 58, 70
usury *(Ribā)* 100, 134

violent 34–5, 101, 104–5, 144, 147–9, 161, 170

war
  1967 44, 12, 113, 167
  1973 51–3, 77, 112–13, 167

Zaghlul, S. 149–50
Zionism/t 58, 59, 124

www.ingramcontent.com/pod-product-compliance
Lightning Source LLC
Chambersburg PA
CBHW071834300426
44116CB00009B/1537
9780755653195